The Stranger
She Loved

ALSO BY SHANNA HOGAN

Picture Perfect: The Jodi Arias Story

Dancing with Death

The Stranger She Loved

A Mormon Doctor, His Beautiful Wife, and an Almost Perfect Murder

SHANNA HOGAN

St. Martin's Press ❧ New York

www.stmartins.com

Designed by Anna Gorovoy

The Library of Congress Cataloging-in-Publication Data is available upon request.

ISBN 978-1-250-05750-1 (hardcover)
ISBN 978-1-4668-6808-3 (e-book)

St. Martin's Press books may be purchased for educational, business, or promotional use. For information on bulk purchases, please contact the Macmillan Corporate and Premium Sales Department at 1-800-221-7945, extension 5442, or write to specialmarkets@macmillan.com.

First Edition: April 2015

10 9 8 7 6 5 4 3 2 1

TO LOVING MOTHERS
LIKE MICHELE MacNEILL AND
TO MY AMAZING MOM,
DEBBIE HOGAN

AUTHOR'S NOTE

This book is a journalistic account of a true story. The quotes used to compile the narrative were taken from trial testimony, court documents, personal interviews, television programs, and newspaper articles. Conversations portrayed in this book have been reconstructed using trial testimony, extensive research, interviews, and press accounts. All of the dates and locations mentioned throughout are factual. However, the names of some of the inmates who testified for the prosecution were changed, including George Martinez, Von Harper, and Frank Davis. For these people, identifying characteristics were also altered. Although Martin MacNeill has been convicted by a jury of his peers of first-degree murder and sexual assault, he has filed notice that he plans on appealing the verdicts.

A stray drop of water fell from the faucet and trickled across her cold, pallid skin.

Her body lay crumpled inside the drained bathtub, a long-sleeved black shirt clinging to her wet torso. She was tilted on her side, her nude lower half curled against the tub's slick porcelain wall.

The woman's ashen face—beautiful even in death—was marred by sutured incisions across her eyelids and around her scalp. Blood from the ruptured stitches wept into damp blond hair.

Hovering over the bathtub, a slim man with a tanned face and gray hair was wailing. "I need help! Help!"

From the doorway of the master bathroom, Kristi Daniels gaped wide-eyed at her next-door neighbors—Martin and Michele MacNeill. "I'll call nine-one-one," Kristi said, spinning away.

"I've already called nine-one-one!" Martin howled. "I need help getting her out of the tub."

But Kristi had already fled the bathroom, dashing down the hallway and out of the house. On the front porch she brushed past a little girl dressed in a khaki skirt, white-collared blouse, and blue blazer—a school uniform. She was the youngest of the MacNeills' adopted daughters, Ada.

Just moments earlier the doe-eyed six-year-old had knocked on Kristi's front door. "My dad needs some help." Kristi had followed Ada back toward the MacNeills' open front door. By the time she was halfway across the driveway, she had heard Martin's screams and had taken off running, leaving Ada outside.

Following the cries down the hallway and into the bathroom off the master bedroom, Kristi had discovered Martin and his dead wife. Her first thought was that she and Martin would not be able to lift Michele out of the tub by themselves. So Kristi—a petite blond flight attendant—had run to find help.

Crossing the shared driveway separating their properties, Kristi rushed back into her house and found her neighbor Angie Aguilar crouching in the foyer, tying her own daughter's shoes. A half hour earlier—around 11:20 A.M.—Angie and her daughter had stopped by the Danielses' house to drop off Kristi's son, as part of the neighborhood carpool. Following a brief visit, Angie was preparing to leave when Kristi burst back through the front door, her face contorted with panic.

"What's wrong?" Angie asked.

"I need you to come with me!" Kristi gasped. From a table in the front room, Kristi grabbed her cell phone and pressed a button to speed-dial her husband, Doug Daniels, who was just a few houses away, assisting another neighbor with a basement renovation.

"Martin needs help. Martin needs help," she said breathlessly. "Hurry, come fast . . ."

"Where are you?" Doug interrupted.

"The MacNeills'!"

Doug emerged from his neighbor's house, catching a glimpse of his wife and Angie slipping through the MacNeills' front door. He chased after them, sprinting through the gated subdivision of Creekside in Pleasant Grove, Utah. The usually peaceful community about thirty-five miles south of Salt Lake City is nestled in the foothills of the snowcapped mountains of the Wasatch Range.

The MacNeills' one-story home with its brick façade sat on a grassy lot dotted with hedges. The MacNeills, with their eight children, had one of the largest families in the neighborhood. Martin was a fifty-one-year-old practicing physician, law school graduate, and a former Mormon bishop. Fifty-year-old Michele was a stay-at-home mom who spent her days carting her youngest daughters to school and ballet practice.

Although Kristi and Doug had lived next door to the MacNeills for more than a year, the families didn't associate beyond exchanging the occasional pleasantries. Up until this day, Kristi hadn't even been inside their house.

Stepping into the master bathroom, Kristi and Angie found Martin kneeling beside the tub, cradling his wife's head in his hands. The sleeves of his lab coat were drenched. He had just reached into the basin to drain the murky brown bathwater in which Michele had been immersed.

The raised Jacuzzi tub in the center of the bathroom was inset in an elevated travertine tile deck. Sunlight streamed through a window next to the shower, illuminating a vase of lavender flowers on the tub's ledge.

Michele was clothed only in a long-sleeved black shirt worn over a white Mormon undergarment and bra, with no pants or underwear. Thick, cloudy mucus glazed her face, oozing from her nose and mouth onto her cheeks and onto the gaping gashes across her hairline.

"Angie and I are here," Kristi told Martin.

Martin craned his neck and shook his head. "I need a man's help to get her out of the tub."

"I called Doug," Kristi said.

Seconds later Doug burst into the bathroom. At a glance he knew the situation was dire. Instinctively he passed to the far end of the tub, near Michele's feet.

"Let's get her out!" Martin shouted.

Doug scooped up Michele's legs under the knees, Martin grabbed his wife under her arms, and together they lifted. As Martin lifted her torso, Michele's shirts and bra were pulled up to her neck, exposing her breasts. The two men gently placed her on the floor beside the tub. Michele's arms splayed at her sides. Beneath her, a puddle of water began to spread across the taupe tile floor.

Martin's eyes darted around the bathroom, horror etched across his face. "Oh my God! Oh my God!" he choked.

Shaken, Angie ran her fingers through her long dark hair, then clapped both her hands over her mouth and backed away from the body, into the bathroom closet.

"I know CPR," Kristi said to Martin. "I'll do the compressions if you do mouth-to-mouth."

Martin nodded in agreement. Doug grabbed a rag and passed it to Martin to wipe the mucus from Michele's face. Because Michele was naked from the waist down, Angie found a pink towel and draped it lengthwise to cover the exposed lower region.

Kneeling and placing one palm on top of the other, Kristi pumped on Michele's bare, damp chest in succinct compressions, silently counting to herself, attempting to keep a pace of one hundred beats per minute. When she paused, Martin sank down, pinched his wife's nose, and placed his lips over hers, blowing twice into her mouth.

After one round of compressions, Doug tapped on Kristi's shoulder. "I can do that. Go outside and wait for the ambulance so they can find us."

Nodding, Kristi stood, stepped over Michele's body, and left the bathroom. Outside she found Ada MacNeill and escorted the girl into the Danielses' house, to be supervised by another friend who had also been visiting. "You can go stay at my house for a while," Kristi told Ada.

In the bathroom, Doug bent his burly frame over Michele and—on Martin's command—resumed pumping on her torso. Mindful that his neighbor was a physician and experienced with life-saving procedures, Doug deferred to him for instructions.

"Stop," Martin told Doug after several beats. Once again he put his lips over Michele's, passing two breaths. Kneeling lower, Martin tilted his head and placed his ear on her chest.

There was no heartbeat. Michele wasn't breathing.

"Oh my God. Oh my God. Oh my God," Martin mumbled to himself. He sat up and touched his face. "She shouldn't have done this." Sighing heavily, he directed Doug to continue.

As they performed CPR, Martin alternated between moments of fear and fury, calmly puffing air into his wife's mouth, then exploding, "Why, why? All for a stupid surgery!"

"His demeanor would change, which we thought was a little bit different," Doug Daniels later recalled. "He was very analytical sometimes, telling us what to do, and then would tell us to stop, and then he would have a bit of an outburst over the situation."

When Martin once again breathed into his wife's mouth, Doug noticed that Michele's chest did not rise or fall.

CPR was not being performed properly. Strangely, the doctor didn't seem to notice.

Another round of compressions: Doug pumped on Michele's chest. Martin gave rescue breaths and then paused to check her heartbeat, but again found none.

"Why? Why? Why would you do this?" Martin threw his arms into the air.

Martin suddenly slammed his fist on Michele's chest. "All because of a stupid surgery?"

Perplexed, Doug looked closer at Michele's face. Her cheeks were swollen, her jawline bruised. The bloody stitches were obviously the result of a recent face-lift.

How did she end up unconscious in the bathtub? Doug wondered.

Examining Michele, Doug noticed something else strange. Greenish mucus still coated Michele's face. But none of it had transferred to Martin as he performed mouth-to-mouth.

Minutes passed. The two men continued their efforts to revive Michele. More chest compressions and rescue breaths. Michele remained motionless, her pale skin growing increasingly cold.

Once again, Martin put his ear to his wife's chest, checking for a heartbeat. Recoiling, he slammed his palm on her sternum with a sharp clap.

"Why?" Martin roared. "Why did you have to have the surgery? I told you not to do it!"

Peering up, Martin and Doug saw two uniformed Utah police officers standing in the doorway of the bathroom.

Pleasant Grove police officer Ray Ormond was midway through an uneventful Wednesday patrol shift when the call came in at 11:48 A.M. that a woman had been found unresponsive in her bathroom and had possibly drowned in the tub.

Tall and brawny, with a shaved head and goatee, Ormond was dispatched to the scene. Flicking on his car's lights and sirens, he sped toward the home. Turning down Millcreek Road, Ormond pulled next to the curb outside a house addressed 3058 and parked behind another cruiser, its red and blue revolving lights still flashing. Ormond's partner, Joshua Motsinger, had arrived just seconds ahead of him in a separate car.

From the trunk of his cruiser, Ormond grabbed a handheld masked ventilator—known as an Ambu bag—and followed Motsinger up the natural-rock steps and across the grassy front yard. Kristi Daniels met them on the driveway, guiding the officers into the residence and toward the bathroom. "It's back here."

As the two officers entered the bathroom, Ormond's view was briefly obscured by his partner's broad build. Once Motsinger stepped aside, Ormond saw the woman on the wet tile floor. Ormond's gaze fell to Martin MacNeill, who had just whacked his wife's chest. Exchanging a glance, Ormond and Motsinger darted to the woman's side.

"I'm her husband. I found her in the bathtub," Martin blurted to the officers. "She just had surgery. She had a face-lift. She was on a lot of medication."

"Okay," Motsinger said, taking over compressions for Doug. "We got this from here."

At the officers' request, Doug and Angie exited the room and left the house. Martin stayed, looming over his wife's body. "Why, God? Why?" he cried.

As Ormond placed the Ambu bag over Michele's mouth, he noticed her lips were blue. He began hand-pumping the ventilator and heard a gurgling noise emanating from her chest—an indication of water churning in her lungs or stomach.

Because the bathroom was narrow, the officers decided to move Michele's body. Together they carried her into the master bedroom and laid her on the carpet. The bedroom was tidy and elegantly decorated with large wooden dressers and an armoire holding a flat-screen TV. A couch was centered in front of the bay window. A dozen decorative pillows were neatly arranged atop the king-size bed, which sat next to a narrow hospital-style bed bordered with railings.

To create space in the room, Ormond pushed aside a rollaway nightstand, making note of a pink container filled with eight to ten orange pill bottles. The name on the prescriptions: Michele MacNeill.

In the bedroom, the officers switched positions around Michele. Ormond took over compressions and Motsinger delivered rescue breaths. After several rounds of CPR, Michele's skin regained a pinkish hue. Blood gushed from the incisions on her face—a result of the CPR manually stimulating her circulatory system.

Meanwhile, Martin paced nervously from the bedroom to the bathroom, shaking his head. "Why? Why?" he shouted, jerking his arms. "I told her not to do it!"

Minutes passed. The guttural gurgling noises emitting from Michele grew louder. Motsinger removed the mask from her face and tipped Michele on her side. Her head fell next to Motsinger's lap, her cheek near his left leg. Michele suddenly spewed several cups of clear liquid, dousing Motsinger's arms and pants. The water dribbled down from his arms into his latex gloves and from his pant legs into his boots.

The officers resumed CPR. Moments later, Michele regurgitated more fluid. Leaning over her body, Motsinger removed the mask and Ormond turned her head toward his right knee. This time the vomit spilled onto Ormond. The expulsion was frothy, thick, and tinged with blood. Mixing with the blood on Michele's face, the fluid dripped onto the carpet.

Nearby, Martin continued pacing, his voice growing louder. He turned to Michele. "Why did you do it? Why'd you have the surgery?"

He stormed out of the room, down the hallway, and out of the house.

Around noon—fourteen minutes after the first 911 call was placed—the ambulance arrived. From the porch, Martin waved his arms to alert medics to his location. Around the same time, the fire captain pulled up to the house, parking his emergency vehicle along the curb. As the captain grabbed his equipment from the back of his car, Martin yelled from the porch, "What's taking so long? Get inside!"

Firefighters and paramedics soon swarmed the property, police cruisers and fire trucks lining the block. Inside the bedroom the paramedics, police, and firefighters crowded around the prone woman. Assessing her condition, the medics determined that she was in full cardiac arrest.

An intubation tube was inserted down her throat. One paramedic cut off her shirt, bra, and undergarment top, while another applied padded sensors to her chest to check for signs of life. No activity registered—Michele was flat-lined.

Stomping back into the bedroom, Martin looked up at the ceiling and cursed God. "After all I've done for you? After all the time I've spent in church? Why have you done this to me?" he ranted. "I've been a bishop. I paid tithing and this is the way you repay me? This is what I get for it?"

Desperation transformed to wrath as Martin circled around his wife's body. "Why did you take all those medications?" He glared down, hissing, "Look what it did to you!"

Martin's increasingly aggressive outbursts drew the attention of the medics. Struck by the man's animosity, Ormond tensed, wondering if he might have to restrain Martin or defend himself. Others—distracted from the woman—asked for Martin to be removed from the bedroom. It was beyond the typical reaction of an anguished spouse and unlike anything most of them had encountered during a rescue.

"He was very angry," Ormond remembered years later. "It was uncomfortable, honestly, to have him come back and forth into the room yelling at us."

Pleasant Grove fire chief Marc Sanderson pulled Martin aside. "Can you come with me so we can gather more information?" The slim firefighting veteran escorted Martin out to the front porch. As they spoke, Martin offered various explanations for what might have happened to his wife, saying he believed she may have slipped, tripped, or fallen in the tub and hit her head.

Martin claimed he had only been gone about ten to fifteen minutes, and when he returned, Michele was bent over the tub's ledge, submerged facedown in a pool of bloody water.

It was not the position the neighbors had found Michele in.

"Did she take any medication?" Sanderson asked Martin.

"She was . . . she was taking a lot of medications!" he stammered, adding that Michele may have overdosed on pain pills.

Meanwhile, in the bedroom, resuscitation efforts continued. Paramedics inserted an IV in her arm and administered emergency drugs—epinephrine, atropine, and sodium bicarbonate—in an attempt to restart her heart.

Martin wandered in and out of the bedroom, down the hall, and into the living room, flailing his arms and mumbling to himself, "Why? Why, God?" He stopped only to answer questions and offer brief statements to passing officers.

Sanderson followed Martin as he returned to the bedroom, seemingly to supervise the paramedics.

"What are you doing to her now?" Martin demanded. "What medications did you give her?" Making it known he was a doctor, he barked orders for her treatment. "Did you give her epinephrine? You need to give her epinephrine!"

Pulling him aside, Sanderson assured the doctor that everything possible was being done, although not necessarily in the order Martin requested. Reaching for his phone, Sanderson asked Martin to speak with the emergency room physician at the nearby American Fork Hospital, where Michele would be transported. Because Martin was a doctor—and because it was routine for medical professionals to consult with one another—Sanderson believed it would be helpful for the two men to speak directly. Martin, however, refused.

"No. No." Martin shook his head, his focus drifting from Sanderson. Instead, he wanted to speak to a different doctor, one he'd worked with previously.

Sanderson pressed Martin, explaining that it would be more useful for the doctor treating Michele to speak to him, rather than the information being relayed through a third party.

"I'm a doctor!" Martin pronounced. "She's dead!"

Puzzled, Sanderson asked another patrol officer on scene to monitor Martin and try to keep him away from the bedroom. The officer tailed the distraught doctor, attempting to quiet him.

"You need to calm down, sir," the officer said. "You need to take some deep breaths. You're going to hyperventilate."

"Don't tell me what to do!" Martin shouted. "I'm a doctor. I know I'm okay."

For twenty minutes paramedics attempted to revive Michele before strapping her body to a gurney to take her to the hospital.

Outside of the house, concerned and curious neighbors had gathered on the front lawn. Standing on the driveway beside her husband, Kristi Daniels hugged herself around the waist and shuddered. As paramedics loaded the gurney into the back of the ambulance, Kristi caught a glimpse of Michele, blood streaking her cheek. Somehow she knew she would never see Michele MacNeill again.

The gurney barreled through the double doors of American Fork Hospital at 12:24 P.M. Flanked by one paramedic pumping the resuscitator and another steadying the IV, Michele was wheeled down a short hallway into the nearest trauma bay.

Nurses circled the patient and lifted her onto the hospital bed. An ER tech took over chest compressions. A nurse suctioned the airway clear of any possible fluid or blood.

When the attending physician, Dr. Leo Van Wagoner, first laid eyes on Michele, he knew she was dead. Her face was blanched, her chest mottled with discoloration. Blood had begun to pool in the lower parts of her body, causing blotchy purple bruising known as lividity on her back and buttocks.

Van Wagoner skimmed the paramedic report, questions flying through his mind. What had caused her heart to stop? If she had been unconscious for only fifteen minutes, why were the revival efforts unable to produce any signs of life?

At fifty, Michele was fairly young, and she was healthy, with no known history of heart problems, chest pains, or shortness of breath, according to the medic's report. Between the medication, compressions, and ventilation, first responders should have been able to regain some sort of cardiac activity.

Because Michele had been unresponsive for such an extensive period by the time she reached the hospital, the emergency room doctor knew resuscitation efforts were likely futile. But Van Wagoner, an experienced physician in his fifties with a stern face framed by cropped gray hair, would exhaust every medical option in an attempt to revive Michele, as he would for any patient in her condition.

Shortly after Michele arrived, her husband traipsed through the trauma bay. Van Wagoner knew Dr. MacNeill as the director of a state-run facility for people with intellectual disabilities. Van Wagoner treated some of MacNeill's patients, and they spoke about twice a month.

Martin told Van Wagoner about his wife's plastic surgery and her prescriptions. Contrary to what Martin had told the first responders, he said she was taking just two prescriptions. "She was down to just one Percocet a day," he said. "And an antibiotic."

As the doctors and nurses worked to revive Michele, Martin roamed the corridors and paced around the nurses' station, causing a scene. The nurses watched as Martin put his hands on his head and screamed at no one in particular, "Why did she do this? I told her not to do this!" At one point, he stomped out of the room, kicked at the door, and threw a stack of papers. Security was called to monitor him.

In the trauma bay, nurses inserted an IV into Michele's left shin and taped a catheter to her forearm to administer medications. She was dosed with more epinephrine, calcium, and sodium bicarbonate.

Because her body was cold—her temperature had dropped to 96.26 degrees Fahrenheit—nurses used tepid fluid and a heated blanket called a Bair Hugger to try to warm her.

Since Michele had recently undergone a surgery, Van Wagoner considered whether she'd suffered a blood clot. The bluish pattern on her skin appeared consistent with a burst pulmonary embolism—a blood clot that travels to the lungs. Van Wagoner administered a medicine used to break up blood clots, called a tissue plasminogen activator.

Through all the procedures, the heart monitor continued to hum with a low, flat tone.

For thirty-eight minutes, hospital staff tried to resuscitate Michele. As the nurses slowly ceased working on his wife, Martin became hysterical. He approached Van Wagoner.

"I'll give you ten thousand dollars not to stop," he begged. "I'll give you all that I have if you just save her!"

Van Wagoner balked, astounded.

"It was the oddest request that I have ever had doing emergency resuscitative efforts," Van Wagoner said years later. "He offered me ten thousand dollars if I would not cease resuscitation efforts. He offered me ten grand! It put me in a tough spot."

Van Wagoner knew that Martin, as a physician, must have realized his wife was dead. In fifteen years of working in the ER, Van Wagoner had never heard such an unusual outburst, especially from a fellow doctor.

Van Wagoner didn't respond to the new widower. "I'm calling time of death," he said somberly, then turned and walked away.

Martin collapsed, sobbing.

Michele Marie MacNeill—former beauty queen, devoted wife, and loving mother of eight, including four adopted children—was pronounced dead at 1:03 P.M. on April 11, 2007.

Days after her passing, the Utah State medical examiner would declare Michele's death due to natural causes from a heart arrhythmia. It appeared that her passing was tragically inevitable.

But nothing in this case was as it seemed.

It would take six long years and the unrelenting dedication of Michele's children to solve the mystery of her death, unraveling a lifetime of duplicitous deceit, searing betrayal, and an unfathomably cruel murder.

Martin led a life of contradictions. While he portrayed himself as a loving husband, devoted father, and compassionate doctor, it was all a carefully concocted façade. In nearly thirty years of marriage, Michele never knew her husband.

Perhaps no one ever really knew the real Martin MacNeill.

2.

From the moment Martin entered their lives, Michele's family feared her life would end tragically. But for three long decades, they were forced to observe from a distance, silently bearing witness to her agonizingly slow descent toward death.

"We all knew in our family that it wasn't going to work out well for Michele," remembered her youngest sister, Linda Cluff. "There was nothing really we could do—no way to stop it."

It shouldn't have ended this way. Michele's life had begun with such promise.

Born on January 15, 1957, Michele Marie Somers was one of seven children of Milton and Helen Somers. She had three older brothers: Stephen, Richard, and Mick. And she had three sisters: Susan, Terry, and Linda.

The children were raised in Concord, California, a scenic suburb about thirty miles east of San Francisco in the shadows of Mount Diablo. Comprised of quiet, middle-class neighborhoods, Concord is the largest city in Contra Costa County. The Somers children ranged vastly in age. Helen had her first son, Stephen, when she was just seventeen. By the time Michele was born, some twenty years later, all of her brothers were grown men. Because of the gap in their ages, Michele wasn't as close with her brothers.

But she grew up tight with her three sisters. And her bond with her youngest sister, Linda Cluff, would endure throughout her life.

Helen was a stay-at-home mom, while Milton worked various sales jobs. Milton also struggled with alcoholism and wasn't active in his children's lives.

"He wasn't a good father—I hardly ever remember him being around," Linda recalled. "My mom pretty much raised us."

In addition, their maternal grandmother was very involved in the rearing of all seven children.

Despite her father's absence, Michele's childhood was mostly wholesome and carefree. She was an adorable girl with wide blue eyes and light blond hair. "She was like a princess," younger sister Terry Pearson remembered. "She was outgoing, very kind. She was very sweet to everybody that she came in contact with."

Although Terry described her as a princess, Michele was also a tomboy. Instead of playing with dolls, she rode bikes and pulled wagons with her sisters. Her siblings recall fond memories of her upbringing: piling on the couch with their mom to watch their favorite TV shows, munching on dill pickles from the grocery store, and playing with their dog Daisy's puppies.

Michele was a happy, sweet girl with a big heart and a generous spirit. Once she and her sisters secretly collected glass bottles for months, hauling them around in a red wagon, to raise money to buy their mother a brown teapot for hot chocolate. Decades later the pot remained in Helen's kitchen.

Michele was bright and had a love of learning. "I just remember how excited she was to turn five, to get to start kindergarten," older sister Susan Hare recalled. "That enthusiasm for school never left her. She adored school."

As she reached her teens, Michele blossomed into a stunningly gorgeous young woman. Standing at five foot seven, she was slender with a curvaceous figure. She had long blond hair, flawless ivory skin, small feminine features, and a perfect smile.

It seemed she led a charmed life. She was a straight-A student who played the violin and learned to speak French. She enjoyed theater, classical music, and the ballet.

"Out of everybody in our family, Michele had it made," Linda later said.

"She had everything going for her. She was super smart, happy, beautiful. Everyone liked her."

Helen raised her children to be devout Mormons, and Michele and her siblings grew up studying the gospel of the Church of Jesus Christ of Latter-day Saints. Michele spent much of her life at church, studying the Book of Mormon. She never used alcohol or drugs, which are forbidden in the church. At the end of a long day, she loved to relax in a hot bath, flipping through magazines.

She attended El Dorado Intermediate School and Concord High School. In high school she was a popular cheerleader who acted in school plays and was voted homecoming queen. For the homecoming dance she wore a long, lacy dress and white elbow-length gloves, her blond hair falling loose around her shoulders. She was crowned with a bejeweled tiara. A photo taken for the student paper was captioned, "Queen Michele reigned over her court."

Classmates remember Michele as soft-spoken, beautiful, and not at all pretentious. She went out of her way to be friendly and helpful. Everyone seemed to like her, especially the boys. She always had more guy friends than girlfriends, and had several suitors. During her senior year of high school she spent a semester abroad in Switzerland as a foreign exchange student. Shortly after returning, a smitten Swiss boy flew to California to see her.

There was a particular type of guy Michele favored. She was attracted to flashy guys with big personalities. Her sisters remember shaking their heads at her sometimes pretentious choice of partners. "She liked different types of guys—real dramatic types," Linda recalled.

In 1975, Michele graduated from high school. She planned to continue her education and had a desire to attend Brigham Young University, the famed private Mormon institution in Provo, Utah.

While contemplating college, she spent her late teens and early twenties working as a professional model and competing in beauty pageants—and was crowned Miss Concord in 1976. In her modeling photos she appeared sensual and sultry, her eyes lined with dark makeup, her hair wavy and feathered.

Around 1977, Helen and Milton divorced. After that, Milton didn't have much to do with his seven children. Milton would later remarry. Helen never would, instead devoting her later years to her children and grand-children.

Helen moved with her daughters to Mission Viejo, a suburban city in the Saddleback Valley in Orange County, California. Known for its tree-lined streets and picturesque neighborhoods, the city is largely residen-tial and is considered one of the largest master-planned communities in the country.

Michele was then twenty, and still lived at home. In Mission Viejo, Mi-chele became a fixture at the Mormon church, where as a young adult she was a member of the singles' ward, which hosted regular events facilitating opportunities for young, unmarried LDS members to meet.

One night in late 1977, she was attending one such event at church when a man approached her. He was tall and handsome with thick blond hair and icy gray eyes. He flashed a wide, charming smile and reached out his hand. "Hi. I'm Martin."

3

As Michele would soon discover, Martin was a peculiar young man with a mysterious past. Having grown up in the slums of New Jersey, Martin's background could not have been more different from Michele's. His early upbringing was bleak, consumed by extreme poverty, mental illness, abuse, alcoholism, and death.

Born on February 1, 1956, Martin Joseph MacNeill was one of six children born to Albert MacNeill and Lillian Woodie. He had two older brothers, Albert Jr. and Rufus Roy, and one younger brother, Scott. His sisters were Alice and Mary.

Their father, Albert Sr., a navy veteran, was twenty-three years older than Martin's mother. The couple married when Lillian was just a teenager. Albert Sr. was fifty-eight years old when Martin was born.

The children were raised in Camden, New Jersey, an impoverished, densely populated city located across from Philadelphia's Delaware River. Infamous for its high crime rate, Camden is considered one of the most dangerous cities in the country. Camden neighborhoods are blighted with crumbling asphalt streets, shuttered warehouses, and dilapidated apartment buildings, their broken windows boarded with plywood.

Martin would later describe his family as "the definition of dysfunctional."

His parents had violent arguments, often fueled by alcohol. They divorced when Martin was a boy. Following the split, Albert Sr. moved to Long Beach, a seaport city in Southern California.

Left in the care of their mother, the children lived in a cramped apartment. Martin would later say that Lillian turned to prostitution to support the children. Divided from where the children slept by nothing more than a sheet, she entertained clients as the children were forced to listen to the muffled grunts of sex, Martin claimed.

It is impossible to know exactly what went on inside the MacNeill household. By 2007, the year of Michele's passing, nearly every member of Martin's family would be dead, several the victims of suicide or drug abuse. Whatever occurred had left each of the children deeply scarred and suffering from various maladies.

In her early twenties, Martin's sister Alice MacNeill committed suicide by strangling herself.

Martin's oldest brother, Albert MacNeill Jr., was an alcoholic. He suffered a stroke and died in a nursing home on March 11, 2005, at the age of sixty-four.

Rufus Roy MacNeill became a heroin addict. He married and had children, but drugs eclipsed his family. On April 3, 1986, he was found dead of an apparent drug overdose inside his mother's bathroom in Camden.

Following a stint in the marines, Scott MacNeill married and had three children. He was employed as a maintenance worker at an apartment complex when he committed suicide on July 30, 2006, at the age of forty-five.

In the end, Mary MacNeill was the only one of Martin's siblings who seemed to sidestep the family's failings. After her parents' divorce, she moved to Mission Viejo, California, where she later married.

By his midteens, Martin had also developed a ruthless determination to escape Camden and make something of his life. Around then he moved to Long Beach to live with his father, who was in his seventies.

Years later, Martin would look back at the dysfunctions in his family with disgust. He considered his parents and siblings weak, pitiful, and pathetic. But Martin faced his own deep-seated issues.

Only his were more carefully concealed.

As a young man, Martin was handsome—tall and broad-shouldered with high cheekbones and a strong jaw supporting a prominent chin. Highly intelligent, he excelled in school and read voraciously, including classic literature and poetry. He enjoyed theater and acted in school plays.

Over the years, Martin developed a flamboyant, almost theatrically dramatic personality. He had a strange, stilted manner of speaking and used broad hand gestures in everyday conversation, as if he was delivering a monologue. Because of his eccentric personality, classmates called him "Martin the Martian."

Beneath the quirky behavior, Martin was also mentally unstable. His moods fluctuated wildly from manic episodes to bouts of paranoia and depression. When he became enraged, his cold glare was penetrating and terrifying.

As a teenager he was diagnosed with bipolar disorder. After his diagnosis, he became fascinated with understanding the human mind and began studying psychology and psychiatry. He developed a keen ability to read others, instantly discerning one's motives and weaknesses. He would use that ability to manipulate those around him.

In 1973, Martin enlisted in the army. He was just seventeen, but claimed he was eighteen. Martin's commanders and fellow recruits soon noticed his curious behavior. He was often insubordinate and got in trouble with commanders. He spoke of hearing voices urging him to kill and seemed deeply disturbed.

About two years into his service, Martin's commanders sent him for psychiatric testing. After a battery of tests and evaluations, psychiatrists deemed Martin a "latent schizophrenic" with "other mental and psychological infirmities." In 1975, at the age of nineteen, Martin was discharged from the army due to his mental illness. He applied for and was granted financial benefits through the Veterans Benefits Administration and also through Social Security.

Around this time, Martin was introduced to the Mormon religion through missionaries. Despite never having been particularly spiritual, he integrated himself in the LDS community, attending services at the local Mormon church. He even went on a mission to spread the Mormon message, a typical practice for young LDS members, especially males. But while missions usually last two years, Martin's term ended after just a few months. The other missionaries became fearful of Martin's mercurial moods and erratic behavior. It was determined that his mental issues were too severe to complete a mission. Martin flew back home, escorted on the plane by another missionary.

Despite his apparent mental illness, Martin had lofty goals and ambitions, including becoming a psychiatrist. He moved to Olympia, Washington, a bustling governmental hub located in the Pacific Northwest, encircled by historical landmarks and lush evergreen trees.

Martin enrolled at Saint Martin's University, a private Catholic college located in neighboring Lacey, Washington, where he studied psychology. Because he was able to transfer sixty-five educational credits he claimed from the army's extension program, he graduated from Saint Martin's in just two years, with degrees in psychology and sociology. He planned to continue his education and become a doctor.

After graduating in 1977, he moved to Mission Viejo, where his sister Mary was living. There, he attended the same Mormon church and was a member of the same singles' ward as Michele Somers.

Martin possessed a dangerous combination of intelligence and callous ambition. For such a brilliant but twisted mind as his, boredom was insufferable. The sheer monotony of life seemed so corrosive and thick, it drove him to extreme, risky behavior. Despite the consequences, he seemed intent on creating turmoil.

In the summer of 1977, he was watching an episode of the news program *60 Minutes* that included a story about check forgers and how they operated. He was fascinated with the simplicity of the scam and told friends he could execute the con with fewer risks. "I could do it better," he said.

For reasons even he would later consider inexplicable, Martin decided to commit check fraud. Selecting a random name from the county recorder's records, he hired a friend to go to the Office of Vital Records and obtain a copy of that individual's birth certificate by swearing to be that man's father.

Using the birth certificate, Martin went to the DMV and was able to obtain a temporary driver's license, which he used to open a checking account. He deposited fifty dollars and received a set of blank checks.

On Labor Day weekend in 1977, when he knew the banks were closed, Martin used the checks and phony license during a three-day shopping spree. Dressed in designer slacks and a collared shirt, he brashly strolled into fourteen different stores, spending thousands of dollars on extravagant purchases including furniture, appliances, jewelry, and clothing.

Business owners and sales clerks would later remember him as affluent-looking, smooth, confident, and not at all nervous. Martin purchased diamond rings, watches, couches, chairs, a grandfather clock, a refrigerator, TVs, bicycles, car tires, sixty pairs of socks, two dozen pairs of shoes, a wardrobe of clothing, and even a year's supply of chocolate-covered cherries. By the time a store employee became suspicious, he had spent about thirty-five thousand dollars. The employee alerted police, and Martin was arrested and charged with fourteen felonies.

After consulting with a lawyer, at first Martin pled not guilty by reason of insanity, based on his previous diagnosis of schizophrenia. As part of his defense he was evaluated by two court-appointed psychiatrists. He tried to explain why he felt compelled to attempt the scam. "I don't know why I did it," Martin told one psychiatrist. "I didn't want the stuff. I didn't need the stuff."

Martin also spoke of his homicidal urges and the voices in his head. While the psychiatrists believed he was deeply damaged, they deemed him mentally fit to stand trial. "The patient has gotten into trouble with the authorities due to his desire to kill people at the command of voices," a psychiatric report stated.

The case was prosecuted by the then assistant district attorney of Orange County, Gary Ryan, who remembered the young delinquent as intelligent and full of potential. "He was bright and he was a con," Ryan explained. "He should have been a success. He had all the talent in the world."

As Martin fought the charges, he continued to go to church, and he confided his legal troubles to a bishop. Throughout the fall of 1977, he attended church-sponsored activities for young single Mormons, where he first caught a glimpse of Michele. Confident in his approach, Martin asked her on a date and she said yes.

Just a few months later, Michele Somers would become his bride.

4.

Martin's initial lust for the young beauty queen flourished into a domineering desire. He seemed to love Michele with a selfish intensity—he wanted to possess her.

Shortly after they first met, he began to govern every aspect of her life. In the beginning, Michele was smitten with her handsome, ambitious, and extraordinarily attentive new boyfriend. Their relationship was passionate and exciting.

But Michele also had doubts about Martin. At times his controlling manner seemed to frighten her. After one of their dates, she expressed her concerns to her sisters. "I don't know about Martin," she said, shaking her head.

On one occasion, Martin and Michele were arguing in his car when she suggested they break up. Suddenly, Martin grew frantic. From the center console of his car, he retrieved a pistol and placed it against his temple, as Michele would later tell her sisters.

"I can't live without you," Martin screamed at Michele. He cocked the weapon, his finger on the trigger. "If you leave me I'll kill myself." After several minutes, Michele convinced him to set the gun aside, and they continued dating.

But the stress of their dramatic relationship seemed to weigh heavily on

Michele. Over the course of their courtship, she lost weight and seemed fraught with worry. Reflecting back, Linda Cluff wondered what Martin must have said to convince Michele not to leave him. "There were fights and she couldn't take it. You could see the stress in her face," Linda recalled. "I don't know what happened. Her whole world changed in a few months after meeting him."

Maybe Michele mistook Martin's obsession for love. Or perhaps he used her compassion against her. During their relationship, Martin told stories of his traumatic childhood, claiming his mother was a prostitute. Michele's tender heart seemed touched by the wounded young man with the tragic past.

Soon after they met, Martin made plans to introduce Michele to his then seventy-nine-year-old father in Long Beach. On Halloween 1977, Martin and Michele were attending a play when suddenly he claimed to experience a dark foreboding. "I feel like something happened to my dad," he said to Michele.

The next day, November 1, Martin went to his father's house and knocked on the front door, but there was no reply. Finding a key, he entered the home. Inside he discovered Albert MacNeill Sr. dead. When he later informed Michele of his father's passing, she was convinced her boyfriend had experienced an astonishing premonition of death.

Albert MacNeill Sr.'s death was ruled natural, relating to age and health problems. Martin seemed devastated, and Michele was sympathetic. He collected a few thousand dollars from his father's insurance policy—money he desperately needed due to his impending legal troubles from the check fraud.

Soon it seemed Michele had fallen deeply in love. But while she had strong feelings for Martin, her friends and family were far from impressed. Once the couple had become serious, Michele brought her boyfriend home to meet her mom and siblings. Martin strolled brashly through the front door, pausing to admire his reflection in the mirror hanging on the wall. He spoke haughtily of his own educational background and career ambitions. He seemed cold, disingenuous, rude, and arrogant. Helen had a bad feeling about Martin, and Michele's siblings believed there was something off about his demeanor. The more time Martin spent with Michele, the more her family grew concerned.

"I thought he was just a big actor—he just gave me the creeps," Linda Cluff said years later. "He was self-absorbed. It became more and more apparent each time I saw him that he believed he was more superior than anyone else and he thought very highly of himself."

Weeks later the Somerses' bishop came to the house to warn Helen about her daughter's blossoming romance with Martin. "I can't tell you why exactly," the bishop said. "But there are some things in his background that are concerning."

Around this time Martin confessed to Michele about his arrest for check fraud. While she seemed worried, Martin simply shrugged. "It's no big deal," he insisted. "It was just a dumb mistake I made in the past."

When Michele spoke to her family about the arrest, they tried to convince her to end it with Martin. But Michele defended her boyfriend. "If you only knew about his childhood," she said.

By the time anyone in Michele's life learned the true extent of the criminal charges, she would already be his wife.

Over the course of their relationship, Martin tried to isolate Michele from her family and friends. He had a way of twisting situations to paint her family as the villains. During one argument at the Somerses' home, Martin turned to Michele, pointing at her mom and sisters. "Look at them, Michele. They're crazy."

As Michele's friends watched her slip further into Martin's grasp, they were troubled as well. "We were all very concerned for Michele," childhood friend Cynthia Crosby Woods explained. "She very much loved Martin but she was very much dominated and very much controlled by Martin."

But despite the concerns of her loved ones, just a few months after they met, Martin and Michele were wed. On February 21, 1978—a Tuesday—they went to the justice of the peace and eloped.

For a while Michele's mom and siblings had no idea about the marriage.

Weeks later, Martin came to the Somerses' home with the intent of collecting Michele and her things, to move her into his apartment, Linda remembered. Helen protested, a blowup ensued, and the police were called. As Martin frantically grabbed Michele's possessions, he sneered. "It's too late, we're already married!"

Helen was distraught.

Soon after, Helen spotted a newspaper article in the *Orange County Register* with the headline: BRILLIANT FORGERY SPREE INSPIRED BY TV. Scanning the article, she realized it was about Martin. Her new son-in-law was facing fourteen felony counts for forging over thirty-five-thousand dollars' worth of checks.

Compelled to investigate, Helen drove to the courthouse and obtained all the records related to Martin's prosecution, including two psychological evaluations. She was horrified to learn that Martin was a diagnosed schizophrenic and heard voices urging him to kill. "I wouldn't be surprised if he killed her someday," Helen told two of her daughters.

Helen tried to speak with Michele about her findings. But now that she was married, Michele was determined to make it work with Martin.

"We have no idea how or what he said to explain everything to her, but we just know whatever we said made her draw further from us and closer to him," Linda recalled. "There was no talking to her. He had a hold on her. There was nothing we could do."

Around that time Helen discovered something unusual in her car. Martin had recently borrowed her vehicle and he had left his briefcase in the trunk, which Helen discovered while loading groceries. Helen peaked inside the briefcase and found blank stationery and an official seal from Saint Martin's University. Helen knew it was the college Martin had attended, and it struck her as odd. She showed everything to Linda, who made an impression of the seal. Helen added the seal to her collection of news clips, court documents, and psychological evaluations.

"I want to keep ahold of these because I just have a feeling we may need them someday," Helen told her daughters. There would be no way she could have known then how important that evidence would eventually become, but on an incredible hunch, she would store those documents for three decades.

Fearful of losing their relationship with Michele, the Somers family made an attempt to embrace Martin. "It was from that point on that we just had to move forward to keep a relationship with Michele," Linda later said. "We, as Michele's family, tried our hardest to accept Martin. What else could we do? We had to deal with the devil, as we saw him, or lose what we had left of a relationship with Michele."

But while Michele's family tried to make amends, Martin only seemed to widen the rift. The Somerses watched helplessly as Michele drifted farther away from her family.

Facing years behind bars for forgery, theft, and fraud, Martin took a plea and was sentenced to 180 days in jail and three years of felony probation. Four months after tying the knot, he served the six-month sentence in a California jail. He used the money he had collected from his father's insurance policy and his army benefits to pay for expenses while he was incarcerated.

Once released, he reunited with his wife and they moved into an apartment in Hollywood.

After serving his time in prison, Martin seemed intent on changing his life. Whatever mental illness had driven him from the military and Mormon missionary work was suddenly no longer an issue. The disturbing voices in his head seemed to lower to a whisper and then, quite curiously, go silent.

5.

Martin sat at his wife's bedside as she rested in the delivery room of a hospital in California. She wore a sleeveless white gown, her feathered blond hair cascading around her shoulders. In her arms she cradled a baby bundled in a blanket. As she glanced down at her new daughter, a peaceful grin spread across Michele's face.

It was October 11, 1979, and Michele had just given birth to a girl she named Rachel Renee. Following Martin's stint in jail, the young couple had wasted no time starting their family. Just one month after her husband's release, Michele learned she was pregnant. She was twenty-two.

Once Rachel was born, Michele's world revolved around motherhood. Over the next five years she would give birth to four children. By all accounts she was an exceptional mother. "Above all, her kids meant everything to her," her sister Susan recalled. "Her life pretty much circled around whatever they were involved in doing. That's what her days were really filled with . . . her children."

Meanwhile, Martin enrolled in medical school and began working toward a career as a doctor. He abandoned his plan of being a psychiatrist, aiming instead for a career as a physician. He pursued his degree through a little-known program launched in 1972 for American medical students attending foreign universities. The course of study requires students to complete four years of schooling at a foreign college, perform clinical work at American schools, and complete a residency. Before being licensed, students must pass the same exams and requirements as American-trained physicians. Thousands of doctors have become licensed through the program, most attending schools in Mexico.

At the age of twenty-three, Martin enrolled in a college in Guadalajara, Mexico, known as the Universidad Autónoma de Guadalajara School of Medicine.

In early 1980, Martin, Michele, and baby Rachel briefly moved to Mexico. After just one semester, however, Martin left the school for reasons unknown. The family returned to California, where they lived in Walnut, an affluent suburban city in eastern Los Angeles County.

Martin transferred his credits from Mexico to the College of Osteopathic Medicine of the Pacific in Pomona, California. The school was later renamed Western University of Health Sciences. For the next three years, Martin studied osteopathic medicine, a holistic field focusing on the musculoskeletal system and based on the principle that a person's health is reliant on the skeleton, muscles, and ligaments functioning together.

Meanwhile, the MacNeill family grew. The couple's second daughter, Vanessa Marie, was born on September 16, 1981. Fourteen months later, on November 19, 1982, Alexis Michele came along.

In 1983, Martin graduated from medical school and was licensed as an osteopathic surgeon in California. More than a year later, Martin and Michele's only son, Damian Alexander, was born on January 31, 1985.

Martin then landed a residency at a hospital in New York and moved his family of six to Flushing, a residential community in north-central Queens.

After completing his residency, the MacNeills settled in Utah. Martin was licensed as an osteopathic physician in Utah in 1987. And over the next twenty years Dr. Martin MacNeill, D.O., worked as a physician at hospitals and clinics across the state.

No one knew then that his entire career was based on lies.

———

From the pictures in their photo album, the MacNeills appear to be the perfect, wholesome Mormon family.

In one picture the children are piled on the couch with their parents, the girls wearing frilly dresses and bows in their hair. Michele holds baby Damian on her lap. Martin, wearing surgical scrubs and oversized eyeglasses, has one arm draped around his wife.

In another photo, the family is huddled in front of a fishing boat during an excursion at the lake. Michele is surrounded by her toddlers, her hair blowing in the wind.

A Christmas portrait one year shows the children posed together in front of a pile of tattered wrapping paper and shiny new toys. Rachel's arms are wrapped around her sisters, who are clad in matching red pajamas. In the middle, a beaming Damian has donned a tiny Santa hat.

There were birthday parties and family vacations. Dance recitals and backyard barbecues. As they were growing up, the MacNeill children say, their life seemed truly blessed. "I had a wonderful childhood," Alexis remembered. "My mom was always there and just the best person."

The girls remember their upbringing as idyllic. Both parents were warm, affectionate, and loving, they say. Michele was the heart and soul of the family. And despite working long hours as a doctor, Martin was a doting father who was very active in their lives.

Rachel, who shared her father's love of books, grew up closest to Martin. "I adored him," Rachel recalled. "We were very much a devout Mormon family. I thought of my parents as having the ultimate love story."

As a girl, Alexis had ambitions of following in her father's footsteps and becoming a doctor. Each year on her birthday, Martin brought his daughter with him for the day to whichever hospital or clinic he was working in. As an adult, Alexis would pursue a career in medicine.

"I had a very close relationship with my father. I kind of tagged along with him a lot at work," Alexis would testify years later in court. "He was someone I loved and respected and relied on, and someone I always wanted to be proud of me."

While her father was a role model, Alexis was most connected to her mother, whom she considered to be her best friend. "I was always around her. She was kind of like my superhero and I tried to be her sidekick," Alexis remembered. "She was someone that I adored. She confided in me a lot. I did the same with her. She was my mom."

Church was at the center of the MacNeills' life. In each city in which they lived, they were actively involved in the local LDS community.

While Martin had a tendency to come across as brash and egotistical, he was also a well-respected professional and was considered a pillar in the Mormon community. He taught Sunday school and acted in church plays, once cast in the role of Jesus. While living in California, he had also served as bishop for a small LDS congregation. In the LDS church, bishops preside over worship services and are called to serve from among members of their congregation, without pay, for a term of four to seven years.

For Mormons, marriage is sacred, and is a prerequisite for the highest degree of being in the afterlife. Beyond a legal marriage, Mormons believe in a divine union known as a celestial marriage, which endures beyond the grave. To seal their love for all of eternity, Martin and Michele were wed in a Mormon temple in a ceremony known as a sealing. The MacNeill children were also each baptized into the faith.

Each Sunday, Martin led the children into the church. For services, Michele dressed the girls in lacy pink and purple dresses, their hair tied with ribbons. Damian wore tiny suits with suspenders and bow ties. Martin stood at the center of his brood, chest puffed out, bursting with pride.

Church congregants often commented on how perfect the family seemed. "He'd walk into church, he'd march in and line up his children, who were perfectly dressed," recalled a family friend. "Everybody had to be perfect. They'd even hold their bodies and heads like [they were] marching in. Everything had to be just so."

As Martin's career took off, he worked at various hospitals and clinics across Utah. In 1988, he treated patients at an emergency room in Blanding, Utah, a small city flanked by two Native American reservations. After a short stint at the hospital, Martin took a part-time job at Brigham Young University. Martin worked as a physician at the college's health center, treating students and faculty for a variety of ailments. At the same time, he enrolled at BYU's law school, where he pursued a law degree.

In 1990, he graduated from law school, although he never passed the bar or practiced as an attorney. That year he took a director position working in medical law and moved his family to Washington, where they lived in Friday Harbor, a quaint town located on the east side of the San Juan Islands, only accessible by plane or ferry.

Lived on SJI in 1988

The MacNeills were there less than a year before returning to Utah, where Martin found full-time work as a physician at BYU's health center. Over the years he also took various side jobs in the medical field to earn extra money.

In addition, Martin acted as the family's primary care physician, writing prescriptions if the children were sick. "We never went to any other doctor growing up," Alexis later said. "I don't remember going to any doctor. It was always my dad."

While Martin worked long hours as a doctor, Michele was a homemaker who kept busy volunteering and participating in after-school programs with her children. Because of her lifetime love of the ballet and classical music, she enrolled the children in dance classes at a ballet studio called the Petite Neat Academy in American Fork, a city at the foot of Mount Timpanogos in the Wasatch Range, north of Utah Lake. Their ballet teacher, Jacqueline Colledge, trained Rachel, Vanessa, Alexis, and even Damian to dance, and she would be part of the MacNeills' lives for twenty years. For performances, Michele volunteered to sew costumes, create props, and prepare meals. While their relationship started out as business, over the years Michele and Jacqueline became the best of friends.

Eventually Jacqueline introduced Michele to the Utah Regional Ballet, a professional ballet company that performs around the world. Because of her knowledge of ballet and her eloquent public speaking skills, Michele became a spokesperson for the arts in Utah. She also served as president of the guild boards before becoming a member of the board of directors of the Utah Regional Ballet.

"She had wonderful ideas," remembered Jacqueline, a full-figured woman in her fifties with olive skin and shoulder-length black hair. "She wasn't afraid at all to stand for something she believed was a good direction for the company to go."

Martin also pursued his love of the fine arts throughout his adult life.

Over the years he performed in community theater, acting in a number of plays and musicals. With his booming voice and flair for the dramatic, he was a natural thespian.

As time would prove, Martin was, indeed, a talented actor.

In 1993, the MacNeill family settled in Salem, a small suburb known as "the city of peace" on the south end of Utah County in the Provo-Orem metro area. They purchased a four-thousand-square-foot house at 15 East Center Street. Built in the early 1900s, the six-bedroom, two-bathroom home was painted beige and brown, with custom molded woodwork and a porch overlooking the grassy front yard.

By then, several members of the Somers family had also settled in Utah, including Michele's mother, Helen. Her youngest sister, Linda Cluff, who had since married and had children of her own, lived in nearby American Fork, while Michele's older brother Richard Somers had settled with his family in Salt Lake. Sadly, Richard passed away at the age of fifty-two on October 25, 1994, after a long battle with cancer. He left behind a wife and two daughters.

A few years later, Michele's estranged father, Milton, also died of natural causes.

Despite the Somerses' attempts to repair their acrimonious relationship with Martin, he remained distant. While Martin and Michele didn't often see her family in California, Linda was often around the couple. When Linda divorced her first husband, she and her two children, Ryan and Jill, lived for a period in the MacNeill home. Linda, who was slender and pretty with long, blond hair and big blue eyes, later remarried and had another son, Adam.

Though Linda remained close with her sister, the rest of Michele's family became further alienated from the MacNeills when Martin accused one of her relatives of molesting Damian. The Somerses believed it was an outlandish lie and just another way of turning Michele against them.

Martin seemed to despise Michele's family. Later he would claim that he never felt accepted by the clan and thought they were always judging him. Linda, however, believed the conflict existed because the Somers family knew Martin's true character. "He was always really standoffish," Linda later said. "He hated us because we knew all of his secrets."

When the MacNeills intermittently attended get-togethers with the Somers family, Martin would inevitably create a scene and storm out of the celebration. "Michele, let's get out of here," Martin would pronounce. "Children, we are leaving!"

"We'd go to family gatherings and Martin would act all superior," Linda recalled. "Meanwhile, the kids would be crying; he would be acting like a lunatic. It was really weird."

In December 1998, the MacNeill family moved to Orem, the fifth-largest city in Utah. About forty-five miles south of Salt Lake City, Orem is a major metropolis in the northern-central part of the state. The conservative city has a high Mormon population and has been ranked one of the best places in the country to raise a family.

The MacNeills purchased a sprawling estate at 19 West 620 South, located at the end of a cul-de-sac in a neighborhood known as Stonewood. The six-bedroom, eight-bathroom, eleven-thousand-square-foot home was built in 1994. Michele, who always had a knack for design, decorated the home with warm earth tones, dark wood furnishings, and antique fixtures. Once complete, the house looked like something out of a catalog.

The MacNeills quickly made friends in their new neighborhood. One such friend was Lani Swallow, a Mormon mother with a full face and long, dark hair, who had a son close in age to Damian. "Damian and my son bonded. They were the two new boys in the neighborhood," Lani later said. "Whenever I needed to plan things with Michele, I would often be at her house doing that, and they would roughhouse and play."

The MacNeills became prominent figures at the Mormon church in Orem. Michele regularly volunteered her time and always seemed willing to help out anyone in need. Church friends described her as one of the most kind, generous, loving people they had ever met.

In 2000, Michele was called to serve as president of her church's Relief Society, a philanthropic and educational organization for women in the LDS church. Each congregation in the church includes a Relief Society, and all female Latter-day Saints over the age of eighteen are members of the organization. Every Sunday the Relief Society hosted meetings consisting of various kinds of lessons. As president of her congregation's chapter, Michele held one of the highest-ranking callings for women in the church's hierarchy. As part of the position, she appointed two other female congregants as counselors: Loreen Thompson and Cheryl Radmall.

Cheryl was slender with shoulder-length golden hair. Loreen had short graying hair, deep-set eyes, and olive skin. Karen Klinger, who was a thin brunette, served as the Relief Society's secretary. As the women worked together and met for lunchtime planning meetings, a close friendship blossomed. Two and a half years later, when they were released from their commitments, the four women remained the best of friends. And when Karen was later diagnosed with breast and uterine cancer, the other women rallied around her.

In the summer of 2002, Karen was going through one of her final surgeries to remove the uterine cancer, after which she planned to undergo several rounds of intensive chemotherapy. The night before the operation she was nervous, and Cheryl, Loreen, and Michele wanted to be there for their friend.

They took her to see the film *Divine Secrets of the Ya-Ya Sisterhood,* a movie based on the 1996 novel about four women with an enduring friendship that lasts decades. "And from that point on, Michele called us the 'Ya-Ya Sisters,'" Loreen recalled. "There were four of us and we had a very tight, close relationship. . . . It was unusual because we were all very different, but we developed a strong bond very quickly."

Although life eventually took Michele and the other women in different directions, their friendship would endure until the day of Michele's death.

In 2000, Martin was appointed by Mike Leavitt, governor of Utah at the time, to a prestigious position as the medical director of the Utah State Developmental Center.

Located about fifteen minutes from Orem, on the outskirts of American Fork, the center provides twenty-four-hour supervised care for 265 mentally disabled individuals. The facility was established in 1932 and operates under the Utah Department of Human Services.

As the medical services director, Martin was in charge of health care for the residents. He had a private office at the Developmental Center's medical services building and oversaw a team of doctors and nurses. He served a dual role, working in administration in addition to his duties practicing in urgent care. Heavily involved at the job, Martin often arrived early, stayed late, and worked weekends. For several seasons he also played on the company softball team.

Although working with mentally disabled patients can be stressful, Martin provided treatment with cool, detached professionalism. Amongst his colleagues, however, Martin was considered demanding and difficult. Coworkers described him as intimidating and a bully with a profound lack of medical skills. He terrorized vulnerable medical residents, and his management tactics chased competent nurses and doctors away from the facility.

Nurse practitioner Steven Nickelson worked closely with Martin for seven years. "He has a very strong personality," remembered Nickelson, a slight man with thinning red hair. "I didn't give him reason to be defensive, but I knew that was something I had to manage—swimming through rough waters. I just approach it differently."

Over the years, as Martin grew more successful and accomplished, his already engorged ego swelled. Associates and former friends described him as a braggart and a brute who dominated every conversation. In social situations he was known to be openly condescending, contemptuous, and unapproachable. Michele's friends were often fearful to call the house because of concerns that Martin might answer the phone.

As Martin's children grew older, they realized that he was not a typical father. Embarrassed by his pompous outbursts, his daughters seemed to frequently be apologizing for their dad and making excuses for his moods. "I was constantly trying to explain my father," Alexis said years later. "He thought anyone that was not at his educational stature was very beneath him. He treated them very poorly."

The children knew Martin was eccentric, with a dry wit and macabre sense of humor. He told his family that right after medical school he had worked with infamous pathologist Dr. Jack Kevorkian, known as "Dr. Death" for his physician-assisted suicides, his daughters recalled. "He didn't start killing people until after I worked with him," Martin joked.

Even so, the girls felt they knew their father's true character. While he could put on an air of superiority, at home he seemed warm and earnest. They all believed their family was normal and that their dad loved their mom.

"I thought he was rough around the edges but sweet," Alexis recalled. "When he would come home, he was a completely different person. So we thought we knew the real person."

6.

On the deck of a cruise ship, Martin leaned close to his wife, wrapped his arm around her shoulder, and squeezed affectionately. He was dressed in a dark suit and checkered bow tie, a jubilant grin spread across his face. Michele wore a silk gown and a triple string of pearls, her hair elegantly swept to the side.

Michele turned her gaze to the camera lens, her smile soft and subdued, as the flash brightened the area. They were a portrait of staid sophistication—the reputable doctor and his lovely wife. The MacNeills seemed to have it all: wealth, education, class, and beauty. Vacations were extravagant: cruises and beach trips. Parked in their garages were luxury cars including BMWs and Jaguars.

Their home in Orem was grand, with dark hardwood floors, soaring ceilings, tall picture windows, and a fireplace accented with green marble. The space had an elegant quality—heavy mahogany bookcases, antique table lamps, couches covered in muted fabrics, oil paintings and family photos hanging on the beige walls.

A sense of hushed class—no discernible signs of trouble. Just a lingering hint of gloom, so subtle it existed only in the corners of the rooms, hiding beneath the accent rugs, hissing behind the curtains.

Michele spackled and painted over any flaws in the family with such expert precision that they were almost imperceptible. No one could tell that secrets and lies infiltrated every aspect of the family's existence. But the absence of overt turmoil spoke to its own troubles too dangerous to acknowledge. Any hint of distress was kept behind bedroom doors. Late-night disagreements were heard only as muffled voices pulsing through the walls of the master bedroom.

There were certain rules the children were expected to follow. They were to do well in school, value education, go to church, respect their elders, and above all, not embarrass the family.

The outward appearance of perfection—the refined images captured in the framed family photos—was perhaps more important than the unsettling truth. Churning behind the deceptive smile was a Martin MacNeill the family did not know existed.

"It wasn't a normal family," remembered Linda Cluff. "They were so used to portraying what they wanted people to believe. Their house was crazy. There would be these great big fights. But then they'd all walk out the door and they'd be like perfect."

When a new neighbor or friend came by the house, Martin always made an entrance and provided a tour of his stately home. Then he would quickly disappear into the confines of his office.

While Martin appeared to be a loving, attentive father, his connection with the children seemed more like ownership. They were an extension of his carefully cultivated image, not individuals. He cared less about his family than about guarding his reputation. And if his children challenged that status, he excluded them from family functions and rarely spoke of them.

Those close to the family knew something was very wrong.

In his marriage Martin was a dictator who dominated Michele. She did nothing unless he approved and wasn't even allowed to speak to neighbors without his permission. Their arguments were dramatic and sometimes turned ugly.

If Michele was bothered by the problems in her marriage, she didn't confide in friends. Instead, she bore the burden in silence. When Linda tried to speak with her sister about any problems, Michele acted as if everything was fine. "You knew things were going on in the house because you'd hear arguments. But she'd never say anything," Linda said years later. "It was a very secretive family."

It's impossible to know how much Michele understood about her husband's true character. But over the course of their nearly thirty-year marriage, she caught glimpses of the stranger she'd married. At times the mask he wore inevitably slipped.

Throughout his medical career, Martin always seemed to be leaving jobs, often abruptly. His explanations were inconsistent, which seemed to bother Michele. And there was something else deeply unsettling. Pornography is forbidden in the Mormon faith, and Michele found the act of viewing explicit images to be a betrayal. Periodically over the years, however, she caught Martin looking at X-rated material. They had several nasty fights, but every time it seemed he might lose Michele, Martin threatened to commit suicide.

The couple's most vicious confrontation took place in August of 2000. Michele caught Martin looking at pornography, and another nasty argument ensued. Shrieking irately, Martin picked up a butcher knife. He threatened to kill his wife and then himself. As he madly waved the knife, Damian, who was fifteen at the time, confronted his father. Damian lunged at Martin, wrestled him to the ground, and pried the knife from his hands.

A neighbor heard the screams and called the police. When officers arrived, Michele said she didn't want to press charges, but a police report was filed. Martin was placed on a temporary psychiatric hold and spent the night at Wasatch Mental Health in Provo.

Over the years there were dozens of similar fights. But each time, Michele forgave her husband and he promised to change.

Such instances hinted at much deeper problems in the marriage.

Unbeknownst to Michele, Martin was a serial philanderer who engaged in numerous affairs. He frequently used his position as a doctor to prey on his female patients. Martin also had liaisons with women he met at church, online, and at his job. He chose vulnerable partners—new divorcées and single mothers.

After Michele's death, several women would come forward with disturbing allegations. One woman from church claimed Martin propositioned her over the Internet. A man said that in the eighties he had witnessed Martin raping a girl.

In 1996, while working at the BYU health center, Martin had an affair with one of his patients, a forty-two-year-old recently divorced mother of eight named Karen Wright. When Karen first met Martin, he was seductive and charming, bragging about his dual degrees and luxury cars. He made her feel beautiful and desired, and explained that he didn't have a good sex life with his wife. Soon they engaged in an affair, once having sex in his office. The encounters left Karen racked with guilt.

"He manipulated me," Karen later said. "But he managed to do it in a seductive way. I didn't tell anyone because I thought it was my fault. I think he knew I wouldn't report it. That's why he made me think I was so attractive."

Over the years, Martin's reckless and irresponsible behavior often got him in trouble. His entire medical career was punctuated with disturbing allegations of sexual assault, misconduct, and misdiagnoses. In 1990, Martin was accused of Medicaid fraud after he tried to bill for treatment and services that were never actually performed. He pled no contest and was banned from Medicaid billing for twelve years.

Four years later, he was accused of having sex with one of his patients at BYU. Around that time the MacNeill children remember a violent altercation between their parents where Martin once again threatened to kill himself.

In 1998, shortly after purchasing the Orem house, Martin abruptly resigned from the BYU health center following a long list of complaints filed against him. He briefly returned to BYU in 1999 for three months but left again after more unseemly allegations surfaced.

At each hospital and clinic that employed him, Martin faced troubles, but he always found another job as a physician, another group of unsuspecting patients who placed their trust in him. Fellow doctors and colleagues grew wary of Martin. But no one ever suspected his most sinister and deepseated secret.

It was only after his wife's death that his lies would be exposed.

7.

Being raised in a household stewing in such insidious treachery scarred each of the MacNeill children in various ways. Once they became adults, their lives took very different directions.

By 2000, Martin and Michele's firstborn, Rachel, was twenty-one. She grew up slender and statuesque, with dark brown hair that contrasted with her alabaster complexion. She had Michele's wide, warm eyes and Martin's high cheekbones and angular chin. Unfortunately, she also inherited her father's mental illness and was diagnosed as bipolar. At times she was exuberant and energetic; on other occasions she sank into depression.

Shortly after graduating high school, Rachel married in the church. Martin and Michele paid for the ceremony, reception, and honeymoon. But the marriage didn't last, and Rachel soon divorced. She spent her twenties drifting from job to job, moving around the country. She lived twice in Seattle, Washington, before moving to California, where she wed a second time.

After her second marriage also ended in divorce, Rachel returned to Utah, where she rented an apartment in Salt Lake City, which Michele decorated and furnished. She returned to school, where she studied to be a dental hygienist. At the time of her mother's passing, she was working at a dentist's office.

Vanessa MacNeill's life was fraught with more serious problems. Out of all the MacNeill children, their second daughter most closely resembled her mother. She was slim and tan with long blond hair, green eyes, a small nose, and pouty lips. As a teen she was troubled, and she suffered from anxiety. She abused drugs and alcohol and engaged in premarital sex. In the summer of 2000, at the age of eighteen, she discovered she was pregnant.

On March 25, 2001, Vanessa gave birth to a daughter named Ada. Given her troubles, she knew she wasn't ready to be a mom. Shortly after Ada's birth, Martin and Michele adopted their granddaughter and raised the girl as their own. Michele doted on Ada, spoiling her with dolls, toys, and a princess bed. All of the MacNeill children adored the little girl, and Alexis was particularly close with Ada.

After she'd given up custody of Ada, Vanessa's drug abuse escalated and her life spiraled downward. By 2005, she was a heroin addict. Michele, who adored Vanessa, spent years trying to get her daughter into drug treatment programs. Vanessa detoxed and had intermittent bouts of sobriety, but she inevitably relapsed. She rarely held a job for long, and months passed where she was essentially homeless and stayed with friends. Contemptuous of her drug abuse, Martin excluded Vanessa from the family. Privately, he fumed about her problems, calling her "an embarrassment."

At age twenty-six, Vanessa was living in an apartment in Bluffdale, twenty miles south of Salt Lake City, and attempting to turn her life around. Her mother's death would leave her shattered.

Of all the children, the MacNeills' youngest daughter, Alexis, seemed to possess the best traits of both her father and mother. Like Martin, she was wickedly intelligent, determined, and ambitious. Like her mom, she was generous, warm, kindhearted, and had a natural desire to help others. She blossomed into an attractive young woman with narrow brown eyes and a square face framed with straight, dark hair. Although she was the youngest of the MacNeills' biological daughters, she would become the most responsible and accomplished in the family. After high school, she set out to become a doctor.

Alexis attended Brigham Young University for her undergraduate degree, before moving to London to study medicine at the Imperial College of Science, Technology, and Medicine, where she received her master's. In 2006, she enrolled in medical school at Touro University Nevada College of Osteopathic Medicine. She rented an apartment in Henderson, Nevada, an affluent city in Clark County, about fifteen miles from Las Vegas.

As she navigated through her early twenties, Alexis remained extraordinarily close with her family and often spent weekends and school breaks at her parents' home in Utah. Alexis's bond was especially strong with her mother, whom she considered to be her best friend. They spoke several times a day and were so close Michele once commented that they must have been best friends in the "pre-existence." Their connection would endure beyond her mother's passing.

Damian MacNeill was perhaps the most disturbed of the children. Like his father and his sister Rachel, he was diagnosed as bipolar. But his bouts of depression seemed more severe. At times he disappeared from the world and sank into despair.

As a young man he was handsome, with shaggy dark brown hair, blue eyes, and a pointed chin. He was intelligent and funny with a wry sense of humor and a deep love of music and movies. After graduating high school, he went on a two-year mission to spread the Mormon message, which is considered a rite of passage for young Latter-day Saints. The church assigns each missionary a designated area in which to serve.

On the day Damian received the letter informing him of his assignment, he was in the front room of the house, surrounded by his family. After ripping open the envelope, he silently read the letter. He then threw back his head and jumped out of his chair.

"I'm going to Hiroshima." He danced. Alexis leapt toward her brother, squealing with delight, and threw her arms around him.

When he left for Japan, all of his sisters were in tears. Two years later, Damian returned to Utah and enrolled at Utah Valley University, intent on becoming an attorney.

In the spring of 2006, he began dating a beautiful young woman named Eileen Heng, also an aspiring attorney, who had long, silky black hair, full lips, and petite features. The MacNeill family embraced Eileen, and she was a frequent guest for Sunday dinners and social gatherings. As the only son, Damian remained closest with his father.

Their enigmatic bond would ultimately destroy Damian's life.

Once the MacNeill children were grown and had moved out of the Orem house, the place seemed empty. Martin and Michele were raising Ada. But Michele, who was accustomed to juggling a family of four children, found herself with much more free time. Having since undergone a hysterectomy, she was also facing the symptoms of early menopause and was taking prescription hormones. Martin and Michele were both in their midforties when they made the surprising choice to adopt three more girls in 2003.

While Michele always had a big heart and adored children, the decision confounded some family members. Never before had Michele expressed an interest in adoption. Years later, Linda would question what exactly had inspired the decision. Had Martin pressed for more children to consume Michele's time? Was the grand philanthropic move just another way for him to seem more impressive?

"She loved kids but her kids were grown up and out of the house," said a family friend. "I think he wanted her to be monopolized with kids, being busy taking them places. Because if everyone was out of the house it was just him and her. He couldn't live his separate life."

Regardless of the motivation, Michele began the adoption process, searching overseas in Ukraine. By 2003, Europe's largest country had become a popular destination for Americans wanting to adopt Caucasian children, where the waiting period was only about five months to one year. Ukrainian law requires orphans to be at least five years old before they are eligible for adoption by American parents, with exemptions made for children with special needs.

Orphanages in Ukraine are austere cement buildings, housing thousands of children in dreary conditions. Orphans are assigned daily chores, given one outfit to wear, and permitted to bathe just once a week. After touring the facilities, Martin and Michele selected three girls from two separate orphanages. As they went through the adoption process, the couple hired a translator named Yulia Shust, who would later come to play an un-usual role in the MacNeills' life story.

In 2003, Noelle, Giselle, and Elle became the newest members of the MacNeill family. The eldest, Noelle, was a thirteen-year-old waif of a girl with cropped dark hair. She had grown up in the same orphanage as Giselle, a diminutive twelve-year-old with a light complexion. Elle, age ten, had a heart-shaped face framed with light blond hair.

Michele truly adored her new daughters, dressing them in the same type of girly dresses as she had her other daughters. The girls attended Orem Elementary School, and Michele enrolled them all in ballet classes. "She told us we were her princesses," Elle said during her mother's funeral.

But it wasn't all bliss. After growing up abandoned, the girls faced dif-ficulty adjusting to their new lives. As the youngest, Elle had the smooth-est adjustment—she picked up English easily and did well in school—whereas Giselle could hardly write in English and had a pronounced Ukrainian accent. Noelle, however, was the most troubled and disconnected from the family.

For the first few months after the adoptions, there appeared no obvious signs of distress with the girls. Then, without warning, Noelle disappeared. Linda Cluff recalled visiting with Noelle at family gatherings. Then one day she was at the house when she noticed the girl was gone.

"Where's Noelle?" Linda asked.

"We couldn't deal with her," Linda was told. "We had to send her away."

Linda was shocked. "Everything was going fine. No one says 'we're hav-ing trouble.' And all of the sudden she sort of disappears," Linda recalled years later.

Noelle had been sent to a treatment facility in Michigan for children who suffer from reactive attachment disorder, a rare but serious condition in which a child lacks any attachment with caregivers. Eventually, Martin and Michele unraveled the adoption and Noelle became a ward of the state of Michigan. Years later, as an adult, Noelle would reach out to her siblings on Facebook and reconnect with the family. Michele, however, would never see Noelle again.

In 2004, shortly after Noelle departed the home, the MacNeills adopted another daughter from Ukraine. An adorable brunette, Sabrina was just seven when she and her sister were placed into an orphanage in the Eastern Ukraine city of Gorlovka—the same facility where Elle had lived. Growing up together, Sabrina and Elle had been close friends.

Around the time of Elle's adoption, another American woman had adopted Sabrina, then ten, and her younger sister. But once Sabrina had settled with the family in New York, it became clear to her that her new mother only wanted her five-year-old sister. Sabrina felt unwelcome and unloved.

In the summer of 2004, Sabrina traveled to Utah to visit her friend Elle. During her monthlong stay, Sabrina bonded with the MacNeills. When Sabrina told Martin and Michele of her life in New York, they decided to adopt her, reaching out to the girl's adoptive mother to complete the process.

The MacNeill family now consisted of Martin, Michele, Rachel, Vanessa, Alexis, Damian, Giselle, Elle, Sabrina, and Ada.

Sabrina blended easily into the MacNeill family, excelling in school and taking ballet with the other girls. After so many hardships, Sabrina's life with her new family was everything she had ever hoped for. "It was wonderful," Sabrina remembered. "I had always dreamed for a family like the MacNeills when I was first adopted. My mom was just wonderful. It was exactly what I dreamed of—just perfect."

While the adopted children loved Michele, they all recall Martin as being largely absent. While Martin had a connection with his biological kids, the adopted girls seemed more like window dressing or props on the stage of his life. "I saw him every once in a while," Sabrina said years later. "He worked a lot. He was gone all the time, but I saw him sometimes."

But while Sabrina and Elle said life with the MacNeills was happy, Giselle's recollections were more unsettling. She remembered Martin as cruel and malicious, and claimed the girls all feared him. Giselle said he once molested her while they were together in the living room alone. "He was touching me in weird places. I don't know what it was about me. He was always touching me," she explained with a thick Ukrainian accent. "I always felt weird."

Following the incident, Giselle retreated to her bedroom in the basement. She later spoke to Michele about the sexual assault, but her mother told her not to speak of it again. "You can't actually have this conversation with him right now," Michele told Giselle. "He's under a lot of stress."

For Giselle, it seemed like once Noelle was gone, all the tension in the MacNeill home transferred to her. "I felt like I was loved for a couple of months," Giselle would recall years later. "But then afterward I was more of a troubled girl and it was more that I felt weird about that whole family."

While both Sabrina and Elle enjoyed ballet, were straight-A students, and embraced the Mormon faith, Giselle never really fit in with the Mac-Neills. She didn't do well in school, hated ballet, and refused to take dance classes. And she expressed little interest in converting to the Mormon faith. Feeling like an outsider in the home, Giselle became further withdrawn from the family.

She was subsequently punished and forced to spend hours completing chores. "It was more happy, but miserable at the same time. I was more of a slave girl who always cleans up, always gets in trouble, always does something," she recalled. "I was one of the girls who was not part of the family. I was part of the side girl . . . I decided to back off just a little more because they never wanted to be around me. That's how I looked at it."

But perhaps Martin ostracized Giselle for more perverse reasons. While Sabrina and Elle were private and reserved, Giselle had a nasty habit of revealing family secrets. "The problem with Giselle is she told things," explained a family friend. "And you don't tell what goes on in that house. You have to keep the secrets."

8.

By 2005, a precipitous shift had occurred in the MacNeill marriage. While Martin had never remained faithful, he had always seemed intent on keeping Michele. But over time, he seemed to become weary with the life he had so meticulously constructed. Martin grew distant, contemptuous, and verbally abusive toward his wife. His mood swings were volatile and unpredictable—alternating from bitter and cruel to strangely kind and affectionate. At the end of each day, Michele never knew which version of her husband would be walking through the door.

Martin, meanwhile, continued to cheat on his wife. And in 2005, he had two sordid affairs with two very different women. One would steal his heart. The other may have learned his most monstrous secrets.

Anna Osborne Walthall was in her early forties, raising two young boys, and embroiled in a bitter divorce when she first met Dr. MacNeill. Voluptuous, with a round face framed with shoulder-length brown hair, Anna was outspoken and educated, with degrees in music and business. In 2005, she was living in Park City, Utah, and running a laser hair removal franchise in Salt Lake City called Sona MedSpa.

Utah law required a licensed physician to oversee operations of cosmetic medical facilities. And that March, Anna hired Martin as her medical director.

As they worked together, Anna opened up to Martin about the details of her imploding marriage. He offered support and legal advice, and eventually volunteered to assist as a liaison between Anna and her husband.

Soon an attraction developed, and Martin and Anna began a torrid sexual affair. After sex the couple would lie in bed, engaging in deep, intimate conversations. They discussed religion, ambitions, love, and family.

But most of the time, they spoke of death.

Martin's mind was more morbid than most, yet few ever saw the depths of his depravity. But for whatever reason, he seemed willing to confide in Anna. He told her of his lifelong struggle with homicidal urges. At times, he said, he surrendered to those demons.

He said he tried to kill for the first time when he was just eight years old, Anna later reported in court. It was 1964 and his mother, Lillian, had drunkenly passed out on the couch. Sorting through the cabinets, Martin gathered all the medication he could find. He grabbed a beer from the refrigerator and fed the pills into the can. Jostling his mother awake, he helped her raise her head, and put the can to her lips.

"I helped her sit up and drink it," Martin told Anna. "Then I watched as she stopped breathing."

Just as his mother's heart ceased beating, Martin's sister Mary came home and found Lillian unconscious. Mary called 911, ambulances arrived, and the paramedics revived her. Later, everyone, including Lillian herself, believed she had tried to commit suicide.

As Anna listened to the story, a chill ran down her spine. "Later, did you regret trying to kill her?"

"I regret there wasn't more medication in the house," he quipped. The casual amusement in his voice unnerved Anna.

Years later, Martin said he murdered his older brother, Anna testified.

Rufus Roy MacNeill was a drug addict who wasn't suicidal but cut his wrists for attention, Martin claimed. While Martin was visiting New Jersey, Rufus Roy called to say he had hurt himself and wanted to die. Martin went to their mother's place in Camden and found Rufus lying unconscious in the bathtub, with superficial cuts on his wrists. Stooping next to the tub, Martin told Anna, he dunked his brother's head underwater and held him there till he stopped struggling.

"Were you ever worried that you'd get caught?" Anna asked, sitting up in bed.

"No. No one would ask me about it." Martin shook his head. "It's not unusual for a cutter to drown because they lose enough blood that they don't have the strength to stay above water."

Although Anna was disturbed, she was also intrigued with the doctor's twisted mind. She both loved and feared Martin. As their dark sexual entanglement escalated, discussions of killing became more frequent. When Anna complained of her ex, Martin offered to murder him. He also mentioned a desire to kill his daughter Vanessa because he said her drug use had become a "family embarrassment," according to Anna. Once, during a violent sexual episode, Martin even proposed ending Anna's life to put an end to her woes.

Martin said that throughout his medical career, he had murdered several patients, Anna later testified. And he claimed to have published an anonymous article on mercy killings. The 1988 article published in the *Journal of the American Medical Association* is infamous in the medical community. Entitled "It's Over, Debbie," the piece, written by an unknown medical resident, recounts the treatment of a twenty-year-old woman dying of ovarian cancer. Because the patient was in pain and not responding to chemotherapy, the doctor gave her an overdose of morphine with the intent of ending her life.

"I injected the morphine intravenously and watched to see if my calculations on its effect would be correct. Within seconds her breathing slowed to a normal rate, her eyes closed, and her features softened as she seemed restful at last," the doctor wrote in the article. "With clocklike certainty, within four minutes, the breathing rate slowed even more, then became irregular, then ceased."

Throughout the summer of 2005, as Martin's affair with Anna grew more impassioned, his marriage further disintegrated.

In August, suspicious that he had been unfaithful, Michele searched her husband's computer and found pornography. They argued and Martin bitterly announced he regretted adopting their daughters. "I don't love you anymore," Martin told his wife. "I don't want to live here with you."

Weeks later, during a counseling session at church, Martin also confided to the bishop that he no longer loved his wife and adopted children.

Meanwhile, Anna was planning for a future with Michele's husband. Her MedSpa business was floundering, and she made arrangements to move to Oklahoma with her children. She wanted Martin to leave his wife and join her. In October, Anna's business went bankrupt and she closed the doors to MedSpa, angering customers who had purchased prepaid laser hair removal packages worth thousands of dollars.

Later, Anna was ambushed by a local television reporter doing a segment on the shuttered business. With tears in her eyes, Anna told the reporter she was broke but promised to somehow refund her customers' money.

As she prepared to move, Anna spent her last few weeks in Utah tangled beneath bedsheets with her lover. And they continued to discuss Martin's tales of murder and mercy killing.

Martin told Anna of his favorite method of murder: injecting a person with potassium to induce a heart attack. An injection of too much potassium is lethal and would quickly cause heart failure, Martin explained. But the chemical also occurs naturally in the human body, and when a person dies from a heart attack their potassium levels elevate. Because of this, he said, high potassium levels do not seem abnormal in an autopsy.

Martin said he would never get caught killing, but on the off chance he was arrested, he would never plead insanity.

"Why not?" Anna asked.

"Because." Martin's stare bored into Anna. "I always know exactly what I'm doing."

9.

Martin's stony gray eyes idly flitted across his computer screen. Trolling the Internet, he clicked through member profiles on a service connecting users with similar interests. A picture of a young brunette caught his attention. She was pretty, with a round face, high cheekbones, wide brown eyes, and pouty lips. Her screen name was "phoenixsheba." Under her interests she listed astrology, sphinxes, and, oddly, quantum physics.

Chuckling to himself about the woman's seemingly strange and diverse interests, he typed out a message. *What do you know about quantum physics?* Martin wrote, jokingly accusing her of trying to seem smarter than she was.

In a house forty miles away in Salt Lake City, the message popped up on the computer screen of a twenty-nine-year-old divorced nurse named Gypsy Jyll Willis. She sent a quick reply—a basic definition of quantum physics. *I have an interest in anything I can learn more about,* Gypsy added.

The message spurred a long online chat about their respective lives. Martin told the woman he was a thirty-nine-year-old married pharmaceutical representative named Joe.

For the next three weeks, they continued to send instant messages back and forth, and during the last week of November 2005, they met for lunch at a Thanksgiving Point restaurant.

When Martin approached Gypsy in the restaurant's parking lot, she was immediately impressed. With graying temples and fine wrinkles around his eyes, he looked much older than thirty-nine. Still, she was attracted to his handsome good looks, bright smile, and deep voice. Plus, the chemistry they had online carried over in person. "I was kind of taken aback, I guess. I was not expecting to feel so impressed and overwhelmed," Gypsy said years later. "His personality is very strong, he's really terrifically intelligent, very handsome, very tall, just great. In my mind he was the perfect combination of qualities."

Soon "Joe" confessed his name was actually Martin, and admitted he was a forty-nine-year-old doctor and lawyer. Although he was twenty years her senior, Gypsy was infatuated. "I thought he was amazing," Gypsy explained. "I thought, 'This is really an awesome person.'"

He was also married—a detail Martin was quite candid about. Martin also mentioned to Gypsy he was dating a few other women, although she didn't ask for details.

During one of their first dates, Martin spoke about his wife. "She's very beautiful—a former beauty queen," he said. "She's a great, very capable mom."

"He said he had the perfect life and the perfect wife," Gypsy recalled.

At that comment, Gypsy's brow had furrowed. "If your life is so perfect, what are you doing here?" she asked.

"Boredom." Martin shrugged. "Everything is so consistent and perfect and boring."

Gypsy realized why *she* was there—she was meant to be his excitement.

Throughout the latter part of 2005, Martin and Gypsy met in person several times and talked frequently online and through text messages.

Meanwhile, Martin also spoke with Anna, who was then living in Oklahoma. Anna pressed him often about leaving Michele. For a few weeks she even expected to hear that Martin's wife had died mysteriously, perhaps of a heart attack caused by an undiscovered potassium injection.

But with Gypsy in his life, Martin no longer seemed interested in Anna. Soon, he had ended their affair and ceased all contact. "I would never leave Michele," he told Anna.

When Anna realized it was over, she was hurt and angry. "I hate him. I hate him," she scribbled in her journal. "I want to hurt him."

Although they never spoke again, Martin haunted Anna. Her mind kept replaying their discussions of murder. Filled with dread, Anna saw her psychiatrist in January 2006.

"I had an affair with a serial killer," she said.

10.

Gypsy captivated Martin. The bored doctor, disenchanted with his perfect life, was bewitched by the much younger woman. For Gypsy, the romance was simply intoxicating.

By January 2006, their affair had grown sexual. They met for trysts at her apartment, in motel rooms in Orem, and in his office at the Utah State Developmental Center. They spoke or texted dozens of times a day, often late at night when Michele was asleep. To entice Martin, Gypsy's texts often included provocative pictures of herself. "It was very passionate and very sexual," Gypsy said years later. "It was so fun—this beautiful, handsome doctor taking time out of his life for me."

It seemed such an unlikely pairing. Martin was a traditional Mormon doctor, while Gypsy was free-spirited and unconventional. And Gypsy couldn't be more different from Michele.

Born on October 8, 1976, Gypsy Jyll Willis was the first child of conservative Mormon parents, Howard and Vicki Willis. She had two brothers, Ben and Matthew, and a sister, Julie. Gypsy got her unusual name when she was a baby and her mother placed a red cap on her head, remarking she looked like a little gypsy. "That should be her name," her father said.

As a little girl, Gypsy's favorite bedtime stories were the ones that told of a knight in shining armor who rescues the beautiful damsel in distress. She dreamed that someday a dashing prince would sweep her off her feet and take her away from her mundane life, growing up poor on a farm in Idaho.

The Willis family lived a sheltered existence in the small rural city of St. Anthony, in the county seat of Idaho's Fremont County. Both parents worked, but they never seemed to have enough. In 1985, when Gypsy was nine, Howard decided he wanted better for his family and went back to school to work toward a degree as a doctor. As the eldest of the four children, Gypsy was always expected to be responsible, and was often left in charge of her siblings.

In high school, Gypsy became fascinated with her father's medical books and decided she wanted to become a nurse. During her junior and senior year she enrolled in a vocational high school that offered a program in nursing. She graduated at the age of seventeen as a licensed practical nurse, or LPN. That same year her father also completed medical school and became a physician. While Gypsy worked as a nurse, she continued her education at Idaho State University.

As she blossomed into a young woman, Gypsy attracted a lot of attention from the opposite sex, and always seemed to have a boyfriend. Vicki worried her daughter was growing up too fast. "When Gypsy was perhaps in her early teens she was going at a breakneck pace toward adulthood. And intellectually she was absolutely where she wanted to go. But emotionally these things take time to develop. And that was her major flaw," Vicki said years later. "Her intellectual ability outstripped her emotional maturity."

In 1994, a few days before her second year of college was set to begin, Gypsy discovered she was pregnant. When Howard and Vicki learned their daughter was going to be a teen mom, they chastised her. Sex before marriage is forbidden in the Mormon faith, and Gypsy felt shunned by her religious parents.

Dropping out of college, Gypsy worked throughout her pregnancy to save money, and in 1995, she gave birth to a little girl she named Heidi Marie.

Throughout her pregnancy she had dated Heidi's father, an engineering student who lived out of state. But on the day she went into labor, she couldn't get ahold of him. After delivering her baby she called again and reached his new fiancée—her boyfriend had left her for another woman. Gypsy was devastated.

Now a single mom, Gypsy turned to her parents. Howard's attitude toward his eldest daughter was dismissive. "You're used goods now," Gypsy said her father told her. "No one is going to want you. You need to give up any hope of finding your own guy for your own preference and just find a guy willing to take you and your child."

At age twenty, Gypsy married a man she met at church named Jayson Jensen. She would later say she hadn't been ready for marriage but had believed it would redeem her in the eyes of her parents. "I didn't want to get married," she recalled. "But I wanted to fix things with my family. So I got married and tried to patch it up and make it all better."

Gypsy and Jayson moved to Nebraska to raise Heidi. She worked while he studied to be a chef. But shortly after they wed the relationship became tumultuous.

Two years after marrying, Gypsy filed for divorce, moved back home with her parents, and took a nursing job at a home for retired veterans. But her relationship with her family was strained. "As far as I know, I became the first person on either side of my family to have a child out of wedlock and be divorced," she remembered. "I felt a lot of judgment from my parents."

By the time she'd turned twenty-three, Gypsy had fallen in love again, this time with a man named Eric Blair. And when she decided to move with her boyfriend to Salt Lake City, her parents took temporary custody of three-year-old Heidi. On the understanding that she would still be a part of Heidi's life, Gypsy signed away parental rights, and Howard and Vicki later adopted their granddaughter.

For a period of time, Gypsy returned to Idaho every few weeks to see her daughter. But tension grew over Gypsy's relationship with Eric. After one nasty argument with her parents, Gypsy was told not to return home.

In 1999, Gypsy sued her parents for custody of her daughter. Howard and Vicki then took Heidi and moved to Wyoming.

When her finances were depleted by the legal fees, Gypsy dropped her custody bid, knowing Heidi was getting older and it would be traumatic for her to be taken from the grandparents who had been raising her.

Years passed before Gypsy ever saw her daughter again.

Estranged from her family, Gypsy became disenchanted with the Mormon faith. "I tried really hard to be a good Mormon. I think I was just inherently a little bit different," she said years later. "I think I could have been a very good married Mormon. I definitely had some failings there. I obviously got pregnant."

Trying to come to her own understanding of the world, Gypsy explored other religions and grew spiritual. She embraced her whimsical birth name, and her interests became bohemian. She got a tattoo of angel wings on her shoulders, drove a silver Volkswagen Beetle, and attended Renaissance festivals and colorful cultural events. "I was having a happy-go-lucky life living on my own," she recalled.

But she still longed to see her daughter.

Though she had no contact with her parents, she had remained close to her paternal grandmother. Through that connection, she learned that her parents and Heidi were going to be in Utah for a blessing of Gypsy's brother's new baby. Gypsy decided to go to the church to try and see her daughter.

When Gypsy sat next to her parents and Heidi in the church's pews, she was worried they might cause a scene. Instead, Vicki patted her on the shoulder, and after the ceremony invited Gypsy to a picnic.

Over the next few years, the family slowly developed a relationship, and Gypsy was able to reconnect with Heidi.

Throughout her twenties, Gypsy continued to live in Utah and work at various nursing jobs. She purchased a small white house in Bountiful, Utah, a bedroom community on the outskirts of Salt Lake City. In 2004, a friend she had met at a medieval culture event became her roommate. Michelle Savage was a divorced single mom in her thirties, with short brown hair and a round face. Savage's daughter, Brandi Smith, also lived at the Bountiful house.

But the living arrangement didn't last long. After a vicious argument, Savage and her daughter abruptly moved out.

Years later, Gypsy's and Savage's lives would bisect in an unusual way.

Soon after her roommate moved out, Gypsy had a financial setback and sold the house. For seven years she hadn't paid taxes, and eventually the government came after her for the money. By then the debt had accrued with interest and she owed nearly fifty thousand dollars. Gypsy later explained the debt by saying that she had unwisely protested paying taxes.

After selling the home in August 2005, she moved into an apartment in north Salt Lake City. She would eventually return to medical school to work toward a registered nursing degree, in order to earn more money and improve her financial situation.

Meanwhile, her relationship with Eric Blair had ended, and she dated varied types of men, some of whom she met on the Internet. She had no interest in being a wife again, and many times had affairs with married men, deciding it was their responsibility to be faithful to their spouses.

"I've been married. I've had a baby. I've been kind of traumatized by that whole experience," Gypsy explained. "I don't really want to get married again."

By the time she met Martin, an affair with a handsome doctor seemed thrilling. "I knew it wasn't going anywhere, and that was fine. It was just fun and exciting," she recalled. "I was just living my life and doing whatever I wanted to do. I came to realize that wasn't the best attitude. It hurt people, because inevitably they found out."

During the last year of her life, Michele seemed deeply distressed. Her marriage was crumbling, and while she couldn't fathom the true breadth of her husband's betrayal, she began to suspect that he was having an affair.

Throughout 2006, Martin became increasingly icy toward his wife. At home he was possessive of his cell phone—rarely letting it out of his sight. He was also secretive with his computer, consistently deleting his e-mails and search history. Even more alarming, he disappeared for long stretches at a time. On several occasions he claimed to be working late, but when she called the office or drove by the Developmental Center to check for his car, he wasn't there. When Michele confronted him about it, Martin changed the topic.

During a marital counseling session at church in 2006, Martin once again confessed to his bishop that he no longer loved his wife and wanted a divorce. Michele confided to at least one friend that she feared her marriage was over.

In the grip of depression, she gained weight. When she spoke to her family, they heard the sorrow in her voice. "Toward the end of her life, my impression was that something seemed to be bothering her," Linda remembered. "You'd sense an underlying sadness."

———

Meanwhile, Gypsy's relationship with Martin intensified. While he had to play the part of the Mormon family man in every other aspect of his life, he felt he could be himself with Gypsy.

"He had a lot of demands in his life—church stuff, a large family, daughters in dance, and he and his wife being social figures . . . I was the only aspect of his life that didn't drain him," Gypsy explained. "I know he felt liberated in my presence, as I did not ask, expect, or judge anything about him."

Soon Gypsy too had fallen deeply in love with Martin. He was everything she'd ever wanted in a partner. He was wealthy, handsome, intelligent, and seemed sincere. The traditional Mormon doctor seemed to reignite the deeply held desire she'd had since childhood—to be rescued by her own handsome prince. She would later describe Martin as "the American version of Prince Charming, coming from his glorious castle."

While she may have started out with thoughts of a casual affair, it appeared that Gypsy fell under the mistress's curse—wanting her lover to leave his wife. With her heart belonging to Martin, she stopped dating other men. But late-night phone calls and clandestine motel room trysts soon became unsatisfying.

After a few months of dating, Gypsy spoke to Martin about their potential future. At that point, it seemed Martin wasn't ready to leave Michele. He told Gypsy they couldn't be more than just lovers. Disheartened but still enamored, Gypsy continued her affair with Martin, but also reestablished her profile on a dating Web site and saw other men.

Later, she informed another suitor about a conversation she'd had with the doctor. "I guess he felt the way you do, like the friendship was too good to tempt fate and go anywhere else with it," Gypsy wrote in an e-mail. "After we had a conversation to the effect . . . I went back to dating and being available."

But Martin would come to have a change of heart about Gypsy, deciding he wanted to make her his next wife.

———

Middle age seemed to trigger something in Martin.

On February 1, 2006, he celebrated his fiftieth birthday. Around that time he made several abrupt changes in his life. He became consumed with his physical appearance and preoccupied with improving his looks. Perhaps to keep up with his much younger girlfriend, he exercised compulsively, running and lifting weights at the gym. In a few months he'd shed about thirty pounds and had begun frequenting tanning salons.

"He became obsessed with the way he looked," Alexis recalled. "He'd start exercising just all the time, just in the middle of a conversation, jumping and doing push-ups, things like that. It was really bizarre. Really strange. Very out of the ordinary."

Martin's children believed he was going through a midlife crisis. To Michele, his newfound focus on physicality felt like another sign of an affair.

In early 2006, Martin also insisted on moving away from the family's longtime home in Orem. Michele didn't want to move, and she told her daughters she feared it was his way of preparing for a divorce.

In February, they closed on a house at 3058 Millcreek Road in Pleasant Grove, about three miles from Martin's job at the Developmental Center. Built in 2002, the five-thousand-square-foot, six-bedroom, five-and-a-half bathroom estate had a large basement, marble floors, and a private den. Although their new house was expansive, it was about half the size of their previous place in Orem. Martin and Michele paid for the house in cash: $571,500.

All of the homes in their new master-planned community of Creekside encircled a five-acre park, where the residents' children congregated. The neighborhood was occupied with affluent young families, including airline pilots, attorneys, and even one professional baseball player. Many of the young families were Mormon and attended the Mount Timpanogos Utah Temple in American Fork.

The MacNeills' older adopted daughters enrolled at John Hancock Charter School. Ada attended a private elementary school, American Heritage.

As the MacNeills got to know their neighbors, many of the residents were put off by Martin's brash, boorish behavior. "He's always felt like he's a little bit above everybody intellectually," one neighbor said.

Sharing a driveway with the MacNeills, Doug and Kristi Daniels couldn't help but notice the stark contrast between Martin and his wife. While the MacNeill and Daniels families never became close friends, Kristi thought of Michele as a lovely person. "She was very quiet, was always very pretty and very well kept," Kristi remembered. "All the girls were just dressed perfect, like a tea party."

Doug, however, recalled how Martin seemed condescending from their first meeting. "He just made sure to say that he was downsizing into his home, and that he was a doctor and a lawyer," Doug said years later. "You could tell that he had a huge ego."

Michele settled into Pleasant Grove, decorating, organizing, and arranging the new home to suit her sophisticated style. The house featured large original paintings and sculptures, ballet-themed artwork, and elegant furniture. On weekends, Martin worked on construction projects to complete the home.

Straddling two different worlds, Martin continued to juggle his wife and his mistress. By this time he had become skilled at compartmentalizing his life.

But as Michele's suspicions strengthened and she sank further into depression, Martin began to find his wife and adopted girls insufferable. And the more time he spent with Gypsy, the more he seemed to realize that was where he preferred to be.

During the summer of 2006, Gypsy escorted Martin to a medical conference in Atlanta. At night they explored the city, visiting an aquarium and getting sushi at one o'clock in the morning. Months later they also took a trip to Detroit, where they toured a museum and saw the popular Body Worlds exhibit, which features preserved human bodies.

Each night they returned to their hotel room and made love. After returning to Utah, Gypsy bragged to her friends about the exciting trip and her exhilarating sexual escapades.

Martin's and Gypsy's lives would grow oddly tangled. Martin confided thoughts and desires to Gypsy that he could not reveal to anyone else in his life. In turn, she grew fiercely loyal, later going to great lengths to protect him.

It's impossible to know what occurred during those romantic getaways, late-night phone calls, and covert sexual trysts.

Had Gypsy gotten a glimpse of Martin's malevolent side? Like Anna Osborne Walthall, was she one of the few to learn his abhorrent truths? Did Gypsy ever meet the real Martin MacNeill?

It is a mystery that would be fiercely debated, dissected, and examined in court. What is known with certainty is that Gypsy was a paradox.

And she was a woman with her own secrets.

12.

A cryptic ailment afflicted Martin in late 2006. It began with a pain in his foot. His big toe swelled grotesquely and became inflamed for weeks at a time, often so severely that he limped or walked with a cane. Perplexed, Martin consulted several doctors and specialists in an attempt to diagnose the condition. Over the next few months he would undergo three surgeries on his toe.

Martin seemed consumed by his health problems. He spoke about them to anyone who would listen—his coworkers, church congregants, and family. With various colleagues at the Developmental Center, Martin's explanations about his condition were often contradictory. In December, he limped into the office of human resource manager John David Laycock.

"Hey, Martin," David said. "How's it going?"

"Well, I'm having some issues with my toe." Martin sighed, slumping into the chair on the opposite side of the desk.

Without prompting from Laycock, Martin slipped off his shoe, tore off his sock, and propped his foot on top of the desk. Laycock glanced down at Martin's toe, noticing it was indeed swollen. Later, Laycock observed Martin using a cane.

Martin's toe problem seemed to progressively worsen. That December,

Martin told his family his prognosis was grim. "I don't have long to live," he said somberly.

That Christmas the MacNeills gathered at the new house to celebrate the holiday. No one knew it at the time, but it would indeed be their very last Christmas as a family.

Over the next few months, Martin seemed to be living as if he were gravely sick and dying. He made plans for his final arrangements. On January 28, 2007, Martin took out a two-million-dollar life insurance policy on himself, including Michele and Alexis as beneficiaries. In addition, he signed the house into Michele's name.

But even Martin's family was confused about his illness. In December he told his wife he had cancer. Later, he said he also had multiple sclerosis.

Michele told her friends about Martin's ailments. On January 15, Michele had turned fifty. To celebrate, she had gone to lunch with her "Ya-Ya Sisters," Cheryl, Loreen, and Karen. They had spent much of the afternoon discussing Martin's health. "We would frequently discuss Martin's health because he had told her he was diagnosed with MS," Cheryl said years later.

Neighbors in Pleasant Grove also heard about Martin's impending death. He told the Daniels family that his condition was rapidly deteriorating and that because of the diagnosis, he had put all of the family assets in Michele's name. "I'll be dead in six months," he said.

On Sunday, February 4, the MacNeill family attended church at the Mount Timpanogos Temple. Alexis and Rachel, who were both in town, also attended the services.

During Sunday school class that day, Martin taught a lesson. He stood before members of the congregation and discussed his incurable illness. "I've been diagnosed with terminal cancer." Martin's voice was husky with emotion. "I'll be dead soon."

Looking at his wife in the front row, he told the congregation how he had been preparing Michele to take over the financials of the household. Tears welled in Michele's eyes.

One of the MacNeills' neighbors, Angie Aguilar, was seated with her family behind the older MacNeill children. "He taught a lesson in which he discussed his deteriorating health in a Sunday school class," Angie said years later. "It was a very heartfelt, tearful lesson. And the family was there as well, and tearful."

But while church friends, neighbors, and Martin's own family believed he was dying, no one at his work was under the impression that his condition was terminal. Martin explained to John David Laycock that he was having two separate health concerns—one was related to his nervous system, and the other was cancer. "He said he had cancer in his toe—he shared that with me," Laycock explained, adding that Martin never said he had a few months to live.

Martin also showed his toe to Guy Hale Thomas, the Developmental Center's director of nursing. However, this time he had a different explanation. "He told us he had Charcot-Marie-Tooth syndrome," Thomas recalled. "From what I understand, it was a neurological atrophy–type problem similar to MD [muscular dystrophy] and it affected his toe and he had to have some surgical work done on it."

Steven Nickelson heard yet another story. Martin told the nurse practitioner he had a genetic problem, possibly "peripheral neuropathy," a nerve condition causing pain and numbness.

During her relationship with Martin, Gypsy noticed his injured toe on a number of occasions. "It was huge. The toe was half the size of his foot. It was red and it looked like it was coming down with cellulitis half of the time. It was bad," Gypsy recalled. "Some days were better than others. Some days he used a cane and some days he didn't need it."

At first Martin told Gypsy he'd broken his toe and it hadn't healed correctly. Later, he said he had briefly been concerned about cancer but that blood tests proved he didn't have the disease. Eventually, Martin explained to Gypsy he had been diagnosed with a genetic nerve disorder.

As Martin sought out medical answers for his toe problems, he made two separate trips in February to Scottsdale, Arizona, where he underwent medical testing at the Mayo Clinic, the prestigious medical and research practice. On February 12, he went alone, staying for three days and undergoing a battery of physical and psychiatric testing. For his second trip, Gypsy accompanied him to Scottsdale. The date of that excursion would hold a special significance for Martin and Michele.

While planning for his impending death, Martin simultaneously prepared for a future with Gypsy. During the last few months of his wife's life, something changed between Martin and Gypsy. He decided he wanted more than just simply an affair—he wanted a life with Gypsy. And by January 2007, their relationship had grown serious.

By then Gypsy had decided to go back to school. She had enrolled in a program to further her nursing education and earn a registered nurse degree at AmeriTech College in Draper, about twenty miles south of Salt Lake City.

Gypsy gave notice at her apartment and lived cheaply by staying with friends, sleeping on their couches. "I didn't have a lot of money saved up because I didn't do that well," she later said. "It was a very intensive nursing program. I was very overwhelmed. It was a very hard time."

Her schedule made it difficult to see Martin as often, which he lamented. And without her apartment they had little privacy. Once, they actually arranged a rendezvous at a vacant building in American Fork that was scheduled to be demolished, and a stranger walked in while Gypsy was nude.

Searching for a place nearby for her to stay, Martin asked neighbor Angie Aguilar for a favor. A few houses north of where the Aguilars lived was the home of pro baseball player Jeremy Guthrie. The Baltimore Orioles pitcher and his family were currently away for spring training. Martin asked Angie if they needed a house sitter.

"There's a gal who works at the Developmental Center who is also going to school to be a nurse," Martin said casually. "She needs somewhere close by to stay."

"I'll ask if they are interested," Angie replied.

The Guthries declined, which Angie informed Martin of a few days later.

Martin then came up with another solution. In January, he told Gypsy he had a duplex he had leased for construction workers he hired to complete a renovation on his home. Martin said the workers had skipped out on the job but that he still had to pay the lease. The duplex was located in

Lehi, a small suburb about eight miles from Pleasant Grove. "You're welcome to stay there," he said.

Gypsy agreed, and moved in weeks later. The accommodations were not luxurious—there were holes in the carpet and dated seventies décor. But having a place to stay meant a lot to Gypsy.

Martin paid for rent and utilities. He also provided Gypsy with a debit card to use for all personal expenses. With Gypsy closer by, they met more frequently for sex; at least twice a week. "We communicated more, and just being closer to him, we had more visits," Gypsy later said.

Although she had been dating other men previously, Gypsy now seemed exclusive to her married boyfriend. When a potential suitor she met on the Internet e-mailed her for a date, she told him it would be inappropriate given her current relationship. "A very good and best friend of mine has recently become much more than that," she wrote in March 2007. "I met him online a year and a half ago. We've always been great together . . . And just recently his reasoning and views changed and we are together now."

Meanwhile, Michele could no longer ignore the signs of infidelity. Six weeks before her death, her suspicions had heightened. She confronted Martin more and more often. In February, Michele confided in her daughter Alexis.

"I think your dad is having an affair," Michele said, before bursting into tears.

13.

Martin and Michele's twenty-ninth wedding anniversary was on February 21, 2007. On that day there was a romantic getaway, a candlelit dinner, passionate sex in a hotel room, and professions of love. But Martin was not with his wife.

Instead, he spent his wedding anniversary with his mistress.

The trip was to Scottsdale for Martin's second appointment at the Mayo Clinic. With Gypsy accompanying him, they turned the medical visit into an amorous adventure. The couple first drove to Nevada, where Martin stopped in Henderson to visit Alexis and exchange vehicles with her, because he said the convertible she owned would be more fun for him to drive on his trip.

Before seeing his daughter, Martin dropped Gypsy off at a nearby restaurant, in order to conceal the fact that he was traveling with another woman. Still, Alexis was suspicious of her father's unusually exuberant mood when he stopped by her place. Knowing her mother's concerns of infidelity, Alexis decided to secretly investigate.

While Martin was inside the apartment, Alexis went out to his vehicle and opened the trunk. The luggage she found there included a few bags she didn't recognize. Unzipping one of the bags, Alexis found makeup, women's clothing, and lingerie.

Her stomach sank.

She closed the trunk and didn't say anything to her father. Minutes later, Martin came outside, transferred the luggage to the other vehicle, gave Alexis the keys to his car, and left in the convertible to pick up Gypsy.

As soon as he drove off, Alexis called her mom and told her what she had found.

Horrified, Michele phoned her husband.

"Who are you with?" Michele cried. "What is this about?"

Martin denied to his wife that there was anything nefarious linked to the extra luggage, claiming the bags belonged to a colleague at the Developmental Center. Hanging up the phone, Martin turned around and returned to Alexis's apartment. On the way he discreetly called Gypsy and explained what had happened. To allow Martin time to deal with his family, Gypsy made arrangements to stay the night with friends in Nevada.

When Martin returned to the apartment, he berated Alexis, acting indignant that she could possibly think he would be unfaithful. To erase his daughter's lingering doubts, Martin stayed overnight at Alexis's place.

Early the following morning, Martin picked Gypsy up from her friends' house and they continued the trip to Arizona. For the remainder of their getaway, Martin and Gypsy stayed together in hotel rooms, where they could be intimate.

In March, Michele had plans to meet with her "Ya-Ya Sisters" for lunch. But that morning she called Loreen, sobbing. "Martin really needs me to do some things," she said through her tears. "I can't come to lunch."

"We can do it another time," Loreen said.

"But I really need my Ya-Ya Sisters," she cried. It broke Loreen's heart to hear Michele so upset.

Michele would never get a chance to see her three close friends again.

Martin, meanwhile, continued to speak of his impending death. He remained oddly inconsistent as to the cause of his illness. Intermittently throughout the month of March, he used a cane, while at other times he seemed healthy and physically fit.

One weekend, Rachel was at the house while Martin was working on a home improvement project, enlarging Elle's bedroom in the basement with drywall. Rachel watched as Martin singlehandedly carried the heavy materials down the stairs. Offering to assist, Rachel raced him down the steps. But Martin did not slow down and refused her help, snapping at his daughter, "I got it."

On Friday, March 16, Alexis had come home for the weekend. While Martin was at work, she helped her mom snoop through the house, searching for anything that could connect him to an affair. Instead of hotel receipts or love letters, they discovered an envelope from the Mayo Clinic. Inside were the test results from Martin's visits in February—and the contents of the reports were stunning.

Contrary to what he had told his family and congregation, he was not dying of cancer, MS, or any other life-threatening disease. In fact, Martin was in good health. Tests that were performed on his big toe had determined he had a simple hereditary condition. He had been diagnosed with a rare genetic disease known as "hereditary neuropathy with liability to pressure palsies." This nerve disorder causes pain, numbness, and paralyzation in the limbs. It is not, however, life-threatening, and can be treated by simple lifestyle adjustments, such as avoiding excess pressure on the nerves.

A wave of relief momentarily washed over Michele—her husband was going to live. But she was also perplexed. If Martin was healthy, why hadn't he told anyone in the family? Why was he continuing to tell people he was dying?

That night, after Martin returned from work and they all sat around the kitchen table, Alexis implemented her plan to expose her father's adultery. Earlier she had plotted with Michele, concocting a ruse to get ahold of Martin's cell phone and gain access to his call records.

"Hey Dad," she said. "I want to download a new ringtone to your phone. Can I see it?"

Reluctantly, Martin handed over his phone.

While he wasn't looking, Alexis slyly connected to the T-Mobile Web site and requested that the password to his account be texted to his phone. When she received the text seconds later, she memorized the password and deleted the message so Martin wouldn't know what she had done. She then downloaded a ringtone and handed the phone back to her dad.

Later that night, Michele and Alexis signed on to the T-Mobile Web site and reviewed his phone records from January. They quickly identified one number in particular that they didn't recognize—a number Martin had called frequently all month, often late at night. Some of the calls were placed in the middle of the night, at 2 and 3 A.M. Alexis wrote down the number and told her mom she would investigate further. That Sunday she flew back to Nevada.

On Monday—March 19—Alexis called the number. At first no one answered and the call went to voice mail. It was not a personal greeting, and Alexis couldn't determine much about the owner's identity. An hour later she called again, but there was still no answer.

At 5:41 P.M., she called a third time, and finally someone answered.

"Hello," the woman said.

Alexis's heart sank. The voice clearly belonged to a young female.

"Hello," the voice repeated. "Hello?"

Alexis hung up without saying a word.

Heart racing, Alexis immediately called her mom and told her the distressing news that Martin had indeed been phoning a woman.

The following day Alexis ran a background check, conducting a reverse phone number lookup on the Web site Intelius, which provides access to public records. She paid the seventy-dollar fee and entered the suspicious phone number. The results produced a name: Gypsy Jyll Willis.

"Gypsy? What kind of name is Gypsy?" Michele asked her daughter when Alexis called her with the results of the search.

"It sounds like the name of a stripper," Alexis commented.

When Martin came home from work that night, Michele confronted him, admitting she had seen his phone records. "Who's Gypsy?"

Martin immediately became defensive, claiming the calls were innocent.

"She's nobody. Just a nurse I had worked with," he said dismissively. "She's renting one of our properties."

"Well, why have you called her at all these strange hours?" Michele asked. "Like three o'clock in the morning?"

There was no reason for a married father to be speaking to a young woman in the middle of the night, Michele said. Martin claimed they spoke at night because Gypsy worked the graveyard shift as a nurse. Michele doubted her husband's tale, and told him it seemed implausible. She insisted that he cease contact with Gypsy immediately. After a contentious argument, Martin agreed.

But he had no intention of keeping his word.

He immediately changed the password on his T-Mobile account. And in a subsequent conversation with Gypsy, he told her they needed to be more discreet—they would no longer be able to speak on his cell phone, because Michele was monitoring his call records. Martin, however, had an idea to get around the problem.

"From now on we can only text from my cell," he said. "I'll call you from my office phone."

Over the next few weeks Martin saw Gypsy several times and they texted frequently—often exchanging more than a dozen texts each day.

"You need a face-lift," Martin told his wife, cocking his head as if he were examining her appearance.

"What?" Michele was taken aback, aghast.

Martin softened his approach. "I want to get you a face-lift, as a gift."

It was the day after the fight about Gypsy when Martin made this unusual suggestion, seemingly out of nowhere.

Michele wasn't sure how to react. She didn't feel like she looked old, and she considered invasive cosmetic surgery indulgent. As he had been throughout their marriage, however, Martin was persuasive. He told her it would make her feel better about herself.

"After you are all healed, we can take a cruise," he said.

Michele examined herself in the mirror, scrutinizing the lines on her face. At age fifty, she was still a striking beauty. But time, as it has a tendency to do, had caused her looks to begin to fade. Fine wrinkles surrounded her eyes; her skin sagged slightly around her jaw. The thought of erasing a decade from her face was enticing. But more than anything, Michele desperately wanted to save her marriage. Martin had lost weight, was tanning, and she suspected he was sleeping with another woman. Perhaps if she looked younger, Martin wouldn't be tempted to stray. It took some convincing from Martin, but eventually she agreed that she would see a surgeon, to learn more about the procedure.

With haste, the very next morning, Martin began the hunt for a plastic surgeon. Searching through the newspaper, he found an ad for a surgeon offering a coupon for discount Botox. Martin called and scheduled a consultation.

Dr. Scott Kent Thompson was fairly new to Utah, having opened his practice just nine months prior. A recently board-certified facial plastic surgeon with offices in Bountiful, Draper, and Layton, Thompson had completed medical school at the University of Rochester and a fellowship in New York before opening Scott Thompson Facial Plastics in 2006. Thompson's main office was in Layton, an urban bedroom community about sixty miles from the MacNeill home in Pleasant Grove. Although there were dozens of qualified surgeons close by, Martin seemed intent on selecting one outside the area, who would not know his professional reputation.

On March 22, Martin and Michele met with Dr. Thompson. Introducing himself, Martin lied to Thompson, saying he was an attorney and licensed psychiatrist. "Don't worry. I've never sued anyone," Martin said with a chuckle.

Martin and Michele took a seat at a large wooden desk across from the surgeon. Thompson was in his thirties with a narrow, boyish face, sandy brown hair, and thick-framed glasses. He appeared young for a plastic surgeon, but his knowledgeable demeanor seemed to instill confidence.

Michele spoke with the doctor, expressing concerns that she was now middle-aged and starting to see some changes in her face. They discussed various procedures and options. The hollows in her cheeks could be corrected by a mid-face lift. A brow lift would smooth the wrinkles in her forehead. A lower-face lift would tighten the skin around the jawbone to reduce jowling. And droopy eyelids and bags could be fixed with an eyelid surgery.

Martin and Michele went back and forth, playfully discussing options. To Dr. Thompson, Martin seemed very protective of his wife, saying he was concerned about her high blood pressure and that he was going to have it checked out by a physician. Michele also expressed some hesitations, saying she was concerned about the risks, recovery, and downtime.

At the end of the consultation, Martin told the doctor they wanted all the procedures they had discussed—a forehead lift, mid-face lift, lower-face lift, and an upper and lower eyelid surgery. "We just want to address this all at once." Martin smiled at his wife.

The surgery was scheduled for April 3—just twelve days later.

After booking the surgery, Michele told Alexis about the face-lift.

"Mom," Alexis said with concern in her voice, "you don't need that. You're beautiful."

"I don't really want to do it," Michele said. "But if your dad's getting all fixed up and looking good, maybe I should too."

Amid the growing suspicions of an affair, Alexis was terribly bothered that her dad would convince her mom to change her appearance. Cosmetic surgery was never something she thought her mom would consider, Alexis later said. "She'd never been into plastic surgery," Alexis said years later. "My mom had never talked about that before or anything."

Because Martin would be busy at work, Alexis volunteered to assist in her mother's recovery. The surgery date corresponded with her spring break from medical school.

Still, it was alarming how quickly the operation was moving forward.

Later, Alexis spoke to her dad about the surgery. "When I talked to him initially he said he was giving it to her as a present," Alexis recalled. "He surprised her with the plastic surgery as a present."

Perhaps embarrassed, Michele didn't mention to many of her friends that she was getting a face-lift. "I don't think she wanted people to know she was doing it," one friend later said. "She was beautiful."

———

On March 25, the MacNeills celebrated Ada's sixth birthday. When Rachel arrived at the house that afternoon for the party, she noticed a silver Volkswagen Beetle parked out front. "Who parked in my spot?" Rachel asked. No one in the family seemed to know who the car belonged to.

The next day was a sacred occasion for Elle and Sabrina. The whole family went to temple for a sealing ceremony, binding the two adopted daughters to the MacNeills for all eternity. Giselle, who resisted converting to Mormonism, declined to be linked forever to the family for which she had no attachment.

Michele wanted the day to be special and purchased presents for the girls. Martin, however, appeared in a foul mood and was particularly nasty toward his wife. Michele spent most of the day in tears.

Later that night, at the house, Alexis and Rachel were passing by Martin's home office when they noticed their father at his desk, flipping through a thick book while jotting down notes. Alexis recognized the book as the *Physicians' Desk Reference,* a guide known as the *PDR* in the medical community, which lists various prescription drugs, their chemical makeup, effects, and common usage.

The book was covered in dust. Over the last ten years Alexis had seldom seen her dad look through it, and was surprised to see him reading it so intently.

"Hey Dad," Alexis said, stepping into the office. "What're you doing?"

Martin looked up from the book.

His tone was curiously cheery. "I just want to make sure I'll have all the medications your mom will need after her surgery."

To ease Michele's apprehensions about the surgery, Martin contacted a doctor he worked with and asked to schedule a physical examination. Dr. Von Welch was a physician of internal medicine at Mountain Clinic in American Fork. Welch, in his fifties, with thinning brown hair, narrow eyes, and sharp features, regularly treated Martin's patients at the Developmental Center, and they had a professional friendship.

At the time of Martin's phone call, Dr. Welch's schedule was hectic and he wasn't currently accepting new patients. However, Martin asked if he would see his wife as a personal favor, to avoid delaying the plastic surgery.

On March 29, Martin and Michele met with Dr. Welch. Martin introduced his wife and explained they were very interested in moving forward with the surgery as scheduled.

Because Michele was a new patient, Welch began the exam by asking about her medical history. Martin spoke for his wife, answering all the questions.

"She doesn't have any history of health problems," Martin said as Michele sat quietly on the exam table.

When Welch asked about heart problems, Michele stared blankly at her husband.

"She has no heart problems," he answered.

Michele softly corrected him. "I have had heart palpitations in the past."

Welch would later say he found it odd how Martin took control of the examination.

"She didn't have very much to say," Welch remembered. "She would answer a question and be quiet. It was very difficult to get much history or information from her."

During the course of the examination, Welch became frustrated by Martin's continuous interjections and asked to speak with Michele alone.

"I asked him to leave the examining room because he was answering all the questions for her and I felt like she could speak more freely if he was out of the room," Welch said years later.

Once Martin was gone, Michele told the doctor that she had been under a lot of stress and had been feeling depressed. While she didn't elaborate or provide details as to what was causing her despair, Welch got the impression that she might have been facing marital problems.

Welch drew blood and conducted various tests, including an echocardiogram, which showed a normal heart rhythm and no sign of defect or disease. As part of the examination, he also took a reading of her blood pressure. The results were 160 over 110, which was considered high, and he diagnosed her with mild hypertension, or high blood pressure.

After conducting the tests, Dr. Welch invited Martin back into the exam room. Because of Michele's elevated blood pressure, he prescribed Lisinopril, a treatment for hypertension. For her mental issues he prescribed sertraline, an antidepressant also known as Zoloft. After writing out the prescriptions, he asked that Michele take the pills for one week and then report back on the results.

Although Welch concluded that Michele was healthy, he suggested the surgery be postponed because of her high blood pressure.

"It would be ideal for her to get that under control before surgery," Dr. Welch said.

At the suggestion of delaying the procedure, the smile faded from Martin's face. "Well, I guess we'll wait then."

Once they left the clinic, Martin told his wife she would be fine and that they would be moving forward with the surgery as planned.

The first week of April, Alexis arrived back in Utah for a weeklong stay. On April 1, she accompanied her parents to their final presurgery consultation with Dr. Scott Thompson at his satellite office in Draper. During the drive, Michele expressed anxiety about the surgery. "I think we should listen to Dr. Welch," Michele told her husband. "Let's just hold off for a while."

"No," Martin snapped back. "You're not doing that."

"Let's just wait until the summer when Alexis will be home for three months," Michele said. "It will give me time to get my blood pressure under control and lose weight."

"You're having it now!" Martin demanded angrily. "I'm too busy and Alexis is here to take care of you."

Michele repeated her concerns about her blood pressure, but Martin was insistent.

"If you don't have the surgery now, you're not getting it," Martin snarled. "I already paid for the anesthesiologist and the operating suite!"

From the backseat of the car, Alexis was shocked by her father's angry outburst.

"She was talking to my dad, saying that maybe we should delay the surgery," Alexis recalled. "He had a very strong reaction . . . He was raising his voice and very animated."

Eventually Michele abandoned her protests, grew quiet, and stared blankly out the passenger window. By the time they arrived in Draper, Martin's fury had cooled.

In Dr. Thompson's office, Michele detailed her past medical history on the patient intake form. Although Martin had told the surgeon that he was a psychiatrist, Michele identified him on the form as her primary care physician. She listed her hysterectomy as her only prior surgery, and stated she had no ongoing health problems.

Dr. Thompson conducted a physical examination and discussed plans for post-op care. Once again, Martin answered all of the questions for his wife.

"She has a little bit of high blood pressure," Martin told Thompson. "I had it checked out and the doctor has her on an ACE inhibitor."

Thompson didn't believe such mild hypertension would be a problem.

"Martin was really the one who directed this discussion," Thompson remembered. "Michele always deferred to Martin on those issues, for example, the blood pressure, the medication; those kind of things were always handled through Martin."

Michele expressed her reservations, and asked the doctor if it would be beneficial to lose weight prior to surgery.

"It would only make a difference if you lost fifty pounds or more," Thompson told her. "And you don't need to lose that much."

Still, Michele seemed hesitant, seemingly fishing for reasons to postpone the procedure. Thompson tried to ease her concerns.

"I know she was nervous about surgery, because I specifically remember saying, 'Okay. We're signed up for a lot of surgery here, for your forehead, your mid-face, and your lower face. But we could do less if you wanted,'" Thompson later said. "'That would be a little easier to recover from.'"

But Martin stated they would proceed as planned.

Toward the end of the appointment, Thompson explained the medications Michele would need to take as she healed. For the pain, he prescribed thirty tablets of Vicodin, also known as Lortab. To reduce swelling, she would take a steroid, Medrol. An antibiotic called cephalexin would stave off possible infection, while Phenergan would prevent nausea. The eye oint-ment erythromycin would help healing. Finally, he prescribed seven tab-lets of Ambien to assist with sleep, if needed.

As they discussed the medication, Martin pulled a piece of paper from his pocket and slid it across the table—the list of medications he had as-sembled after poring through the *Physicians' Desk Reference.*

"I'm really concerned about my wife," Martin told the surgeon. "She doesn't handle pain well. She gets anxious. And I just really want to make sure I have everything I might need in the postoperative period for these issues."

Instead of Vicodin, he asked the surgeon to prescribe her thirty doses of Percocet, a stronger pain pill. In case her jaw was swollen and she had difficulty swallowing pills, he requested a Lortab elixir, a liquid painkiller. And to calm Michele before and after surgery, Martin insisted on a pre-scription of Valium, an antianxiety medication.

"She gets very anxious and I'm concerned that she won't do well with-out these options available," Martin said. "I just want to have all the options available to me."

At the mention of anxiety, Michele looked over at her husband and softly smiled.

Alexis, seated next to her parents, was mortified—her father was basi-cally ordering medication from the surgeon as if he was calling for take-out.

"I was really embarrassed because my dad was telling the plastic surgeon what medication he wanted," Alexis recalled. "He's a plastic surgeon—he knows what medications are appropriate to prescribe. It was not my dad's place, and I just thought it was very, very strange and embarrassing."

Dr. Thompson also found the request abnormal and out of protocol. Per-cocet and Valium were not part of his normal regimen. Under normal circumstances he would never trust a patient with so many dangerous nar-cotics, but because Martin was in the medical field, he made an exception.

Thompson granted all of Martin's requests, under the agreement that he would monitor the administration of the drugs. The surgeon jotted out prescriptions for fifteen Valium pills, thirty tablets of Percocet, liquid Lortab, and increased the dose of Phenergan to treat nausea from six to ten pills. Thompson made a note in his files that the drugs were being prescribed only at the request of the patient's husband, who was also her primary care doctor.

But Thompson also issued a strong warning. The drugs, he said, could have overlapping side effects, and there was no reason for them all to be taken at once. If combined, the medication could dangerously depress Michele's breathing and be potentially deadly.

"This is more medication than I usually prescribe," Thompson said. "Be very careful and only take what you need."

Thompson handwrote all of the prescriptions and passed them across his desk. But when Martin noticed Michele's name had been misspelled as "Michelle," using two Ls, he asked for them all to be rewritten.

Following the appointment, Martin dropped off Michele and Alexis at home and returned to work. He collected the prescriptions from the pharmacy and later had a rented hospital bed delivered to the house to assist in his wife's recovery.

Around 6 P.M. that evening, Martin called home and told his wife he would be working late. As Michele hung up the phone, Alexis noticed the worried look on her mother's face.

"Can you go drive by your dad's work?" Michele asked. "See if his car is in the parking lot?"

Alexis got in her mom's car and drove by the Developmental Center. Martin's car was not there.

Days before the surgery, Martin called a family meeting, assembling Michele, Alexis, Rachel, and Damian. Vanessa was excluded. At the time, Martin was still carrying on the ruse that he was dying. When he began to talk about his illness, Michele and Alexis quickly locked eyes, exchanging a knowing glance. They knew he wasn't dying. Why would he continue this charade?

Martin began explaining the provisions addressed in his will. "If I die," he said, "Alexis will be in charge of the estate."

At that, Michele flinched. "Well, what about me?"

Michele wondered why she, as his wife, wouldn't be the executor of his estate. Martin waved his wife off, dismissing her concern and repeating, "Alexis will be the executor."

"It was bizarre," Rachel recalled. "He wanted to go over each detail of his will and what was in the will. He said that Alexis would be made executor of his will if anything were to happen. And he kept referring to Alexis."

Then he passed out three handwritten checks, to Alexis, Rachel, and Damian, for five thousand dollars each.

"What is this for?" Rachel asked, looking down at her check.

"It's a gift," Martin told his kids. "I just want to give you this money."

"Wow. Thank you." Damian hugged his dad.

But Rachel and Alexis found it strange—there was no apparent reason to give them the money. It was uncharacteristic of their father.

"It was very unusual," Rachel later said. "He had never done anything like that before."

14.

The din of the cardiac monitors reverberated off the walls of the cool, brightly lit operating room at Lakeview Hospital in Bountiful. In the center of the room, Michele lay prone and sedated on the surgical table. She wore a white paper gown, her hair tucked under a cap. A ventilator tube protruded from the side of her mouth, and an IV line was inserted in her arm. Situated on a metallic tray at her bedside, steel scalpels, tweezers, scissors, and other sterilized surgical instruments were primed to carve into her pretty face.

It was Tuesday, April 3, 2007—the day of Michele's fated face-lift and the beginning of the last full week of her life. She had just eight days left to live.

Early that morning Martin and Alexis had escorted Michele to the hospital. Dressed in surgical scrubs, Dr. Thompson greeted the MacNeills in the waiting area.

"I'm really nervous." Michele winced.

"That's perfectly normal." Thompson gently patted her hand. "Most patients are nervous before surgery."

Once again, Thompson tried to ease her anxiety, explaining what to expect during the procedure. The anesthesiologist checked Michele's vital signs. Although her blood pressure registered as slightly elevated, the anesthesiologist said it wouldn't be dangerous.

"Are you sure?" Martin's tone was laced with condescension. "Do you know what medications my wife is on? Are you sure that when you give her the anesthesia there won't be any interaction with that?"

Standing beside her parents, Alexis grimaced, embarrassed by her father's arrogance. "I vividly remember that because it was embarrassing," Alexis said years later. "Because the anesthesiologist obviously knows medication interaction."

Martin kissed his wife and left the hospital, saying, "I have to get to work. See you tonight."

At 8 A.M. Michele was admitted into surgery—a procedure scheduled to last six to eight hours. Scalpel in hand, Dr. Thompson made the first incision, slicing her skin near her scalp, circling behind the ears and around her hairline. He meticulously stretched the skin and lifted the muscles around her jaw upward, suturing them in place. He connected two flaps of skin, trimming off the excess flesh around her jawbone. Carving deeper under the skin around each side of her temple, he lifted the flesh of the cheeks, stitching it securely to her chewing muscles to fill in hollowness. Through the incisions near her scalp, he flattened the wrinkles in her forehead.

Thompson then slashed along the creases in her upper eyelids, removing the extra skin. The bags under her eyes were tightened by going beneath the skin using the incision from the side of her face, correcting the appearance of fatigue.

Throughout the operation, Thompson periodically stepped out of the surgical room to update Alexis on the progress.

By 3 P.M., the surgery was complete. Michele's bruised and battered face was wrapped in gauze and bandages. A drain was placed under the bandages to collect blood and fluid. Cold ice pads shielded her eyes, leaving Michele temporarily blind.

The surgery had lasted seven hours and was considered successful, with no problems concerning Michele's vitals, heart rate, anesthesia, or excessive bleeding.

Thompson placed a call to Martin. "I'm pleased with how it went."

About two hours later, Michele awoke from the sedation and was transferred to a hospital room, where Dr. Thompson went to her bedside to check on her. The surgery had always been intended as an outpatient procedure—and Martin had requested an early discharge—but Michele told the doctor she wasn't ready to return home. "I want to stay here overnight," she uttered groggily.

Thompson and Alexis called Martin on speakerphone to explain Michele's wishes.

"Mom wants to stay the night," Alexis said.

Martin sighed. "We need to go home. I'm on my way to the hospital now."

"What's the big deal?" Alexis asked. "We have good insurance. It's just staying one night for observation."

"We made plans, Alexis," Martin grunted.

By the tone in her father's voice, Alexis knew he was furious. "He was very angry. He wanted her to come home," Alexis recalled. "He was mad at my mom."

Thompson interjected. "Because of how long she was under anesthesia, it would be a good idea to monitor her breathing and vitals overnight."

On the surgeon's recommendation, Martin relented. An hour later, he arrived at the hospital to pick up Alexis, and they headed home so she could pick up items she needed to stay overnight at the hospital. She then drove the Suburban back to Bountiful to sleep at her mom's bedside, propped in a chair.

That night, while his wife slept fitfully at the hospital, Martin and Gypsy exchanged twenty-four texts.

Early the following morning, Dr. Thompson checked on Michele. Although she said her face ached, she was alert and responsive when she answered the doctor's questions. Thompson slowly unwound the layers of bandages, slicing off the gauze, which was sticky with blood. He checked for bleeding under her skin, ensured her facial nerves were intact, and reviewed her vitals before rewrapping her wounds with fresh bandages.

Michele was discharged and released into Alexis's care with a list of instructions.

At home, Alexis guided Michele into the master bedroom, where she tucked her into the rented hospital bed, which was positioned in front of the television. Alexis planted herself beside her mom on the bedroom couch.

For the rest of the day, Alexis was her mother's caretaker—administering medication, assisting her with using the restroom, and feeding her small bites of food and sips of water. Using her medical training, she monitored Michele's vitals. Alexis also rubbed her mother's legs to help her circulation and prevent possible blood clots, which can form during prolonged periods of inactivity.

"I really wanted to do a good job helping her—she was my mom," Alexis said years later. "So I was taking her vitals, blood pressure, pulse, rubbing her legs, things like that."

Late that evening, Martin came home and told his daughter he would take over care. "You need to go get some sleep," he said.

"No, Dad." Alexis shook her head. "I'm just going to stay here with Mom and sleep on the couch."

Martin, however, was adamant.

"At first I said I didn't want to leave my mom," Alexis recalled. "He insisted that I leave. He pretty much forced me out." Exhausted, Alexis went to Ada's room, crawled beside her niece in her princess bed, and fell asleep.

In the master bedroom, Martin handed his wife a handful of pills, telling her to take each one. Once she passed out, he stayed up into the early morning hours, texting Gypsy.

Alexis awoke the next morning at about 6 A.M. and went straight to her mother's bedside. She found Michele asleep in the hospital bed, tucked under the covers with her head lolled to the side.

"Mom. Wake up, Mom," Alexis said softly, stroking Michele's arm. When Michele didn't stir, Alexis nudged her softly. "Mom. Mom. Mom." Seizing her mother gently by the shoulders, Alexis jostled her. "Wake up, Mom. Mom!"

Michele groaned but remained listless.

"I went over and tried to wake her up and she wasn't waking up," Alexis later testified in court. "She was completely sedated and out of it."

Checking her blood pressure and pulse, Alexis found Michele's heart rate low, her breathing shallow. Storming out of the bedroom, Alexis found her father in the kitchen and confronted him. "What happened?"

"Um. Oh. I don't know," Martin stammered.

"She won't wake up. Mom's obviously overmedicated."

"Oh. Well. I . . . I guess I must have done something wrong," he muttered. "I must have given her too much medicine."

They both knew Michele was sensitive to narcotics. While in her daughter's care, she had requested only one pain pill.

"What did you give her?" Alexis asked. "Why would you give her so much?"

"I thought she needed them."

Alexis demanded a list of the medications from her father, grabbing a nearby promotional notepad marked with the insignia for the allergy medicine Zyrtec to write down his responses.

Martin told Alexis that at midnight he gave Michele Valium. An hour later, a pain pill. That caused her to vomit. At 1:30 A.M., he helped her take Phenergan, two Percocet, and an Ambien.

"Well, you're not to give her any more medicine." Alexis glowered at her dad. "I'm taking over."

Alexis remained glued to her mother's side for the rest of the day, regularly checking her pulse, dabbing ointment on her eyes, cleaning her incisions with peroxide, and re-dressing her wounds.

Throughout the morning Alexis periodically tried to rouse her mother. "Are you okay? Mom?"

Michele fidgeted but otherwise did not respond.

By the afternoon, Michele had gained brief moments of lucidity. Alexis helped her sit up to swallow a steroid and her estrogen pill, which she had been taking since her hysterectomy.

By 2:45 P.M., Michele grumbled in pain, so Alexis gave her a Percocet. Later Michele took antibiotics, vitamin C, another steroid, and more pain pills. She never needed an Ambien or the Valium that Martin had requested.

Early that evening she was lucid enough to carry on a conversation. When Alexis told her how long she had been sedated, Michele was alarmed.

"Lexi, I don't know why," Michele said woozily, "but your dad kept giving me medication. He kept giving me things, telling me to swallow."

The pills made her nauseous, but even after she had vomited, Martin had given her more drugs and made her take sips of the liquid Lortab.

"He just kept handing me things," Michele cried. "Even after I started to throw up. He kept giving me stuff."

Michele told her daughter she had protested. "I said, 'I don't need this.' He said, 'Yes, you need this.'"

Fearful that her husband was intentionally trying to overmedicate her for some reason, Michele said she didn't want to be left in Martin's care alone.

"She was upset," Alexis remembered. "I knew my mom—I could hear it in her voice."

Because she still couldn't see and had no idea what her husband had given her, Michele asked Alexis to hand her each pill, tell her what it was, and let her feel the shape and size of the medication.

"She actually had me take out every medication from the pill bottle and she wanted to feel what the pills felt like in her fingers so that if my dad tried to give her anything she knew what he was giving her," said Alexis years later. "Because at that time she could not see."

Over the next few hours, as she began to fully recover from the drug-induced haze, Michele seemed gripped by fear.

That evening Alexis bathed her mother in the same Jacuzzi tub in which she would be found dead five days later.

Throughout her life, Michele's favorite way to relax had been to take a bath. Alexis turned the water as hot as possible, the way she knew her mom enjoyed her baths. Michele leaned her head back under the faucet as Alexis helped shampoo and rinse her hair. When she'd finished, Michele sat up straight.

"Alexis." Michele reached out and took her daughter's hand. "If anything happens to me, make sure it wasn't your dad."

"Mom." Alexis paused, momentarily stunned. "What are you talking about?"

"Make sure it wasn't your father." Michele's voice quivered. Then she began to cry.

———

For the next five days, Alexis dutifully watched over her mother. She maintained a meticulous record of all the drugs, food, and water her mom consumed, along with her vitals, on the Zyrtec notepad, which she stored on top of a pink container holding her mom's medication. Later, she switched to a small black notebook with gray lined paper, transferring the information from the Zyrtec pad so the data would be stored in one place.

Alexis also took over her mother's household duties. She cooked, cleaned, and drove the girls to school and ballet. As Michele healed, her younger daughters gave her get-well gifts, including stuffed animals and cards. The teddy bears and flowers were displayed around Michele's bedroom and hospital bed.

Two days after the surgery, Alexis and Martin both accompanied Michele to her first postoperative appointment with Dr. Thompson in Layton.

Dr. Thompson unraveled the gauze, noting the wounds were healing properly and his patient was in good spirits. Michele's eyelid sutures were removed and replaced with surgical tape.

Once she could see, Michele was no longer confined to her bed. But her mind seemed to be reeling, as if she no longer trusted her husband. She tried to review Martin's T-Mobile phone records, to check if he had contacted Gypsy. But when she tried to log on to his account, she discovered he had changed the password.

Michele confronted her husband, and they argued in their bedroom. Alexis eavesdropped outside the door. Michele told Martin he would not get away with an affair or with hiding his records.

"I want the phone records—I am not going to let this die," Michele shouted.

"I haven't spoken to her!" he bellowed.

"Then let me see your phone records. I want the new password."

Over the last few days, Martin and Gypsy had exchanged twenty-eight texts—he couldn't show his wife the bill.

Inventing a preposterous lie, he said he couldn't provide his wife with his password because his work cell phone was owned by the state of Utah, which runs the Developmental Center, and it would be considered a violation of patient privacy.

"I don't believe your story!" Michele huffed.

Fuming, Martin stomped out of the bedroom as Alexis quickly scurried away from the door. A few minutes later he returned.

"I want to take you on a cruise," he declared. "Once we get clearance from the doctor, let's go away for two weeks so you can relax and recover."

Michele must have known the offer was insincere.

On Easter Sunday—April 8—Michele had a second post-op appointment with Dr. Thompson, where more of the stitches were removed.

That afternoon the children congregated at home to celebrate the holiday, which had always been a big event in the MacNeill house. But Michele wasn't feeling well and stayed in her bedroom, complaining of nausea and a migraine. The next evening, Martin called and said he had to work late. Michele asked Rachel to drive by the Developmental Center and check the parking lot for his car. Rachel did so, then called her mom. "It wasn't there."

When Martin arrived home, Michele confronted him again about the phone records—she wanted proof he wasn't speaking with *that* woman.

"You're lying," Michele said testily. "I know you're lying."

Finally Martin told her he would show her the phone records, but on another night.

On Tuesday, April 10, Michele had another postoperative appointment. It would be the final time Dr. Thompson saw his patient.

By then Michele's swelling and bruising had begun to dissipate. Because she was healing so well, Alexis felt comfortable enough to return to school in Nevada, and had packed her bags before the appointment.

Martin, Alexis, and Ada escorted Michele to Dr. Thompson's office, where the surgeon removed staples from the top of Michele's head. Once they had been taken out, Michele joked, "Good! I no longer have horns."

Dr. Thompson would later say he was pleased with Michele's healing. "She was starting to be able to see the results a little bit because the swelling was going down—she was positive," Thompson recalled. "I was happy with how everything was coming along and I think she was starting to get excited."

Martin asked Thompson if his wife had healed enough to go on a cruise on Sunday—five days from then. "I want her to get away and have two full weeks to recover and relax and heal."

Alexis flinched at that, and gave her mother a sideways glance.

"It surprised me," Alexis later said in court. "He had never said anything [to me] before about taking her on a cruise, but he asked Dr. Thompson." No evidence was ever recovered to show Martin had intentions of planning a vacation with his wife.

Dr. Thompson asked about her medication and Michele said she was down to just one Percocet a day. She had no issues with anxiety or sleep and hadn't taken any Valium, Ambien, or Phenergan since the night she had been left in Martin's care.

"She was taking very little medication," Alexis said years later. "Most of her pain was really under control and she was feeling good."

Despite that, Martin called Dr. Thompson's office shortly after the appointment, requesting thirty additional Percocet and more Phenergan.

Following the appointment, the four went to a nearby Sizzler in Bountiful for an early dinner. Michele ordered her usual—teriyaki chicken with extra chutney. At 6 P.M., they drove to the Salt Lake City airport and dropped Alexis off for her flight, exchanging hugs and kisses. Alexis arrived back home in Nevada that night around 8 P.M. and called her parents. "Just letting you know I got home all right."

In Pleasant Grove, Michele visited with her girls as Martin discreetly texted Gypsy. Throughout that day he and Gypsy had exchanged several texts and one phone call.

Later that evening, Michele curled up in her hospital bed and fell asleep.

Hours later Michele MacNeill would be dead.

15.

On the morning of his wife's death, Martin MacNeill awoke before dawn. He dressed in a pair of black slacks, a dark button-down shirt, and his long white doctor's coat. Sliding behind the wheel of his car, he drove the three miles to the Utah State Developmental Center, arriving at the office at around 6 A.M.

It was April 11, 2007—a Wednesday.

The morning started out like any other.

At 6:48 A.M., Martin called Gypsy from his office phone, but she didn't answer. While they didn't speak then, Martin and his mistress remained in contact throughout the day, exchanging thirty text messages.

Martin's weekly morning management meeting had been supplanted by the annual safety fair—an event organized by management to reduce workers' compensation claims. Martin and his team were expected to receive an award for their department's safety record.

At some point that morning, Martin spoke to his boss, medical services director Karen Clark. He complained about the timing of the ceremony, which was planned for 11:45 A.M., and asked for it to be rescheduled.

Meanwhile, at the Pleasant Grove home, Michele was awake but still groggy. She dressed in a dark jogging suit, sweeping her hair into a loose ponytail. She examined her face in the bathroom mirror. Although her eyes were bruised and cheeks swollen, she could see the early results of the face-lift. She was healing well and not in much pain.

Still weary, she plopped down on the couch in the bedroom and clicked on the TV. A short time later, Sabrina entered the room.

"Hey Mom," she said. "I left my ballet bag at dance class. But I'm going to get it after school. Don't worry."

"That's fine," Michele said.

Michele told her daughter that their father had already left for work but would be back to drive her and her sisters to school. Michele hugged Sabrina. "I love you, princess."

Sabrina knew her mom was still recovering from surgery, but thought she seemed a lot better. "She was normal. There was nothing odd about her behavior at all," Sabrina recalled. "She was tired because she had just woken up, but we had a perfectly normal conversation."

At about 7:45 A.M. Martin left his office and drove back to the Pleasant Grove house, but didn't go inside. Pulling his car into the driveway, he honked the horn, signaling Giselle, Elle, Sabrina, and Ada that he was ready to take them to school. The girls grabbed their book bags and piled into the car.

During the drive, Martin was unusually angry and impatient.

"Is everything okay?" Sabrina asked.

"Your mom's not feeling well," he huffed.

Sabrina found the remark odd, having just seen her mom.

Martin dropped the older girls off at John Hancock Charter School, arriving just before 8 A.M. By 8:30 A.M., Ada was dropped at American Heritage School, near the Developmental Center.

Martin would later tell the pathologist that he didn't return to work until after 9 A.M. From 8:30 until just after 9 A.M. his actions are untraceable.

At 8:41 A.M., Alexis called her mother on the home phone from her apartment in Henderson. Michele answered and said she would call her back. At 8:44 A.M., Michele returned her daughter's call from her cell phone.

"How are you doing, Mom?" Alexis asked.

"I'm good," Michele said, her tone upbeat.

Michele discussed her plans for the day and seemed happy to get back to her normal routine. Around 11:30 A.M. she was going to pick Ada up from school and take her daughter to get lunch at McDonald's. Later, she would drive the girls to ballet practice.

During the call, Michele seemed in good spirits.

"She was happy," Alexis remembered. "She sounded really upbeat . . . I could hear it in her voice."

And while Martin had been angry and impatient with his daughters, he seemed to be going out of his way to be abnormally kind to his wife.

"Your dad is being so, so nice to me. So sweet," Michele told Alexis. "He's taking good care of me."

Toward the end of the conversation, Alexis told her mom what she always told her before hanging up the phone: "I love you."

"I love you, too," Michele said.

It was the last time Alexis would ever hear her mother's voice.

By 9:11 A.M., Martin was back in his office at the Developmental Center. He placed a call to an 800 number. From his work phone, he called Alexis and left a message. He also called Michele's cell but she didn't answer. He left a message for his wife at 9:17 A.M., lasting thirty-six seconds.

"Michele. Don't you dare—don't you dare go anywhere," he said on the message. "Take it easy. Please. I'm very concerned, you just stay where you're at. I'm coming home. I'm going to make you a sandwich and we'll have a lovely lunch together. But just don't call anybody and don't go anywhere."

At 9:26 A.M., Martin also called Gypsy's cell phone, in a call lasting just twenty-four seconds.

From 9:30 A.M. till 11 A.M., Martin disappeared. He was not seen at work; he made no phone calls.

His whereabouts are unknown.

After hanging up with her mom, at around 9 A.M. in Utah, Alexis had gone to her neurology class at Touro University's Medical School.

During a break in the lecture, at around 10 A.M., she glanced at her cell phone and noticed something that left her uneasy—her dad had called from his office and left a voice message.

The missed call felt ominous. Her father almost never called her, especially from his work phone. Worried something was wrong, she immediately checked the voice mail.

Martin's tone was urgent. He said he felt Michele was "doing too much, too soon."

"Alexis. You need to call your mom. You need to call her right away," Martin said. "She's not listening to me. She's getting up. She's out of bed. You need to call her and tell her she needs to rest."

A shiver traveled down Alexis's spine.

"I thought it was strange. It was actually really strange," Alexis said years later. "Because my mom—I had just talked to her. She was doing really well. I had just been with her the day before and she wasn't in bed or bed-bound. She was back to kind of her normal self."

Later the phone call would seem even more peculiar. Reflecting back, Alexis realized her father didn't have her number memorized. To even make the call he would have had to have his cell phone in hand to find her number. And if that was the case, why wouldn't he call from his cell?

At the time, Alexis tried to push the negative thoughts from her mind. Before returning to her lecture, she called her mom at home, as her father had requested. There was no answer. Alexis called several more times but couldn't reach her mother.

By 10:30 A.M., Melissa Frost, the Developmental Center liability prevention specialist, was irritated with Martin. Frost had spent months organizing the safety fair. And now all her preparation was being ruined by one arrogant, demanding doctor.

For several years the Developmental Center had ranked number one in workers' compensation claims, and Frost had been hired to decrease workplace injuries. For three years she had organized the safety fair to promote safety practices. As part of the fair, Frost had planned an award ceremony and had selected two departments with high safety records to receive recognition—including Dr. Martin MacNeill and his staff. The presentation had been scheduled for a time when the greatest number of employees would be present to witness it.

At 8 A.M., Karen Clark's assistant had called, saying that the award ceremony would need to be rescheduled based on Dr. MacNeill's availability.

"You have to be ready to give the award at any moment," Clark's assistant told Frost. "Dr. MacNeill cannot be there at eleven forty-five."

"But no one would be there to see it!" Frost protested. Between 8 A.M. and 9 A.M. the direct-care staff would be assisting patients. "Part of the group that is receiving the award wouldn't even be there!"

"You just need to be ready when Dr. MacNeill is available," the assistant reiterated.

It was a directive and Frost had no choice but to comply. She hung up the phone and sighed. Frost spent the next fifteen minutes making phone calls to recruit employees for the ceremony, apologizing for the inconvenience. She knew Dr. MacNeill was difficult, but this was an egregious demand.

Why does he suddenly care about the safety fair? Frost wondered. *He never seemed to bother with it in the past.*

At around 9:30 A.M., Frost was in the conference room greeting staff as they trickled in and out of the safety fair. Booths were arranged in a circle around the room, each representing an activity considered to be unsafe. As she greeted employees, Frost got another call from Karen Clark's assistant, confirming that the award ceremony had been rescheduled. She advised Frost that they would no longer need to rush, but would instead have the ceremony closer to the originally arranged time. Clark's assistant explained that the doctor's wife was sick and he had to leave to take care of her.

"Dr. MacNeill doesn't have to be there for the ceremony," Frost said. "A member of the department could receive the award on his behalf."

"He will be there," Clark's assistant replied.

Frost made calls from her office to inform employees that the ceremony would take place closer to the previously designated time.

Around 10:40 A.M., Frost received another call directly from Karen Clark.

"We're going to do the award right now," she said. "Get people in the room."

Martin would only be there for a brief time, and the ceremony needed to happen while he was present, Clark said. "We're doing it now."

Just before 11 A.M., Martin made a call from his office to a cell phone—the same 800 number he had called earlier—lasting six minutes.

He then stepped out of his office and headed toward the conference room in the adjacent building. On the walk he would encounter several coworkers, who all remember the doctor was acting strangely.

In the hallway outside the medical area, he passed by the janitorial supervisor.

"Hello, Dr. MacNeill," the woman said with a smile.

"I can't talk," Martin said, brushing past her. "I'm in a hurry. I need to get to the safety fair."

It seemed odd—whenever she encountered the doctor, he always stopped to chat.

"He seemed to me to be very hurried to get over to the safety fair," remembered the janitorial supervisor. "And he did seem very anxious, which I did not understand."

Martin dashed across the campus. Outside the conference room, he passed by the human resources manager, John David Laycock. Martin stopped him.

"Hey. I need my picture taken," Martin announced.

"For what?" Laycock asked. "Why?"

"I won an award and I need my picture taken," Martin said, his tone adamant. Laycock pointed him toward the conference room.

Shortly after 11 A.M., Martin arrived at the safety fair. Frost had managed to gather a few people, quickly scurrying to accommodate the doctor.

When Martin briefly spoke to Frost, he seemed impatient and short-tempered. "If we're going to get this done, we've got to do it now. I've got to pick up my daughter and go check on my wife."

At 11:15 A.M., during a short ceremony, Dr. MacNeill was presented with an engraved plaque. Administrator Roma Henrie was handed a camera and asked to take a picture. With a wide smile plastered across his face, Martin held the plaque as Henrie quickly snapped a photo.

"Did you get me in that picture?" Martin asked Henrie. "Make sure you get me in that picture." He seemed nervous and belligerent.

"Yes, Dr. MacNeill." She nodded. "I got you in the picture."

"Maybe you ought to take a second one," Martin sniped, scowling.

Taken aback, Henrie assured him that he was in the image. Later, Henrie would be so distressed by the encounter that she would file a formal complaint.

After receiving the plaque, Martin stopped at one of the booths, where he chatted with another employee for about five to ten minutes. A few feet away, Frost could barely conceal her frustration.

"After we gave the award—we had this big rush to have it—he kind of stayed and talked to a vendor and I thought that was kind of odd to rush, and not have it when all the people could be there, and then there was no rush to leave," Frost remembered.

By 11:30 A.M., Martin had left the Developmental Center. He called Michele's cell phone again at 11:32 A.M. He left another voice message telling her he was on his way home to make her a "lovely lunch."

At 11:35 A.M., Martin arrived at Ada's private school, about five minutes late. Ada climbed into the car, surprised to see her father. All morning long she had been anticipating an after-school trip with her mom to McDonald's, one of the kindergartener's favorite fast-food restaurants.

"Can we get McDonald's, Dad?" Ada asked.

"No," he said brusquely.

Instead, Martin drove directly back to the house, arriving shortly before 11:45 A.M.

Ada ran inside as Martin leisurely sauntered into the kitchen.

"Mom. I'm home." Ada dropped her backpack in the front room.

Michele didn't answer.

She passed through the living room and peered down the hallway. "I'm home. I'm home. Mom?"

No response.

Entering her parents' bedroom, Ada glanced around. She stepped farther into the room and turned the corner into the bathroom.

A shallow pool of murky, brownish water filled the bathtub. Michele's body was slumped under the faucet. Her head sagged to the side, hair floating toward the drain.

Her glassy eyes were open, gaze fixed toward where Ada stood gawking in the doorway.

Turning away, Ada darted out of the room and found her father in the kitchen. Grabbing his hand, she led him to the bathroom. "Something's wrong with Mommy."

Martin trudged forward slowly. Confused, Ada yanked his arm.

"Come quick." She tugged harder, leading him down the hall. "Come quick."

Martin stepped into the bathroom; Ada stayed in the bedroom. A second later he hollered to his daughter. "Run. Get help!"

Ada's small voice asked, "Where should I go?"

"Go next door," he screeched. "Get help. Quick!"

16.

need an ambulance!" Martin MacNeill roared at the 911 operator.

"Okay. What's the problem, sir?" the dispatcher asked. "Sir, what's wrong?"

"My wife has fallen in the bathtub!" Martin cried as he knelt beside Michele's body and drained the water from the tub.

Dialing 911 from his cell phone, Martin had connected with the Utah County dispatch in Spanish Fork at 11:46 A.M. Seconds into the call, he hysterically spit out his home address in a garbled slur. The dispatcher attempted to map out the location on her computer screen as she assessed the nature of the caller's emergency.

"Who's in the bathtub? Who's in the bathtub?" the female dispatcher asked, the clicking of her keyboard rattling audibly in the background.

"My wife!" Martin cried out.

"Okay. Is she conscious?"

"She's not." His voice cracked. "Actually, I'm . . . I'm a physician."

"Okay, sir . . ."

"I'm in trouble." Martin spoke over her abrasively.

"Okay, sir. I can't understand you," the dispatcher said. "Can you calm down just a little bit?"

"I need help!"

"Okay. Your wife is unconscious?"

"She's unconscious. She's underwater!" Martin's voice rose.

"Okay. Did you get her out of the water?"

"I can't. I couldn't lift her. I let the water out. I have CPR in progress."

"She's under the water?" the operator asked.

"She's under the water. Now when are you going to get me an ambulance?" he spat condescendingly.

"Okay. Is she breathing at all?"

"She's not!"

"Okay, sir. The ambulance has been paged. They're on their way. Okay. Do not hang up."

Ignoring the operator, Martin disconnected the call.

"Sir?" the operator asked, but the dial tone resonated over the phone line.

During the call, Martin's phone number had not been recognized by the dispatcher's caller identification. And because he called from a cell phone, his location could not be traced.

Using the address Martin had given, the county dispatcher narrowed the location of the emergency to the Creekside subdivision, then connected to the Pleasant Grove Police Department, who serviced that jurisdiction and had an ambulance in the area. Pleasant Grove senior 911 dispatcher Heidi Peterson took the call.

"Hey, we got a distressed caller from 305 Millcreek," the county dispatcher told Peterson. "All we could get is 305 Millcreek. He sounded really stressed out. I don't know what it was. It may have been a medical, I think. It sounded more like a medical. He mentioned something about his wife."

Peterson used her computer to search for the address, but the house number the dispatcher heard—305 Millcreek—was not accurate. The MacNeill home was located at 3058 Millcreek Road. Peterson explained to the county dispatcher that she was having trouble finding the address. "Was it 305 . . . ? Did he give a west or south?"

"We tried to get that out of him and then he disconnected. And nothing came up on our caller ID."

"I know it's a gated community we have. So I know . . ." Peterson skimmed the computer screen. "Could it have been 3005 North Millcreek, I wonder?"

"It could have been," the county operator said.

Two minutes after Martin made the call, Peterson dispatched police to the wrong address. They would not reach the MacNeills' property until 11:55 A.M.—a seven-minute delay—due to the confusion over the address. It would take an additional five minutes for the ambulance to arrive.

Meanwhile, precious seconds ticked by and Michele remained unconscious in the tub.

At 11:48 A.M., after hanging up on the dispatcher, Martin dialed 911 a second time. Once again he was briefly connected to the county operator. Then he was transferred to Peterson at the Pleasant Grove Police Department.

"I need help!" Martin shouted at Peterson. "Do you understand?"

"Sir. Sir. They're on their way," she said. "Is your wife breathing?"

"She is not. I am a physician. I have CPR in progress. Do you understand?"

At this point, however, the neighbors had not entered the bathroom. Michele was still in the tub and CPR was not being performed.

"You're doing CPR?" Peterson asked. "Sir, how old is your wife?"

"My wife is fifty years old. She just had surgery here a couple of days—or a week ago."

"What kind of surgery did she have?" Peterson asked.

"She had a face-lift!" He sounded irate.

"She had a face-lift?"

"Yes!"

"Okay. Do you know how to do CPR?"

"I'm doing it!" Martin hollered before abruptly hanging up once again.

"Okay. Do not hang—" Peterson said as the call disconnected.

At 11:52 A.M. Peterson tried to call Martin back, but he didn't answer.

It was an unusual call. In over a decade working as a dispatcher, Peterson had never received an emergency call from someone as angry and emotional as Martin. Years later she would still recall his abrasive shrieks.

"He was just screaming at me," Peterson remembered. "I've taken a lot of calls, but I've never taken one where someone was just screaming at me like that man."

———

Next door, Ada had reached the Daniels family's front door.

When her father sent her for help, Ada had first tried banging on the door of the neighbor to the north of the MacNeill house. When there was no answer, she backtracked toward the Danielses' house.

Kristi Daniels was in the front room visiting with Angie Aguilar and another mother who lived in the neighborhood. As her guests were preparing to leave, there was a low, soft thump on the front door—which Kristi recognized as that of a child's knock. Cracking open the door, she found Ada MacNeill staring back up at her.

"My dad needs some help," the girl said.

What began as a crisp, quiet April morning in Pleasant Grove erupted into an afternoon of chaos and confusion for the residents of Creekside. Patrol cars and ambulances mobbed the MacNeill property, the rotating red and blue lights illuminating the front lawn. Clusters of concerned and curious neighbors gathered outside their homes, flooding into the street.

Inside the house at 3058 Millcreek, paramedics surrounded Michele. Just before noon, Pleasant Grove detective Marc Dana Wright arrived at the scene. Burly and bald with a short goatee and mustache, the twelve-year veteran of the Pleasant Grove Police Department was assigned as the lead detective on Michele's death.

The investigation would be cursory. Scant evidence was collected and only eight photos were taken at the scene. The only witness to be interviewed was Martin MacNeill. The subsequent police report consisted of a few pages.

Detective Wright entered through the open front door of the house and made his way to the bedroom, where he was briefed by one of the first responders.

"She was found by the husband," an officer told Wright, nodding in Martin's direction. "He's pretty hysterical."

Wright attempted to take a statement from Martin, jotting down notes. Martin explained to Wright and to several of the first responders that he'd found Michele slumped over the edge of the tub, her face in the water. He told Wright he wasn't sure who let the water out of the bathtub, but that he thought it was Doug Daniels. On the 911 call, however, Martin had admitted he let the water drain, a detail he would also later confirm to the pathologist.

Martin was allowed to return to his wife's side and Wright began his search of the house. In the bedroom, the detective noted Michele's sopping, bloody clothes strewn on the carpet. He used a digital camera to snap a picture of her shirt, bra, and undergarment, as well as the hospital bed and a tote full of medication.

Wright then scanned the bathroom, scribbling notes about the layout. The tub was affixed to the back wall and flanked by a stand-alone shower stall and closet. Adjacent to the tub was a marble countertop with double sinks mounted atop the wooden cabinets. The bathroom walls were painted taupe, the floors marbled brown tile.

From the doorway, Wright aimed his digital camera toward the tub and snapped a wide view of the bathroom. The flash reflected off the water puddle in the center of the tile floor.

Stepping further into the bathroom, Wright approached the tub. Peering down into the basin, he noticed bottles of shampoo and conditioner tossed near the drain. It appeared as if they had been knocked over in the commotion.

Squatting down, Wright narrowed his eyes and closely examined the tub. A small blood spot blemished the white porcelain ledge across from the faucet. Framing a photo, Wright snapped a close-up of the blood.

Widening his perimeter around the bathtub, Wright discovered two more bloodstains on the tile floor, which he also photographed. Near the tub an amorphous pink blob was diluted with water. A smaller, darker blood pool dripped into the grout.

Meanwhile, Martin continued to dash in and out of the bedroom, barking orders at the paramedics. He grew increasingly erratic, and just before noon, Wright watched the fire chief escort Martin out of the house. While he had investigated hundreds of deaths, Wright had rarely encountered someone as belligerent as Martin MacNeill was that afternoon. But although the detective found his behavior bizarre, at the time he did not view it as suspicious.

If investigators had dug deeper, would they have uncovered Martin's affair with Gypsy? Had they questioned the MacNeill daughters, could they have learned that it was Martin who insisted his wife undergo the face-lift?

Instead, Michele's death was written off as an unfortunate accident. Within days of her passing, the case would be closed.

Since receiving her father's voice message that morning, Alexis had been calling her parents' home and Michele's cell phone, attempting to get ahold of her mother. After each unanswered call, her anxiety swelled.

At 11:59 P.M., during another break in her class, Alexis called her father. By this point, Martin had been escorted outside. He was standing on the front porch with the fire chief when he answered the phone. The moment Alexis heard his voice, she knew something was wrong.

"Your mother's not breathing," Martin bellowed. "She's in the bathtub. I called an ambulance."

Before Alexis could ask a question or make sense of her father's words, he hung up the phone. The color drained from Alexis's face. Dropping her bags, she screamed. She bolted toward her car and drove directly to the airport.

As the police and ambulances sped toward the MacNeill house, Sabrina MacNeill was on campus at her junior high school, having lunch. The warble of ambulance sirens sounded in the distance, growing louder as the minutes passed. Sabrina saw emergency vehicles whiz past the school.

I hope that's not for anyone in my family, she thought to herself.

At the house, Martin phoned the Developmental Center, reaching nurse practitioner Jim Van Zant. "Paramedics are doing a code on my wife," Martin said in a panic, requesting assistance at his house. He also phoned his son Damian and told him to meet him at the hospital.

At 12:05 P.M., Alexis called Martin's cell again and he answered.

"We're doing CPR," he said, then hung up.

At the time, paramedics were the ones actually performing CPR.

Between 12:13 P.M. and 12:17 P.M., Martin and Alexis phoned each other four times, each call lasting just a few seconds.

Soon, Martin's colleague Steve Nickelson arrived at the house. Van Zant had alerted him to the emergency, and Nickelson drove over, hoping to help. When Nickelson pulled up, Martin was on his front porch. He nodded at Nickelson. "Go inside. Michele's in the bedroom."

Nickelson went down the hall and entered the master bedroom. Seeing Michele bloody and unconscious, he quietly gasped. Over the years Nickelson had met Michele and several of the couple's daughters at various charity benefits. Shocked and shaken, Nickelson observed as the medics worked to save her life. Once he realized there was nothing he could do to help, he left the bedroom and exited the house.

Outside, Martin dialed Alexis's number. Before saying a word, he handed Nickelson his phone. "Tell Alexis," Martin whispered. "I can't."

Dazed, Nickelson took the phone and put it to his ear.

"Is she okay?" Alexis shouted hysterically. "Is she okay? Tell me she's okay!"

Despite nearly two decades of handling emergencies, at that moment Nickelson found himself speechless.

"I couldn't bring myself to tell her that her mom looked like she was dead," he recalled. Instead, he told Alexis that Michele had "coded."

"It doesn't look good," he said. "You got to get up here. You got to get up here now."

Alexis was in her car, speeding toward the airport, hot tears spilling down her cheeks. She dropped the phone. At that moment she had no doubt: her father had murdered her mother.

"I just started screaming, 'He killed her! He killed her!'" she said years later. "I just knew, I knew right away that he had done that. My mother had told me that if anything happened to her, make sure it wasn't my father. And I knew it was him."

After hanging up with Alexis, Nickelson turned to Martin. With stilted speech, Martin related that after Ada had found Michele, he rushed to his wife's side and drained the bloody water.

It struck Nickelson as odd that Martin would drain the tub. Both he and

Martin had been on death scenes and knew it was important to preserve evidence.

Strapped to a gurney, Michele was loaded into the back of an ambulance. Police and firefighters trickled out of the house as neighbors continued to mill about, speaking amongst themselves in hushed tones. Doug and Kristi Daniels witnessed the scene from their driveway.

Emerging from the house, Detective Wright approached Doug. "Do you know the MacNeills?" Wright asked.

"Yeah. We're right next door."

"Could you close the place up?" Wright nodded toward the MacNeill house.

"Of course," Doug replied.

Reentering the house, Doug wandered back in the MacNeills' master bathroom. Bloodstains remained on the carpet, along with more blood smeared on the tile floor. Unsure if Michele would live or die, and knowing their children would return home soon, Doug felt compelled to clean up the scene, hoping to minimize their trauma.

Doug glanced around the bathroom and searched for a towel. Oddly, he could find none. He searched the bedroom, where Michele's bloody top and bra remained on the floor. Whatever bottoms she may have been wearing were nowhere in the bedroom or bathroom.

Browsing through the rest of the house, Doug entered the laundry room, where he found three or four damp towels wadded in a pile on the floor. He grabbed the towels, returned to the scene, and wiped the blood from the tub and tile. He dabbed the carpet but was unable to remove all the blood from the fibers. When he was finished, Doug brought the wet towels back to the laundry room.

Meanwhile, Kristi retreated to her house to check on Ada, who was playing with Kristi's son. Ada didn't ask questions and Kristi tried to appear as if everything was normal. She gave the children a box of crayons and some paper, encouraging them to draw. Later she fed Ada a snack and watched over her until a family friend arrived to retrieve the girl.

"Ada stayed in the house to play until someone came and got her," Kristi remembered. "I didn't want to ask her any questions. I didn't want to be involved in what she saw."

When a loved one dies, it's normally a solemn time. But at the American Fork Hospital, Martin's belligerent behavior rattled the nurses and ER staff. Once Michele was declared dead, Martin crumbled. Damian arrived at the hospital to find his mom dead and his father in hysterics.

Damian grabbed Martin by the shoulders. "What happened?"

Because Michele's death had been unattended, at 1:30 P.M. her body was picked up by the Utah State Medical Examiner's Office to be taken to Salt Lake City for an autopsy.

Martin, meanwhile, continued to make phone calls. Among those he spoke with was Dr. Scott Thompson. When Martin told the surgeon his wife was dead, Thompson was dumbfounded—he had just seen Michele the day before. He was deeply distressed, having never lost a patient before.

"I worried she wasn't walking around enough and got a blood clot in her leg—that could have caused a pulmonary embolism," he later said in court. "That's what I was worried about because it was such an acute, sudden thing."

As the last physician on record to see Michele, Dr. Von Welch received a call directly from the emergency room doctor that afternoon. He was astonished to hear that Michele had even gone forward with the surgery.

"I was shocked," he recalled. "At the time I examined her, she was healthy, and it was just unexpected to hear that she would have a bad outcome from surgery."

17.

Martin left the hospital and returned home, where he plopped down on the couch in the front room. He took out his phone and texted Gypsy. *I lost Michele.*

Gypsy was confused. Martin had mentioned his wife was having surgery, and in recovery, but the message was ambiguous. Gypsy said she replied innocuously. *Did she go to the store? You can't find her?*

No. Michele is dead, Martin typed.

Stunned, Gypsy replied, *I'm so sorry.*

Martin also called his sister Mary to inform her of his wife's passing. By then Mary, who was still living in California, was his only remaining sibling. She took the next plane to Utah and would stay with Martin for the next two weeks.

As Martin made phone calls, Damian returned home as well, and sat down on the couch beside his father. Because of Martin's apparent breakdown at the hospital, Damian had assigned himself the unfortunate task of being the bearer of the horrifying news to the rest of the family.

At the hospital he had briefly spoken with Alexis.

"Mom—she didn't make it," Damian had said, his voice husky with sorrow.

Alexis sobbed, her body convulsing with painful tremors.

Damian had then reached Vanessa at her apartment in Bluffdale.

"I don't know how to tell you this, Vanessa," Damian said. "Mom's dead."

Incensed and in anguish, Vanessa chucked her cell phone across the apartment, shrieking. The phone hit the wall, shattering into pieces. "No! No! No!"

Because she didn't have a car, Vanessa got a ride from a friend to her parents' house.

Damian tried phoning Rachel multiple times, but she didn't answer her phone. Over the next few hours, Martin also left several cryptic voice mails on Rachel's phone.

"Rachel. Something happened," Martin said in one message. "Come home now."

While fielding phone calls from family and friends, Damian made arrangements for Giselle, Elle, and Sabrina to be picked up from school. He also repeatedly called his girlfriend, Eileen Heng, who had been in class at BYU. Around 1 P.M., when class ended, Eileen checked her phone and noticed she had a dozen missed calls—all from Damian. She called him back.

"My mom," Damian said, his voice shaky. "She died."

Eileen left campus and drove directly to the MacNeill house, arriving after 2 P.M. Stepping through the front door into the living room, she saw Martin and Damian seated together on the couch. Eileen rushed to their side. She wrapped her arms around Damian and then hugged Martin. "What can I do for you?"

Martin sighed and said somberly, "Let's go to the bedroom."

The three filed into the master bedroom, where just a few hours earlier Michele's life had ended. The three sat on the couch in the sitting area as Martin recounted how he found his wife. Over the next few days, Martin would tell this same account of his wife's death multiple times. The details remained consistent—the facts solidifying—as he repeated the story to friends, family, and coworkers.

Beginning with Ada coming home after school, Martin described finding Michele folded over the tub's ledge, her face submerged in the water, her knees on the tile floor.

"There was blood everywhere," Martin told Eileen.

Because Michele was partially nude, he said he thought she had been getting ready for a bath or had just used the toilet. Martin discussed various scenarios, speculating on how he believed she'd lost her life.

"I just want to know how she died," he said. Maybe she fell and hit her head and fell into the tub? Martin questioned. Or perhaps she overdosed on the medication.

Martin also expressed concerns about his wife's cholesterol and high blood pressure—suggesting she wasn't properly controlling her health problems with her prescription medication. "Michele had high blood pressure and cholesterol," Martin told Eileen. "But she refused to take her pills." He repeated over and over, "She wasn't taking her pills."

After moments of speculation, Martin made a request directly to Eileen. "Can you get Michele's prescriptions from the bathroom?" Martin explained that since Michele apparently wasn't being consistent with her medication, he wanted to review which pills she had been taking. It was important that he account for the medicine in front of a witness, he said.

Eileen readily agreed. Leaving her flip-flops beside the couch, Eileen crossed the bedroom barefoot. As she approached the bathroom, she stepped in a large wet spot on the carpet. Glancing down, she noticed a crimson stain standing out against the beige fibers.

Entering the bathroom, Eileen peered around. Unlike what Martin had said about "blood everywhere," she saw none.

Near the toilet was a plastic container holding about ten prescription pill bottles, just as Martin had described. Retrieving the container, she brought it back to the bedroom and handed it to Martin. Martin asked his son to open each container and count the number of pills. Damian wrote the type of pill and quantity of each on a white pad of paper.

When they were finished, Martin seemed frustrated. "I don't want to do this anymore."

He didn't say if anything was missing.

Martin told his son and Eileen he wanted the drugs destroyed, because he thought they might have contributed to his wife's death. "Flush them down the toilet. I can't bear to look at them."

Eileen tossed the loose pills into the toilet and watched as they disappeared in one flush. Then she took the empty pill bottles to the garage.

"He asked me to and he just lost his wife and I wanted to help," Eileen said later, when asked why she flushed the medication.

Martin then requested that Eileen tidy up the master bedroom before other family members arrived. Although the room seemed clean to her, she straightened up a pile of magazines on the table, stacking them neatly.

The hospital bed in the middle of the room appeared as if it hadn't been slept in. An hour later, when Eileen returned to the master bedroom, the bed was gone.

Word of Michele's death spread like a virus through a series of ghastly phone calls. In hushed whispers, neighbors and friends delivered the news among the church congregation. The MacNeill children spoke to family members, confirming the awful truth: their mother was dead.

Michele's close friend Cheryl Radmall heard about the loss from a mutual friend. Cheryl phoned Karen Klinger, who was still battling cancer. The two women went to Loreen Thompson's house to tell her the news in person.

Opening the door to unexpectedly find two members of her friendship foursome, Loreen's first thought was that something must have happened to Michele's husband.

"Is something wrong with Martin?" Loreen asked.

"It's Michele," Cheryl cried. "She passed away."

"No!" Loreen threw her hand over her mouth in shock.

While friends across Utah were hearing of the tragic passing, no one in the MacNeill family had called Michele's mom or any of her siblings.

That afternoon, Michele's sister Terry Pearson received a call from a friend in California, who'd heard the news through a network of acquaintances in Utah. The friend had phoned Terry to offer her sympathy at the loss of her sister. Having heard nothing from the MacNeill family concerning Michele, Terry was stunned and alarmed.

"What are you talking about?" Terry said. "Who told you that?"

At first she questioned if it was even true. It had to be a rumor, a mistake, a terrible joke. In a panic, Terry called her youngest sister, Linda Cluff. As Terry explained the disturbing phone call she'd received, Linda felt a hot tingling on the back of her neck.

"That can't be true," Linda said. "I've heard nothing."

In shock, Linda could hardly speak. Her daughter Jill Harper-Smith called Michele's cell phone. One of the children answered and confirmed it was true—Linda's beloved sister was dead. Tears flooded Linda's eyes. Blended with the grief, a sick feeling boiled inside her gut. She hadn't yet learned any of the details of Michele's death, but somehow, at that moment, she instantly knew.

"He killed my sister," she whispered breathlessly. "Martin killed my sister."

Michele's family had always known there was something terribly wrong with Martin and had feared that one day he would harm her. For three decades he had stolen Michele from her family through lies and manipulation. Linda knew that her own mother, who by then was in her late eighties, would be devastated. Linda went to her house to inform her of the loss of her daughter in person.

As Linda told her mother the shattering news, Helen's words from thirty years ago seemed haunting. "I won't be surprised if he killed her someday," Helen had once said. Now it seemed that awful premonition had come true.

Evil had prevailed. Michele was dead.

Trembling, Michele's mom called Martin. He hung up on her.

Throughout the afternoon, many of Michele's loved ones congregated at the MacNeill house. The doorbell rang repeatedly as neighbors and members of the church brought casseroles and frozen dinners to assist the new widower. Michele's friends came by to offer condolences and check on Martin. A bishop from the church stopped by to perform a blessing.

At Damian's request, his friend Chris had picked up Giselle, Elle, and Sabrina from school. He also picked up Ada from the Danielses' house and brought the four girls back to his own home.

Huddling together with her sisters on Chris's couch, Sabrina knew something was wrong. She turned to Ada.

"What's going on?" Sabrina asked. "Do you know what's going on?"

Ada whispered to Sabrina, "Something happened to Mom."

The bad feeling in the pit of Sabrina's stomach swelled.

The girls stayed at Chris's house for over an hour, until Damian called to tell them to come back. By the time Chris pulled into the driveway of the Pleasant Grove home, Sabrina's eyes were brimming with tears.

"I remember walking in and I already knew that something really bad . . . I knew that something bad had happened," Sabrina recalled. "I ran into my room and I was already really emotional and crying."

Sabrina collapsed on the floor of her room next to her armchair, throwing her forearms across her face and weeping. Elle plopped down on the bed. Giselle and Ada stood anxiously nearby.

Minutes later Martin entered the bedroom, a towel draped over his face. He swiped away the towel, revealing a somber expression.

"Girls . . ." Martin's voice wavered. "I don't know how to tell you this, but your mom is dead."

Each of the girls began to sob, asking questions. Sabrina gasped, searing tears streaming down her cheeks. She had just found a family. And now, after just three years, she had lost her mom.

"We're so lucky," Martin sniveled. "Families get to be together forever."

He left the room and closed the door.

Just one day after leaving Utah, Alexis MacNeill was back, and desperate for answers.

A friend met her at the airport and drove her to the hospital in American Fork. Alexis spoke to hospital staff and learned that her mother's body had already been transferred to Salt Lake City by the medical examiner's office.

Returning home, Alexis bolted through the front door, finding Damian and his girlfriend in the living room. Alexis gave Damian a quick hug before darting directly to her parents' room.

A poisonous silence filled the bedroom. The lights were off. Martin was on the couch, hanging his head in his hands and staring despondently into the dark.

Ignoring him, Alexis riffled through the bedroom and bathroom, searching for her mom's prescriptions. She needed to know exactly what remained.

Peering around the bedroom, Alexis noticed that the hospital bed was gone. Many of her mom's things were no longer displayed—including the get-well gifts and stuffed animals her daughters had given her. The pink container that had held Michele's medication and the rollaway nightstand that had sat beside the hospital bed were also missing.

Stepping into the bathroom, Alexis noticed there were no towels. The bath mats that usually lay in front of the tub and shower had also vanished.

Alexis looked around, but she could not find the medication. Also gone was the little black notebook that she had used to document all of her mother's vitals. In the armoire that held the TV, however, she was able to locate the Zyrtec notepad, which she had originally used to track the medication.

"The first thing I did was look for the medication. I looked right where I had left them," Alexis said years later. "There was nothing. There was no medication and the black book wasn't there as well."

Alexis turned to her father. "Where's her prescriptions?"

Glancing up, Martin shook his head. "I don't know. The police must have taken them," he lied.

"What happened?" Alexis asked her father.

Speaking slowly and somberly, Martin once again explained how he found Michele, offering various theories, including that she may have died from a pulmonary embolism.

"Show me how you found her," Alexis said defiantly. "Show me."

Martin rose from the couch, and his daughter followed him into the bathroom.

"I wanted to know what happened," Alexis later testified. "He took me into the bathroom and showed me how he found my mom."

To describe the position of his wife's body, Martin squatted beside the tub where the rug had been placed. He draped his body over the edge and stuck his head into the basin.

"I tried to pull her out." Martin peered up at Alexis. "I was too weak."

Alexis could barely look at him.

Continuing to search for the medication, Alexis rummaged through the kitchen and living room. Entering the garage, she found the hospital bed. Piled on top of it were wet towels, the bathroom rug, and her mother's clothing balled in a bloody heap. On the bed she discovered the missing stuffed animals and get-well gifts. In a five-gallon Rubbermaid bucket she also found the medical equipment, including a humidifier and blood pressure cuff.

Touching her mother's things, she was swamped by grief. Suddenly, an overwhelming ache gripped Alexis's chest. She burst into hysterical sobs.

By 5 P.M., Michele's firstborn, Rachel, still hadn't learned of her mother's death. When she went to work that morning, she'd left her cell phone at her apartment. When she returned home that evening, she checked her cell and discovered she had missed a barrage of calls—mostly from her father.

She was overcome by a sickening sense of dread.

Something is obviously very wrong, she thought.

Rachel tried to call her father, but he didn't answer.

Still clutching her phone, Rachel fled her apartment, got in her car, and drove directly toward Pleasant Grove. While driving, she checked her voice mail.

The first message was from her dad—his voice dripping with desperation. "Rachel. Quick. Get to the hospital. It's your mom. Quick."

A molten wave of panic hit Rachel.

She called her dad again. He answered. "Rachel?"

"What's happening?" she blurted. "Is everything okay?"

"Rachel . . ." Martin paused. "Come home."

"What's wrong?" she asked again, her voice rising. "What's wrong? Is mom okay?"

"Rachel. Come home," Martin repeated before hanging up.

"He wouldn't tell me any more," Rachel recalled. "He hung up on me."

As she sped toward the house, she called back repeatedly, but Martin wouldn't answer. Phoning Alexis, Rachel learned the tragic news. At around 6 P.M., Rachel pulled up to the house, jumped out of her car, and rushed inside. The front room was full of strangers.

"Right away I began to look for my father. I wanted to make sure he was okay," Rachel said years later. "He was in my parents' room. He was sitting on the couch. He was there. I just went to hug him and comfort him."

Lunging toward her father, she threw her arms around his neck and bawled.

"Your mom was my rock." He wept.

Once again Martin explained how Ada had found Michele in the tub. He mumbled under his breath, "She's ruined. Ada's ruined."

Holding her father, Rachel tried to find words of comfort when he suddenly made a surprising exclamation. "We need to get an autopsy done."

"What?" Rachel recoiled.

"We need to get it done right away."

"Why?" Rachel didn't understand what he was talking about—it didn't make sense. "Why do we need to get it done right away?"

Martin told her he was concerned about an impending police investigation.

"I don't want anyone to think I murdered your mother," he whispered.

"Why? Why? Why?" Rachel shook her head in disbelief. "Why would anyone think that?"

"It was so shocking to me," Rachel said years later. "It didn't make sense."

Alexis entered the bedroom and Rachel stood to hug her sister. Alexis discreetly pulled Rachel into the closet, away from their father.

"Dad killed Mom," Alexis whispered.

"What?" The words made no sense to Rachel. Nothing made sense at that moment.

Martin joined them, insisting on showing Rachel the position in which he had found Michele.

Rachel, who had always been more emotionally fragile than Alexis, had no interest in seeing how her mom had died. She objected, but against her wishes, Martin stepped into the bathroom.

"He wanted to tell me what happened to my mother," Rachel recalled. "Knowing that she had died, that was not something that I wanted to do. My dad was adamant that he describe what had happened . . . I didn't want to know. He insisted."

Alexis followed her father. Too broken to watch, Rachel stood in the bathroom doorway—not wanting to be in the room where her mother had died. Martin crouched beside the tub.

"He literally bent over and went into the tub to show how she was," Rachel said years later. "He found my mother in a position that he showed us."

Around 7 P.M., Michele's friends Cheryl, Loreen, and Karen arrived at the MacNeill house to offer their condolences. Martin's sister Mary greeted them at the front door.

Inside, a somber silence hung in the air. Giselle and Sabrina were in the kitchen, standing at the counter. Martin was seated on a barstool facing the front door. Rachel was staring at her phone screen, in between making calls.

"When we came in there was a strange feeling," Loreen recalled. "No one was talking."

Cheryl attempted to comfort Michele's children.

"Rachel was upset and emotional," Cheryl remembered. "Alexis was probably more hysterical than I had ever seen anyone at a death."

Karen went downstairs with Alexis, while Cheryl pulled Rachel aside to talk privately. Loreen spoke directly to Martin.

"What can we do?" Loreen asked him.

"I'm doing my best," Martin said. "I know I need to pull it together for the children."

At the appearance of Michele's church friends, Martin reverted to his old regal routines. He began to give Loreen a tour of his house. Room by room he showed off some of his renovations. In the living room, he commented that he had added space for a grand piano.

"I did this all for Michele," he said. Strangely, that was Martin's only reference to his wife or her death.

"I thought it was odd that Martin showed us the renovations of the home," Cheryl said years later. "He never really talked about Michele that night."

While Alexis was distant from her father, Rachel, Vanessa, and Damian remained by his side throughout the night. Martin spoke repeatedly about the autopsy and his concern about being blamed for his wife's death.

"He kept repeating that the autopsy needed to be done. I didn't want to listen to any of it," Rachel later said in court. "My mother had just died—it was so horrible."

Rachel attempted to ease her anguished father's concerns. "Dad, the autopsy will show you didn't do anything."

Still, each time there was a knock at the door, Martin flinched, looking over his shoulder. He was nervous and shaky, as if he expected the police were coming to arrest him at any moment.

As Rachel comforted her father, she felt the reality of life after Michele setting in. She thought of Giselle, Elle, Sabrina, and Ada—who would care for them?

"I'll make sure the kids are taken care of," Rachel told her dad. "Drive them to school and ballet and such." Rachel insisted she would quit her job to be the full-time caretaker.

"Don't you dare do that!" Martin suddenly snapped at his daughter. "We all just need to get on with our lives." Instead, Martin said he would hire a nanny.

Vanessa also volunteered to care for her younger sisters, but Martin declined. "Everything needs to get back to normal," Martin told Vanessa.

Despite her father's wishes, Rachel thought the girls would be better off in her care than with a stranger. That evening, Rachel called her boss at the dentist's office and left her notice of resignation on the voice mail. When Martin found out he was livid.

Later that evening, Rachel wandered around the house, making her way into the garage, where she discovered the wet towels and get-well gifts piled atop the hospital bed. She was disturbed to discover the black top, undergarment, and bra Michele had been wearing when she died. The shirt was sliced down the front. Everything was covered in blood.

"It was just a big bloody mess. All of these things were just thrown in the garage," Rachel said years later. "It was just a big pile. Everything was just thrown in."

Concerned that her younger sisters would discover their mother's bloody clothes, Rachel bundled them up and brought them back into the house. Hands trembling, she presented them to her father.

Martin glanced down at the clothes and glared at Rachel, his face dark and frightening.

"How dare you show me those things?" he said in a hateful voice. "Get rid of it!"

Rachel turned away from Martin, shaking. She couldn't bear the thought of throwing away her mother's things.

"I wanted to keep everything of my mother's," Rachel later said.

Gathering the clothes, she placed them in the washing machine. Once they were clean she stored them in a bag and kept them at her apartment.

Years later those same clothes would be considered state's evidence.

18.

loody fluid had leaked from the yawning incisions on Michele's face, saturating a towel spread beneath her on the autopsy table. The blood pooled around her head, framing the entirety of her face with a macabre crimson halo.

It was April 12, 2007, and Michele had been dead a little more than twenty-four hours. Her remains—cold and stiff from rigor mortis—had been transported to the Utah medical examiner's office in Salt Lake City.

Wearing latex gloves and a long white lab coat, assistant medical examiner Dr. Maureen Frikke began the autopsy at 2:15 P.M. She first jotted notes about Michele's vitals: fifty-year-old Caucasian female, five foot seven, 182 pounds.

Frikke then carefully examined Michele's remains.

Remnants of the revival efforts remained attached to her body. Blood-stained tubes jutted from her right nostril and the corner of her mouth. An uncapped catheter was taped to her left forearm; the tail end of an IV line hung from her left shin. Absorbent gauze was fastened to her right hand, concealing a needle puncture.

Frikke made note of marks left from the plastic surgery, indicating various stages of healing—the purple bruises, the surgical tape on the eyelids, the sutured incisions encircling Michele's ears, and the gaping wounds near her hairline.

Photographs were snapped, tissue samples collected.

Frikke held one of Michele's hands—her perfectly polished French manicure unchipped. Scraping under the acrylic fingernails, Frikke collected the residue in a plastic bag for possible DNA testing.

Frikke inspected every inch of Michele's body. Besides the wounds from the surgery and revival efforts, there were no overt signs of trauma—nothing to indicate how she'd ended up dead and on an autopsy table.

Scalpel in hand, Frikke carved a Y-shaped slice down the chest, beginning at each shoulder and finishing at the pelvis. She peeled back Michele's skin, exposing the ribs and organs.

Examining the chest cavity, Frikke saw no fractures or dislocations of ribs, vertebrae, sternum, clavicles, or pelvic bones. There was no internal hemorrhage around the neck. No obstruction was found in Michele's upper respiratory tract.

Frikke carefully removed each organ, examining and weighing them one by one. Slivers of each were collected for later examination under a microscope. She noted that Michele had previously had her appendix, ovaries, fallopian tubes, uterus, and cervix surgically removed.

Frothy, blood-tinted fluid sloshed around Michele's stomach. A large amount of fecal matter was compacted in her colon, indicating she was constipated—possibly due to the medication she had been taking.

Surveying the liver, Frikke noted it was congested with gobs of yellow sludge—the early signs of fatty liver disease. It was not, however, severe, and would not have been fatal. The gallbladder, spleen, kidney, and pancreas were all normal—smooth and glistening.

Next, Frikke examined the lungs. Because Michele was found in the bathtub, drowning needed to be considered as a possible cause of death.

Drowning is notoriously difficult for pathologists to diagnose after death. There are no laboratory tests to prove drowning. And even if a person dies by drowning, there may be no signs present in an autopsy to prove that particular cause of death.

Furthermore, a person can suffocate in water without ever sucking any liquid into the lungs—a medical phenomenon known as dry drowning. To

diagnose a drowning death when there is no water in the lungs, pathologists check for other indicators, which may include overinflated lungs, heavy
with fluid.

As Frikke examined Michele's lungs, she noticed they were, in fact, heavy.
In an adult female the lungs typically weigh 300 to 400 grams. Michele's
right lung weighed 690 grams; the left was 670.

The extra weight was a result of a backup of fluid in Michele's lungs. But
while it could have been an indication of drowning, this is also a common
finding in an individual who has undergone prolonged resuscitation efforts.

Frikke also found no frothy fluid in the trachea or obstructions in the
airways.

The medical examiner turned her attention to Michele's heart. When
she weighed the heart, she discovered it was enlarged and heavy—390 grams.
An average female heart weighs about 300 to 350 grams.

The muscle walls of Michele's heart were thick, the left side larger than
the right. There was mild blockage in the arteries; her aorta was hardened
and narrowed by fatty plaque. Michele also had inflammation of the heart,
a condition known as myocarditis. Frikke carefully examined the left and
right ventricle—finding no evidence of infection or hemorrhage. There also
was no evidence of a recent heart attack. Although it was not definitively
the cause of death, Michele indeed had heart disease.

An enlarged heart such as Michele's is often the result of high blood pressure—a condition with which she had been diagnosed. But Michele's heart
disease was in the early stage and not necessarily fatal. In addition, for individuals who are hypersensitive to medication, some narcotics can exac-
erbate a heart condition and cause inflammation of the heart.

Seeing no other explanations for a relatively healthy woman to suddenly
drop dead, Frikke suspected Michele's death was related to her heart.

One of the complications of an enlarged heart is a higher risk for an abnormal heartbeat rhythm—known as an arrhythmia. An arrhythmia can
cause the heart to abruptly stop beating, resulting in a sudden, unpredictable death.

There would have been no obvious symptoms or warnings. The arrhythmia causes an instantaneous cessation of breathing. Death would have
been rapid.

There is no way to prove a person died from an arrhythmia. A pathologist can only determine whether a person would have been at risk of having this type of irregular heartbeat.

Considering the condition of Michele's heart, Frikke theorized she died of an arrhythmia. She would wait to rule on the cause of death until the toxicology results came back from the lab.

19.

The days following their mother's death were a blur of agony and anguish for all the MacNeill children.

For Alexis, it was as if her soul had been stolen and was sinking toward oblivion, leaving an empty cavity of grief. Adrift in the sea of despair, Alexis wanted to feel closer to her mom's spirit. She wore Michele's clothes and slept in her bed—anything to smell her scent, feel her presence. Sorting through her possessions, she found a book of poetry her mother had written. She read through the book, marveling at Michele's beautiful writing.

Alexis wrote about her grief.

"I am lost without you. You are my hero, my strength, and my best friend," she wrote on her mom's online obituary. "I will cry for you forever. You are my heart and my life. I will do my best to survive, but right now I cannot breathe. I will try to make you proud. I am broken now, but I will try to be brave like you. I will love you forever."

Vanessa's adult life had been punctuated by problems. But through it all her mother never lost faith that she would turn it around. "I never showed you the love that you showed me. I gave up. I have given up so many times and you never, never gave up on me," Vanessa wrote to her mom. "In the times when I feel like I have lost touch with myself, I always know that you are the one who truly knows who I am."

Staying at the house in Pleasant Grove, Vanessa latched on to little Ada, who had always been so wise beyond her years. As Vanessa wept, Ada took her biological mom's hand.

"Tomorrow will be a little bit easier than today." Ada wiped the tears from Vanessa's face. "Sometimes I will cry. But most of the time I will wipe away your tears."

It was such a touching reminder for Vanessa that she needed to have the same strength, love, and selflessness as her own mom.

"I think perhaps your strength lives on in her," Vanessa wrote. "For Ada, I will be strong. I will do everything that I can to be the mother that I am supposed to be for Ada. I will never be the mother that you have always been for me as well as for her."

To build a tribute for her mother, Rachel used part of the five thousand dollars her father had previously given her to purchase a computer, which she used to create a Web site and video montage in her mother's memory. The video consisted of a collection of home movies and photos of Michele, set to one of her favorite songs, "Thula Mtwana" by Ladysmith Black Mambazo. "My mother always had a special love for Africa, even though she never got a chance to go there in her lifetime," Rachel captioned the video.

Damian was also fractured by the enormous loss. His sisters would later say his mother's death caused him to slowly implode.

On April 13, the family published Michele's obituary in the local paper and online.

"Her life was dedicated to her family. Her life was dedicated to helping all around her. We know her dedication lives on," the obituary read. "Her outer beauty and talents were so great, yet nothing compared to the beauty of her soul—the Light of Christ, a flaming fire that burned so brightly for all to see."

Friends from across the country and as far away as Canada and even Tokyo commented in an online tribute, telling how Michele had influenced their lives.

"Michele had an ability to touch people that no other person could touch.

She was loved and adored by people who shut out the rest of the world," one friend wrote.

"I vow to live my life with passion as she did, to love those in need as she did, and to not judge others but to love them, as she did," wrote another.

Even the Ukrainian translator who had assisted with Michele's adoption of her girls left a comment, posting her condolences. "My thoughts and prayers are with you in your time of grief. May your memories bring you comfort," Yulia Shust wrote.

For Michele's children, it helped to know how much she was loved.

Martin, meanwhile, made hasty arrangements to bury his wife. Without consulting his children and against their desires, he planned for the funeral to be held three days after her death—a Saturday.

"My father was very adamant to have the funeral right away," Alexis recalled.

Martin never spoke to anyone in the Somers family about Michele's death, and forbade his children from sharing any details of her passing.

"I don't want *those* people showing up at the funeral," Martin announced to his family. Michele's youngest sister, Linda Cluff, was one of the few exceptions. Martin told his daughters to contact Linda with instructions about who in the Somers family could attend the funeral. Linda was informed her family's presence would only compound Martin's grief. If they showed up at the church, the police would be there to escort them from the property.

"One good thing about Michele's death is I won't have to deal with *them* anymore," Martin grumbled to his kids.

Michele's older brothers, Mick and Stephen Somers, had already arrived in Utah from their homes in California when they learned they were not welcome at the funeral. Because they didn't want to upset Michele's childrens, they decided not to press the issue.

While making his wife's final arrangements, Martin also continued to text and call Gypsy. The day after Michele's death, Gypsy snapped six suggestive pictures on her cell phone. In one she was topless, with her bare backside turned to the camera. She sent the images to Martin. Later she would admit she'd sent the provocative pictures to keep him interested in her. "I wanted to distract him and I wanted him to still think of me," Gypsy confessed.

On the morning of the funeral, April 14, Gypsy sent two more text messages at around 9 A.M. At the time, Martin was dropping his younger daughters off at neighbor Angie Aguilar's house. To assist the family during their difficult time, Angie had agreed to babysit.

Exchanging pleasantries with Angie, Martin made an odd comment about adding a trellis to his house. He did not discuss Michele.

An hour later Martin arrived at the Manila Stake Center, a meeting place for their local stake, a regional group encompassing several LDS wards. The building was located on the grounds of the Mount Timpanogos Utah Temple, where the MacNeills spent each Sunday. Linda Cluff and her children also arrived at the stake center early. When they pulled into the parking lot, Martin was standing beside his car, unloading boxes of Michele's trophies, pictures, and memorabilia from the trunk. He had set up two tables inside to display the items.

Linda noticed he wasn't using a cane and was walking around without difficulty. She offered to assist with the boxes, but Martin waved her away. "He was extremely rude and refused any help," Linda remembered.

The funeral began at 11 A.M. In attendance were dozens of fellow churchgoers, friends, and neighbors from Pleasant Grove, including Angie Aguilar, Cheryl Radmall, Loreen Thompson, and Jacqueline Colledge. Martin's coworkers John David Laycock and Roma Henrie were also present. Even the plastic surgeon, Dr. Scott Thompson, attended.

Absent from the funeral were most of the Somers family, as per Martin's directive.

Among the sea of heartbroken faces was a dark-haired woman in a form-fitting black dress. She sat toward the back of the church and didn't speak to anyone. Gypsy Willis wasn't there to mourn her former romantic rival, the late Mrs. Martin MacNeill. She wanted to support Martin. Gypsy spent much of the funeral staring at her phone, discreetly sending texts to her lover. *I'm thinking of you,* she wrote.

"I was concerned for Martin," Gypsy recalled. "I wanted to be there for him."

During the funeral, several of Michele's loved ones shared fond memories.

Cheryl and Loreen spoke about the joy their "Ya-Ya Sister" had brought to their lives.

Rachel described the last time she'd seen her mom, on Easter. Alexis told the congregation of the amazing bond she had with her mother and the shock and disbelief of knowing she was gone.

"Last time I spoke to my mom she was happy," Alexis said, her voice breaking.

Martin, who sat near the front of the church, directing the music, was the last to speak. His eulogy would last thirty minutes and leave the audience confounded.

Using a cane, he limped to the podium and began with a joke, before launching into a speech about his difficult childhood growing up in New Jersey. He talked at length about his siblings who died from substance abuse or committed suicide. He mentioned the brother who he said "drank himself senseless" and suffered a stroke, the family members whose bodies were ravaged by years of booze and heroin addiction. As for his brother Rufus Roy, he said his mother found him dead with a needle in his arm. "Ten nickel bags were his ticket out."

Martin also spoke of his personal struggles in life, questioning why he was suffering the loss of his wife. "What have I done to cause this?"

He quoted the story of Job from the Bible and questioned God about why He had taken his wife away. "Lord, I thought I was your boy," he said. "Lord, I thought I was doing a good job. Lord, are you there?"

Later, he vowed that he and his children would survive the terrible fate God had dealt them. "As the hours passed last night, the answer came to me." Martin paused. "I've had such a good life."

Throughout the speech, he didn't speak of Michele as a wonderful wife and mother. Instead, she was only mentioned in passing.

Michele's friends found his eulogy bizarre and insincere. "It was probably the strangest funeral I've ever been to," said one friend. "When Martin spoke, it was all about himself. He talked about past traumas in his life. People he had lost who died of drug overdoses or suicides. And it was all about him. He didn't honor Michele at all. I don't know if he wanted us to feel sorry for him, or amazed that he turned out so well coming up through such difficult circumstances. It was just really bizarre."

At the conclusion of the services, Martin and his children gathered outside the church to greet those who had come to pay their last respects. While Martin had seemed upset earlier in the day, his mood appeared to brighten. At one point Rachel looked over and saw her father grinning as he chatted with a young brunette.

"His emotions would kind of fluctuate," Rachel recalled. "He would be sad and then he'd be smiling. It depended on who he was talking to."

Rachel didn't know it at the time, but Martin was smiling while talking to his mistress. Throughout the day, Martin and Gypsy exchanged twenty text messages, and he later called her from his cell phone.

As Michele's casket was loaded into the hearse, her friend Lani Swallow approached Martin to offer her condolences. Strangely, she noticed, he wasn't crying and no longer seemed mournful. Offering her assistance with the girls, Lani explained she had recently been laid off work, her son had moved out of the house, and she would be happy to serve as the children's nanny.

"My heart was broken. I just loved this family and loved these girls," Lani later said. "And I just thought that it would be really important for them to have someone they knew who cared about them and gave them comfort that knew their mother."

But Martin said he had already found help. "I already hired a nanny," Martin told her. "It's a nurse I work with."

The family gathered at the Highland City Cemetery for Michele's burial. Linda stood near the plot with her daughter, eyeing Martin suspiciously. At first she noticed he was using a cane. But when Ada began to cry, Martin handed the cane to the funeral director and bent down to pick up the girl. Then, as people started to approach, a worried look came across Martin's face. He put Ada down, grabbed the cane, and hobbled to his seat.

"People were starting to come and I noticed him just looking around," Linda said years later. "As people were starting to approach, he sat Ada down and started using the cane again and limped over."

Michele's body was lowered into the ground, dirt shoveled atop her casket. There would be no tombstone or marker on her grave for more than a year.

Once Michele was buried, Martin's demeanor was suddenly jovial. He laughed, smiled, and remarked that he was now a bachelor.

Following the funeral, family and close friends gathered at a restaurant in Pleasant Grove for lunch. Linda sat across from Martin, listening as he made jokes about having to fill his days playing golf with his buddies.

"He was smiling, joking around with some gentlemen," she recalled. "It was particularly disturbing to me. It caught my attention, and I listened because he was joking more about how he would have to get used to living the life of a bachelor."

Even Rachel, who always adored her father, was disgusted by his demeanor. "He was making jokes about being single, and laughing," Rachel remembered. "It made me sick. I just left."

The Somers family, who had been kept from the funeral, held their own private graveside ceremony the following day. Coupled with their grief over Michele's death was an intense anger toward Martin.

When Mick and Stephen heard about the strange circumstances of their sister's death, they both suspected Martin had played a part in her passing.

For Linda, Martin's behavior at the funeral confirmed what she had feared for years. "As soon as I heard Michele died I had no doubt that Martin had killed her," Linda said years later.

She was determined that Martin would not get away with murder.

Linda's years-long quest for justice was just beginning.

20.

If anything happens to me, make sure it wasn't your dad.

Those words kept replaying in Alexis's mind in the days after her mother's death. Following the funeral, she was plagued by awful thoughts. Every time she stepped into her parents' bedroom or bathroom, her mind reeled.

This is where he killed her, she thought. *This house is where my dad killed my mom.*

She couldn't sleep and ate very little. The thought of ever taking a bath again, which she had always enjoyed, was repellent. It would be years before she could dip inside a bathtub again, even in her own home.

While it was difficult to fully accept, she continued to believe that her father killed her mother. "I just had this overwhelming feeling that he had done it," Alexis recalled. "My whole world turned upside down. I am a pretty rational person, but that was the feeling. It was very strange, unsettling, and horrifying to come to that realization."

Hoping to make sense of her suspicions, she questioned her father.

While originally he had told her the police confiscated the medication, Alexis pressed him repeatedly on the issue. Frustrated, Martin snapped.

"They were thrown out!" he shouted. "It was making me too sad to look at it."

Cocking her head, Alexis gave her father a puzzled look.

"As soon as I heard that, things were just starting to add up. Everything was adding up," Alexis said years later.

For a time, Alexis didn't share her concerns with anyone but Rachel. Her most immediate worries were for the welfare of her younger sisters.

Now unemployed, Rachel spent the next few weeks at her parents' house, watching over the girls. Rachel, Vanessa, and Alexis all volunteered repeatedly to be their caretakers, but Martin was firm: they needed to hire a nanny.

Five days after his wife's death, Martin returned to work at the Developmental Center. On that Monday morning he arrived early. Steve Nickelson, who had recently resigned as nurse practitioner and was working his final week, was one of the few employees in the building at the time.

As Nickelson passed by Martin's office, he was surprised to see the doctor. Martin had taken only two bereavement days. It was shocking to see the doctor return to work so quickly after suffering such a sudden and tremendous loss. When Nickelson found Martin sitting at his desk, he stopped to offer his condolences. While sympathetic, Nickelson was also undeniably curious about what had happened to Martin's wife. After about twenty minutes of casual conversation, Nickelson got the nerve to ask. "What happened?"

Sighing deeply, Martin regurgitated the story he had told investigators and his family. "You know she had undergone cosmetic surgery?"

As they spoke, Nickelson noticed Martin showed no hint of emotion.

"I think he let me put the pieces together," Nickelson recalled. "I don't think he told me he thought she hit her head or he thought she drowned. He left it at that and let me draw my own conclusions."

Toward the end of their conversation, Nickelson glanced at Martin's left hand and noticed he was wearing a different wedding ring. For the past six years they had worked together, Martin had always worn a plain gold wedding band. Now he was wearing a ring with a distinctive black stripe.

Administrator Roma Henrie also noticed the new ring that afternoon when Martin arrived, unexpectedly, at the weekly steering meeting.

"Sitting on the steering team for eight or nine years, you recognize the wedding bands of everyone," she said later in court. "And then when someone's ring is suddenly missing or changed, you notice that."

Committee members were seated around the conference table when Martin arrived, much to their dismay.

"What are you doing here?" Henrie asked. "You should be at home!"

In a somber tone, Martin told the others he welcomed the distraction from his grief. "My older children are with the younger girls," he said. "I have nothing to do at home."

Nursing director Guy Hale Thompson remembered that Martin seemed strangely calm that day. "It was pretty much business as usual," he remembered.

Later during the meeting, another coworker pointed out Martin's new ring. Martin explained he had lost his wedding band and had bought a cheap one to wear in its place. "I didn't feel comfortable without a ring on my finger," he said.

Following the meeting, Henrie went to Martin's office to privately offer her sympathies. She hadn't had a chance to speak with him at the funeral. "I just wanted to say how sorry I am," she said. "I didn't realize your wife was sick."

Martin's reply was quick. "Well, she insisted on having elective surgery that I didn't believe she needed. And she thought she did."

Martin also insisted it was Michele who wanted the procedure done covertly, an hour away from Pleasant Grove, where she wouldn't be recognized.

"They missed a heart condition that she had and we didn't know she had," Martin told Henrie. "And she had a reaction to the medication she was taking."

Martin also referenced his own failing health, making a statement that would stick with Henrie for years. "He said the *worst* part was he had signed everything—the house and everything—over into her name, shortly before that," Henrie recalled. "Because he had cancer or something in his foot and he didn't know if he was going to live and he had signed everything over to her, thinking he might not survive. He said now he was in a mess because everything was in her name."

That week Martin also ran into the janitorial supervisor.

"I'm sorry about your wife's passing," she told Martin.

"Everything's fine," Martin said. "Everything will be fine."

"He seemed happy to me. He was just fine," the woman remembered. "I thought he'd still be gone. He seemed fine. He was actually happy."

Following the autopsy, assistant medical examiner Dr. Maureen Frikke spoke to Martin.

Suspicions flying through her mind, Alexis was adamant that she be present to hear everything Martin told the pathologist. Both she and Rachel were at the house when Martin spoke to Frikke on the phone. Rachel, however, didn't want to hear any of the details, and left the room.

Martin placed the call on speakerphone as he explained to Frikke how he had found his wife. Once he had drained the bath, he said, he started chest compressions, until the neighbors arrived to help pull her out of the tub.

He failed to mention that Michele had spewed several cups of water once the paramedics took over CPR. It would be a full year before the medical examiner's office learned of that detail.

Martin asked about the autopsy. "Have you found anything abnormal?"

"Yeah. She didn't have a uterus," Frikke said.

Both Martin and Frikke laughed.

Thirty years earlier, Helen Somers had tried desperately to convince her daughter there was something terribly wrong with Martin MacNeill. Young and in love, Michele wouldn't listen.

On a hunch, Helen had stored the court records from Martin's 1977 fraud arrest—including those disturbing psychological evaluations—for three decades. She'd moved them from house to house, from California to Utah.

With those documents in hand, Linda Cluff went to the Utah County Sheriff's Office just three days after Michele's death.

A sheriff's deputy took down her contact information, but Linda was at the wrong station. The Pleasant Grove home where Michele had died was not in the sheriff's jurisdiction. Linda would need to contact Detective Marc Wright at the Pleasant Grove Police Department.

A few days later, Linda and her daughter Jill met Detective Wright for the first time. Linda expressed her concerns and provided him with copies of the documents concerning Martin's criminal past. Wright flipped through the pages but seemed disinterested.

"We'll need to wait to see what the autopsy turns up," Wright explained. "I'll give you a call when I receive it."

21.

"Everything needs to return to normal," Martin told his daughters.

He repeatedly insisted that his family resume their own lives, and said he would hire a nanny to care for the adopted girls, then sixteen, fourteen, thirteen, and six.

"I want you to continue living your life as you were before," Martin announced. "I don't need your help."

On April 17, Martin asked Rachel to meet him at the temple to "pray about finding a nanny." Rachel found it strange—although Martin had always been involved in the church, he wasn't particularly spiritual and rarely expressed an interest in going to the temple simply to pray.

"My father was adamant that we go to the temple to pray about getting a nanny," Rachel said years later. "It was right away—very soon after my mother's death."

Rachel met her dad outside the Manila Stake Center at Mount Timpanogos Temple, where Michele's funeral had been held just days earlier. As they walked up to the building, they passed by two of Martin's neighbors from Pleasant Grove.

"How unusual to run into them here, huh?" Martin commented to his daughter. Rachel shot her dad a curious look. Many of the Mormon families that attended the temple lived just down the street. It wasn't odd to encounter one at church.

Inside the temple, Rachel expected they would partake in an endowment ceremony where they would be together to pray. Instead, Martin said he just wanted to do an initiatory, a preliminary ritual preceding the endowment proper. They parted ways into the separate male and female quarters, where they would be anointed.

"We'll meet after," Martin said.

Once she had completed the ceremony, Rachel searched the temple but could not find her father. She stepped outside and looked around, but he was not there either.

"I walked out to the right, got into my car. I thought maybe he had gone back to work since it was right across the street," Rachel recalled. "I went to go look for him, so I drove."

Once she arrived at the Developmental Center, Rachel scanned the parking lot in search of his vehicle. Just then her phone rang—it was her father.

"Rachel. Where are you? We were supposed to meet!" Martin sniped.

"I was looking for you," Rachel said. "I couldn't find you."

"I'm outside on the bench," he shouted into the phone. "There's no way you could have missed me!"

"I'm sorry," she replied quickly. "I didn't know you wanted to meet outside the temple."

Never before had they sat outside the building together. Rachel drove back to the temple, parked, and headed toward the stake center, where she found Martin sitting on a bench.

"I went back and my father was very upset, so I had to apologize," Rachel later said in court. "He said he was on the bench outside and there's no way I could have missed him. But I had gone out the other way."

Plopping down beside her father, Rachel apologized again. "I'm sorry, Dad."

Martin spoke to her about nannies for about five minutes before they were approached by a woman dressed in white, her long brown hair flowing loose.

It appeared as if she was headed to the temple. Instead, she walked directly to the bench where Martin and Rachel were seated.

"I am so sorry for your loss," the woman told Martin. "I was at the funeral."

"Oh. Thank you." Martin paused, peering up at her. "I'm sorry. I know you. I recognize you. What's your name again?"

"I'm Jillian," she said, shaking his hand. "We met before."

"Now I remember." Martin smiled. "We worked together."

Rachel studied the woman curiously, vaguely recognizing her from the funeral.

A moment later, Martin rose from the bench. "I'm sorry. I've got to excuse myself and go to the restroom."

Martin turned and walked inside the stake center, leaving Rachel alone with the dark-haired stranger. The woman began to chat about her background. "I'm going to nursing school," Jillian said.

Peering off in the distance, Rachel nodded.

"Your father once told me you were interested in nursing school," Jillian continued. "You look like a nurse."

Rachel half smirked but continued to stare blankly into the distance. The woman prattled on about nursing. So soon after her mom's death, Rachel had no interest in making small talk with this stranger. "This woman kept talking to me," Rachel recalled. "She just kept talking to me about nursing things and I just wasn't interested at all . . . I just wanted her to go away."

"I'm sorry. I can't really talk," Rachel wearily told the woman. "My mother just passed away. I'm just trying to breathe."

But Jillian didn't leave. "I have some pamphlets about my school in my car."

"She just continued to stay there." Rachel later shook her head at the recollection. "I just wanted her to go away . . . I remember thinking, what in the world is going on with my dad? He's been in the bathroom for a while . . . She just kept talking."

After a few more awkward moments, Martin returned.

"What's your name again?" he asked the woman.

"Jillian." She grinned. "I was just telling your daughter about nursing school. I'm taking classes."

"Oh, that's wonderful." Martin glanced down at his daughter.

"I'm not interested." Rachel sighed.

Martin ignored his daughter. "We should get more information about it. Can I get your number?"

As she rattled off numbers, Martin typed the digits into his cell phone. When they parted ways, Jillian turned back toward the parking lot.

"She looked like she was going to go into the temple," Rachel recalled. "But she never went into the temple. I never saw her go in. She came and talked to us and then went back to her car. It was bizarre."

Once Jillian was gone, Rachel expressed her discomfort with the woman. Martin berated his daughter for being rude.

"She seems really nice," Martin exclaimed. "But what's her name again?"

"Jillian, Dad! Her name was Jillian." Rachel rolled her eyes in exasperation.

"Oh," he said. "We should call her about getting together to go to lunch to discuss nursing school."

"I thought we were here to talk about a nanny," Rachel protested.

"Rachel, you're worthless," Martin snapped. "You're never going to amount to anything in life. You think everything's going to be handed to you."

At the nasty comment, Rachel dissolved into tears.

Over the next few weeks, the strange encounter with the dark-haired woman stuck with Rachel. "This was the first time I realized something was wrong," she later said in an interview. "The whole thing had been scripted."

The seemingly happenstance encounter at the temple was, in fact, just another staged scene in the ghoulish third act of the play directed by Martin MacNeill.

Cast in the role of Jillian was Martin's mistress, Gypsy. The setting had been selected to create the illusion that meeting "Jillian" was somehow a sign from God and answer to Martin's prayers. The woman he pretended not to recognize was the mistress he had called and texted more than one hundred times in the last seven days.

Prior to the encounter, Martin had rehearsed the script with Gypsy. "I was supposed to walk up and introduce myself and maybe strike up a small conversation and then leave. It was just an introduction," Gypsy later said. "He wanted me to meet his family on the best possible terms."

The plan had always been for Gypsy to become the nanny and for her to live with Martin in the house, essentially replacing Michele. But first, Martin would need to manipulate his children into welcoming a new woman into his life.

On the afternoon of April 19, Martin called Alexis.

"Alexis," he said enthusiastically. "I found the perfect nanny!"

"Oh really?" Alexis asked. "What's her name?"

"I think it's Jill . . . ," he stammered.

"Gypsy Jillian Willis?" Alexis interrupted. "The woman Mom thought you were having an affair with?"

"Alexis!" Martin shot back.

"Dad!" she spoke over him. "I know that woman! I know Mom was worried you were having an affair with her! You are not to bring her into the home!"

"How dare you!" he yelled indignantly. "How dare you accuse me!"

Martin told his daughter she was no longer welcome at home and was not to have contact with her younger siblings.

"He got irate. He was screaming at me," Alexis recalled. "And hung up on me."

That same day Martin called a family meeting with his other adult children—Rachel, Damian, and Vanessa. Because Alexis had this "ridiculous" notion that he was having an affair with some woman, Martin said, he wanted nothing more to do with his daughter.

"It's ridiculous. If she's going to be this way, Alexis is no longer a member of the family," Martin said.

He also asked his children to assist in the hiring process for the new nanny. He said he had posted flyers around the Developmental Center, local colleges, and the Mormon institute in Orem, advertising for the position. Martin wanted their help interviewing applicants.

Upon hearing that Alexis had been disowned, Rachel refused to participate. Martin dismissed his eldest daughter's apprehensions and asked

Damian's girlfriend, Eileen Heng, to be a part of what he deemed the "nanny hiring committee."

The next day the "committee" expected to interview candidates. Although Martin said three or four women had applied, only one showed up for an interview—a woman calling herself Jillian.

Vanessa, Damian, Eileen, and Martin congregated in the front room of the house; Jillian sat across from them. Martin conducted the interview, asking questions mostly about nursing school. Jillian described her background and experience in the medical field. Vanessa, Damian, and Eileen asked a few questions.

After she left, Martin addressed the "committee."

"What do you think?" he asked. "Should we hire her?"

"What about the other applicants?" Vanessa interjected.

Martin stated the others had all canceled their appointments. Vanessa, Damian, and Eileen were aware of the suspicions of Alexis and Rachel. Because of the turmoil surrounding this woman, Eileen pulled Martin aside and recommended he find another nanny.

"I knew that there was some tension between Alexis and Rachel with Jillian, so I encouraged Martin to not hire her because it could separate them even further," Eileen remembered.

Martin tersely shrugged aside the concerns. "I'm sick of my children trying to run my life." He made it clear he would be hiring Jillian as the nanny.

Later that afternoon, Vanessa phoned Alexis to tell her about the one and only nanny applicant.

"Was her name Gypsy?" Alexis asked.

"No," Vanessa replied. "Her name was Jillian."

Alexis explained she thought Jillian and Gypsy were the same person, but Vanessa insisted there had to be a mistake. "There is nothing to worry about," Vanessa told her sister.

"I was convinced that she wasn't somebody to worry about that my dad might be involved with," Vanessa recalled, "because she was nothing like my mom."

22.

Alexis MacNeill needed to be cunning.

If she was going to protect her little sisters and expose her father as a murderer, being forthright wouldn't work. She would have to resort to duplicitous tactics to take him down.

She didn't have to look far for inspiration to play that part. For twenty-four years she had unknowingly witnessed her father ruthlessly manipulate, scheme, and lie to bend others to his will. Now that she had been banned from the home, she'd employ similar strategies.

To get back in Martin's good graces, Alexis called and e-mailed her father, apologizing for her accusations about Jillian. "These e-mails were strategic for me to get my sisters, to appease the fighting my father and I had, in order to get back into the home and get my sisters and take them out," Alexis explained years later.

Martin quickly relented, and Alexis returned home. Over the next few months, depending on his mood, Martin would alternate from tolerating Alexis to ceasing all communication, banning her from the house.

Dangling on the fringes of her family's life, Alexis was forced to pretend to love the man she was convinced killed her mother.

————

On a chilly day in May, just weeks after Michele's death, Gypsy moved into the basement of the Pleasant Grove home.

That morning, Martin introduced the younger girls to "Jillian."

"Okay, girls, come meet your new nanny," Martin said. "She's going to be living downstairs and taking care of you."

Gypsy would later say she didn't want to move into the home so soon after Michele's death. She claimed she initially declined when Martin first asked if she would be the nanny. But because she wanted to be a part of Martin's life on whatever terms possible, she changed her mind and agreed.

"He was rather insistent that he needed help and that I would be a great support to him and his life," Gypsy later said. "I loved Martin—I really did. I would have supported him any way I could. So I was willing to fill that role."

At the house, in front of the children, Martin and Gypsy both pretended as if they had no romantic relationship. Later, he even called Rachel to explain he was drilling a lock onto the bedroom door in the basement to give the new nanny privacy. Because he was widowed, he said, he didn't want Jillian to worry about living with a "newly single man."

Martin also made a request of Rachel. "I want you to come down and show her around. Make her comfortable."

At that point Rachel was grappling with her own apprehensions about her father. And when she saw Jillian sauntering around the house, gazing lustfully at Martin, she was sickened.

"It was obvious. She was just goo-goo eyes at my dad," Rachel later testified. "I expected her to cook or clean or take care of the children. Nobody was looking after the children. My dad was cooking and she was sitting there staring at him."

Most glaringly, Jillian didn't do anything a nanny should do, according to Martin's daughters. She didn't maintain the household, and rarely drove the children to school or ballet.

"I saw her come and go throughout the day. I never saw her pick up the children," Alexis later said. "I never saw her do any cooking or cleaning. I saw her following my dad around a lot."

Most distressing, Alexis and Rachel claimed the children were being neglected. On one occasion, Rachel said she stopped by to find Ada playing in the street unsupervised.

Over the next few months, Rachel and Alexis found themselves caring for their sisters. While observing the nanny and mourning their mother, both women were distrustful of their father.

While Rachel was guarded, she still clung desperately to hope that her father's frigid demeanor was just his way of grieving. But for Alexis, the bewildering new nanny was further proof that Martin had murdered their mother. Quietly, Alexis began documenting and collecting evidence against her father. While she investigated, she had no idea at the time that Linda Cluff was building her own case against Martin.

But as Michele's loved ones pondered what to do with their blossoming suspicions, the autopsy results were released.

Toxicology results arrived at the medical examiner's office a few weeks after the autopsy. But they did little to solve the mystery of Michele's death. Four different drugs were found in her system: Percocet, Valium, Phenergan, and Ambien. None were discovered at levels considered to be a lethal dose.

Dr. Frikke determined that all four drugs had been administered within an hour of Michele's death. While the Percocet and Phenergan were at a fairly high concentration, all the drugs were within a therapeutic range. Frikke concluded that Michele's death was not the result of medication.

On May 22, 2007, Frikke officially certified the cause of death as natural. "This fifty-year-old Caucasian female, Michele MacNeill, appears to have died as the consequence of natural cardiovascular disease," the autopsy report read.

The mechanism of death was ruled a result of hypertension and the heart inflammation, myocarditis, which led to an unexpected arrhythmia and sudden death.

It was classic heart disease, a cause of death all too common in middle-aged women—especially for one diagnosed with high blood pressure.

The medical examiner had the ultimate say when it came to cause and manner of death. And Dr. Frikke had concluded this was no homicide.

The findings did little to sway the suspicions of Linda and Alexis.

Alexis was most alarmed by the toxicology report. The entire time Michele had been in her care, she had never taken a Valium or an Ambien. And only once was she ever given that specific combination of medicine—Percocet, Valium, Phenergan, and Ambien—the night after the surgery, when she was alone with Martin.

Additionally, all the medication had been administered less than an hour before her death, according to the pathologist. And there would be no reason for her to take an Ambien at 10 A.M.

Alexis was gravely concerned.

But the Pleasant Grove police saw nothing suspicious. Detective Wright called Linda and informed her of the toxicology results. "Sorry," the detective said. "I know it kind of shocks you because she was so young to have a heart attack."

Linda sighed. "Actually, that doesn't surprise me at all. Martin was a doctor. He would know how to cover up what he did to my sister."

But much to Linda's dismay, Wright said he would not be investigating further.

"I'm sorry for your loss, but there's no crime here," Wright said. "We're closing the case."

Linda's stomach sank. She thought to herself, *Martin is going to get away with it.*

2 3.

As the MacNeill children mourned their mother, Martin's relationship with his new live-in girlfriend flourished in secret.

Throughout his workday, he frequently sent Gypsy affectionate text messages: *I love you. I miss you. I wish you were here with me at work.* When at home, Martin and Gypsy would sneak off together for hours at a time to be intimate. And almost every night, once the children were asleep, Gypsy joined him in his marital bed.

While Gypsy kept up the façade that she was Jillian the nanny, it was clear to even the young children that she cared little for them.

"She didn't do much. She made spaghetti once," Sabrina said years later. "That was the only time she really cooked. She didn't do anything. She lived downstairs."

It was a difficult and confusing time for Elle, Sabrina, and Ada, who became sullen and standoffish around Jillian. Perhaps because she never felt as if she belonged with the MacNeills, Giselle reached out to the nanny she saw the other girls snubbing. Of all the children, Giselle was the friendliest and spent the most time with Jillian.

For her part, Gypsy said she tried to bond with Martin's daughters, but felt it was inappropriate when the older children were around. "They were sweet girls. I tried to love them. I wanted to love them. I never really felt like the older children wanted that or approved of that," Gypsy recalled. "When the adult children were home I deferred to them and went back to studying my nursing."

Throughout May, Martin introduced "Jillian" to the neighbors in Pleasant Grove. She also accompanied him and the girls to deliver thank-you gifts to some of the residents who had offered support during the funeral.

One afternoon, Angie Aguilar was in her front yard gardening when Martin pulled up in his car with the nanny in the passenger seat. He rolled down the window.

"This is Jillian. I think I've mentioned her," Martin said. "She's going to help with the girls."

By the way she was referenced, Angie assumed the woman was the nurse Martin had wanted to house-sit for the Guthries. Martin told Angie the arrangement was perfect since he had to return to his job.

"I guess it all worked out." He shrugged.

Angie was relieved to discover that someone would be caring for the children. "I was very concerned about who would watch the girls, especially because in my head Martin was going to be dying soon as well," Angie later said. "It was relieving to me that he found someone, who he described as a quiet nurse, to help with the girls."

On another occasion, after babysitting for Martin one afternoon, Angie walked the girls back to the MacNeill home. Standing in his doorway, Martin told Angie that the autopsy had shown his wife's death was natural.

"It's good to know." Martin shook his head sadly.

Angie was sympathetic.

"He mentioned to me that it had been an arrhythmia, and he seemed relieved that they had been able to find out what was wrong with Michele," Angie remembered. "He was very calm, and smiled."

On a Sunday afternoon in late April, the girls' ballet instructor, Jacqueline Colledge, was cleaning the carpets in her home when the doorbell rang unexpectedly. Peering out the peephole, she saw Martin standing on the porch with Elle, Sabrina, Ada, and a mysterious dark-haired stranger.

Having not had a chance to speak with Martin at the funeral, Jacqueline offered her sympathies the moment she opened the door. "I am so very sorry for your loss. I really can't believe that Michele is gone. I didn't know she had health issues."

"She's had health problems her whole life and refused to take medication," Martin replied coldly.

Jacqueline flinched—she'd known Michele for twenty years and had never heard of any health concerns.

Martin then introduced the nanny. "This is Jillian."

Because Jillian was still in nursing school, Martin said, the new nanny would be unable to take the girls to ballet. To assist with the transition, Jacqueline happily volunteered to bring the girls to their dance classes.

"That would be so great, since the nanny won't be able to," Martin said.

Neighbors Doug and Kristi Daniels soon became accustomed to seeing Jillian around the neighborhood, and her silver Volkswagen Beetle parked in front of the MacNeill home.

One afternoon, Kristi stumbled upon a cell phone at the Creekside community park. Hours later, one of the MacNeill girls stopped by the house to ask if she had found a phone, and Kristi retrieved it.

"It's our nanny's phone," the girl said as Kristi handed it over.

Days later, Kristi and Doug encountered Martin in their common driveway. As they spoke, Martin mentioned the cause of his wife's death, saying, "It was a heart thing."

He referenced an article in the local newspaper about a basketball player who had dropped dead on the court from an arrhythmia.

"When we spoke to the pathologist he made sure to tell us it was no one's fault," Martin said. "It was natural."

Miraculously, in the weeks and months after Michele's death, Martin's own health appeared to improve. He began using a cane less frequently and then stopped altogether. Soon he was no longer limping and seemed as healthy as ever. When asked about his cancer, Martin gave vague updates, telling neighbors, "It's coming along" or "It will be okay."

As she witnessed her neighbor's supposedly deadly disease disappear, Kristi inquired about his terminal diagnosis.

"Martin, how are you doing?" she asked one day in the shared drive-way. "Last I heard, you only had six months to live."

"I'm still here now," Martin replied with a sly grin. "Don't write me off yet."

Top: In high school, the pretty and popular Michele Somers was once elected homecoming queen.
Bottom: Michele was known as a gorgeous, talented, intelligent, and kind young woman.
Both photos courtesy of the Somers family

Top: In her youth, Michele modeled professionally. ***Middle left:*** After meeting Martin MacNeill, Michele fell deeply in love. The couple married in February 1978. ***Middle right:*** In 1979, Michele gave birth to their first child, a daughter named Rachel. ***Bottom:*** During one vacation, Martin and Michele posed affectionately on the deck of a cruise ship. *All photos courtesy of the Somers family*

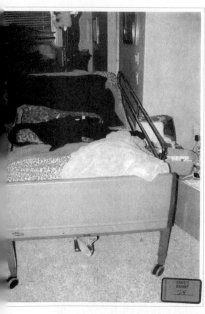

Top: In February 2006, the MacNeills moved into a sprawling estate in Pleasant Grove, Utah. ***Bottom left:*** While recuperating from cosmetic surgery in 2007, Michele slept in a rented hospital bed situated inside her master bedroom. ***Bottom right:*** On April 11, 2007, Michele was found dead in her bathtub by her youngest adopted daughter, Ada MacNeill. *All photos State's Evidence*

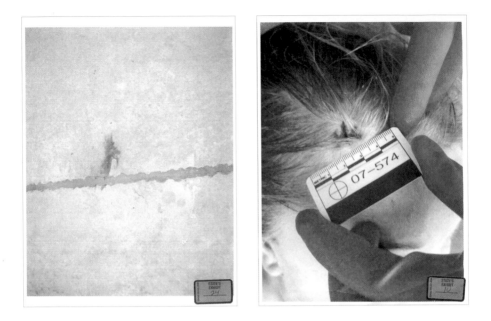

Top left: During a brief police investigation, a detective discovered blood on the MacNeills' bathroom floor. *Top right:* Bloody gashes were documented on Michele's scalp during the autopsy. *Bottom:* Paramedics deposited the bra and shirt Michele was wearing during the futile resuscitation efforts on the master bedroom carpet. *All photos State's Evidence*

Top left: A year after his wife's death, Martin fashioned a makeshift tombstone from cement for Michele's grave. *Photograph by Linda Cluff*
Topmost right: Within weeks of his wife's passing, Martin proposed to his mistress, Gypsy Willis. *State's Evidence*
Middle right: In 2009, Martin and his mistress were arrested for stealing the identity of his sixteen-year-old adopted daughter, Giselle MacNeill. *State's Evidence*
Bottom right: During the investigation, daughter Ada drew a picture of the position in which she found her deceased mother. *State's Evidence*

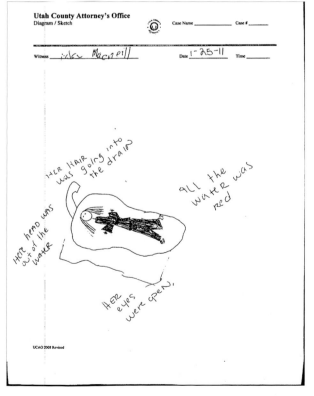

Utah County Attorney's Office
Diagram / Sketch

Case Name _____ Case # _____

Witness _idc MacNeill_ Date 1-25-11 Time _____

HER HAIR was going into the drain

ALL the WATER was red

HER HEAD was out of the water

HER eyes were open.

UCAO 2008 Revised

Top left: Defense attorney Randall Spencer would become Martin's trusted legal advocate for more than seven years. *Courtesy of Randall Spencer*

Top right: In court on identity theft charges, Gypsy wore a distincitive blazer once belonging to Michele. *Al Hartmann/Pool Camera*

Bottom left: When he stood trial for his wife's murder in 2013, Martin seemed to express no remorse. *Al Hartmann/Pool Camera*

Bottom right: Lead prosecutor Chad Grunander would present a complex circumstantial case for murder against Martin. *Al Hartmann/Pool Camera*

Top left: Doug Witney was the first investigator to seriously probe into Michele's suspicious death.
Al Hartmann/Pool Camera
Top right: Jeff Robinson eventually became the lead investigator in the case against Martin.
Al Hartmann/Pool Camera
Middle: Michele's daughter Alexis Somers was a driving force in the arrest and conviction of her father.
Associated Press/Pool Camera
Bottom right: On the stand, daughter Rachel was emotional as she spoke of her father's betrayal.
Al Hartmann/Pool Camera

Top left: Gypsy appeared unrepentant as she testified in court about her affair with Martin.
Associated Press/Pool Camera

Top right: One of Martin's former mistresses, Anna Osborne Walthall, told jurors about her lover's dark discussions of death.
Associated Press/Pool Camera

Bottom left: Defense attorneys Randall Spencer and Susanne Gustin were optimistic before the verdict was delivered on November 9, 2013.
Al Hartmann/Pool Camera

Bottom right: At sentencing, Linda Cluff addressed her former brother-in-law and spoke about the pain of losing Michele. *Rick Bowmer/Pool Camera*

2 4 .

While Martin and Gypsy's relationship had started out as an illicit affair, they now seemed to proceed with their romance quite traditionally. Gypsy decided it was time to bring her new boyfriend home to meet her parents.

Shortly after moving into the MacNeill home, Gypsy called her mom, gushing about her boyfriend, explaining that he was a doctor, lawyer, and former Mormon bishop. She admitted he was a recent widower, but claimed his wife had died months prior—in January 2007. Gypsy said she and Martin had only begun dating after Michele's death. While it had only been a few months, she was in love, Gypsy told her mom. "I'm so excited for you to meet him."

Although Gypsy was planning a trip to Wyoming specifically to introduce Martin to her parents, she lied and said they were traveling through Wyoming and just wanted to stop by.

To prepare for the visit, Martin fabricated another ploy. Gypsy told the girls she had to go to Wyoming to visit with her sick grandmother. Martin said he had to leave town for a work conference. Alexis and Rachel were to be left in charge of the younger girls while they were away.

In early May, just weeks after Michele's death, Martin and Gypsy each slipped out of the house separately. Then they reunited and continued to Wyoming.

By 2007, Howard and Vicki were raising Gypsy's biological daughter Heidi, then twelve years old, in a rural country home on forty acres of open prairie, nine miles north of Cheyenne.

When Gypsy arrived at the house with her new boyfriend, her parents greeted them warmly. To Howard and Vicki, Martin was charming and engaging as he boasted about his schooling and career. As usual, he came across as pretentious—quoting poetry and referencing classic literature in normal conversations. But Martin also spoke fondly of his love for Gypsy.

After observing years of fumbles and false starts, the Willises were thrilled that their eldest daughter had found a proper, moral Mormon man. "Frankly, we were giddy about Martin joining the family," Vicki recalled. "Martin MacNeill is a very impressive person. He's tall, he's got a bright white smile. He holds the title of doctor and also attorney or lawyer, both of which are highly esteemed in American society. We were pleased, of course."

And unlike his apathetic attitude toward the Somers family, Martin was eager to please Gypsy's parents. He shoveled hay, helped Vicki run errands, and paid for dinners in town.

Throughout 2007, Martin and Gypsy would travel to Wyoming half a dozen times to visit the Willises. During each stay, Martin was polite and charismatic. But while it seemed Martin was in love with their daughter, it was also obvious to Vicki that he was the one controlling the relationship.

"It was clear that he was the dominant partner in the relationship. She had a lot of deference to him," Vicki said years later. "She looked after him. She always seemed to me to be very careful about her behavior in front of him."

As they got to know him, Howard and Vicki avoided one subject: Martin's deceased wife.

"We did speak with him about his wife, but we were reticent about asking too much about that," Vicki remembered. "It was my understanding initially that she had passed away in January. It lent more credibility to the relationship of my daughter and Dr. MacNeill."

Assuming Martin was uncomfortable with the subject, Howard and

Vicki never pried. But every so often Martin or Gypsy would make a comment that seemed to contradict the Willises' understanding of the relationship. A few times they would reference time spent together from 2005 or 2006, while he was still married to his wife. Gypsy's parents were hesitant to ask many questions for fear of evoking further pain.

"It was very confusing. Because we don't like to pry into these things," Vicki later said. "They are personal, they're private, and they're painful."

Mother's Day 2007 fell on May 13. It was barely a month after Michele's death and the first of such holidays the MacNeill children would spend without their mom.

That morning Martin attended church with his children. During the services, he addressed the congregation. Because of the occasion, they all expected he would speak of his dead wife. Instead, he launched into a speech concerning single mothers—like Gypsy.

Jacqueline Colledge, who was in attendance for the christening of her new grandson, couldn't conceal her bewilderment. "Most of his talk was about single mothers and how important it was for single mothers to be recognized on Mother's Day because of all the work they do even though they may not be married," Jacqueline recalled.

In celebration of the holiday, Martin sent an original oil painting to Vicki Willis. Attached to the gift was a letter thanking Howard and Vicki for their hospitality during his recent visit and further expounding on his love for their daughter.

"Physical beauty is prized by many but with time it is illusory," Martin wrote. "However, I want you to know that I have seen the beauty of Gypsy's heart and tell you that that is a beauty that will not fade or age or wrinkle."

In the letter, Martin suggested that he knew Gypsy's relationship with her parents had been troubled and fraught with tension, turmoil, and outright antagonism. However, he hoped they could move beyond the past, he wrote. To illustrate his points, Martin included a poem, a Chinese proverb, and quotes from French playwrights and avant-garde writers.

"I am not privy to all of the issues in your relationship with Gypsy, but I see her as a loving, kind, compassionate woman and I will be eternally grateful that she has become such an important part of my life," Martin wrote. "Your relationship with her played such a significant role in the person she has become that I am compelled to give you thanks for raising and nurturing someone such as she."

Throughout May, Alexis stayed at the house in Pleasant Grove. Because the rooms were all occupied, Alexis slept in her parents' bed while Martin slept on the couch in the master bedroom's sitting area. This sleeping arrangement gave Martin and Gypsy no privacy for trysts.

For Alexis, sleeping so close to her mother's killer was excruciating. Leaving her sisters alone with Martin, however, was incomprehensible.

"I was feeling panic, horror, fear that my sisters were not safe and that they were in the home of someone who had just murdered my mom," Alexis later said.

On the night of May 23—six weeks after Michele's death—Alexis was cleaning out her mother's closet and drawers, sorting through her possessions. Emotionally exhausted, she lay down in her parents' bed around 11 P.M. and crawled between the sheets, still wearing jeans and a T-shirt.

A few hours later she awoke to the sensation of fingertips sliding down the back of her jeans, fondling her buttock. A man's lips glided against her left hand, a hot tongue wetting her palm.

Alexis's eyes shot open. She slapped the hand away. Peering up, she saw her own father looming over her.

"I could feel my father's hand rubbing my buttocks," Alexis later testified. "He had one of my hands, my left hand, he was licking and kissing it."

Springing from the bed, Alexis shrieked, "What are you doing?"

Alexis said Martin recoiled and apologized. "Oh. Oh. I'm sorry. I'm sorry. I thought you were your mother."

Repulsed, Alexis bolted from the bedroom and spent the rest of the night in another room, trying to erase the sickening thoughts from her mind.

The next morning she confronted her father. Once again he apologized. "I was asleep. I thought you were Michele."

Later that day, Alexis told Rachel what had happened, and they discussed reporting Martin to the police. But Alexis was hesitant—if she pressed charges, Martin might permanently bar her from seeing her siblings. Alexis decided being tactical was more important, knowing that she now had leverage against her father.

"Please don't say anything to anyone," Alexis pleaded. Reluctantly, Rachel agreed.

Later, Martin called a family meeting, where he admitted he had reached out and touched Alexis inappropriately. He declared that Giselle, Elle, Sabrina, and Ada would no longer be allowed in his bedroom, for fear he might accidently touch them in the middle of the night.

"What if it had been one of the young girls?" Martin said, sounding concerned. "I could have gotten in trouble."

Alexis was now left with the disturbing fear that Martin would sexually abuse his own children. "I was very concerned for my younger sisters," Alexis recalled. "There were a lot of things I was concerned about going on in the home. That was just another horrible thing to worry about."

For the next few days Alexis remained at the house, watching over her sisters. She no longer slept in her parents' bedroom. Gypsy was now able to resume secretly sneaking back into Martin's bed.

By June, the true sordid nature of Martin's relationship with the nanny was becoming obvious to all the MacNeill children. On several occasions, Sabrina caught the two cavorting around the house before slipping into his bedroom.

"I remember her going up into my dad's room at night. And then . . . the door closed," Sabrina recalled. "I remember staying up at night wondering, *What in the world? I thought she was the nanny. Why is she up in Dad's room?*"

Even Damian's girlfriend, Eileen, developed suspicions. On one occasion, Damian, Eileen, Martin, and Jillian went to lunch at a casual, sit-down restaurant.

"I saw Jillian reach over and eat food off of Martin's plate, and I thought that was strange given their employee-employer relationship," Eileen later said. "I told Damian I thought that was weird."

By this point, Rachel could no longer ignore her father's lewd conduct with the nanny.

"Something is very wrong," Rachel wrote in an e-mail to Alexis on June 3. "I know you shouldn't bring it up with Dad. But something is very wrong with the nanny."

Rachel had been monitoring Jillian with increasing concern. What kind of nanny was this woman? She seemed more like her father's girlfriend, Rachel wrote.

"I know Dad is suffering from Mom's death like we all are. But that doesn't mean that something weird isn't going on. Please tell me this lady's full name? Gypsy? Or Jillian? Or what? What is her last name? Where in Wyoming is her family? I know something isn't right and I want it to be taken care of."

Looking back at the bizarre introduction with Jillian at the temple, Rachel also questioned whether it was planned.

"Why was Jillian at the temple that day? She didn't work in that area or live in that area. Why did Dad pretend not to know her name in the temple? And why did she just happen to be outside the temple that day?"

If her father was capable of orchestrating a phony introduction between his daughter and his mistress outside the temple, Rachel could no longer deny he likely had something to do with Michele's death.

The animosity between Martin and his daughters festered throughout the summer of 2007, as Jillian shirked her nanny responsibilities.

One day in June, Rachel had had enough. She confronted her father about the new nanny. Tempers flared, and the argument grew heated. "This nanny doesn't cook. She doesn't clean," Rachel yelled. "She doesn't seem to pay any attention to the girls."

Martin's jaw tightened, and his fists balled at his side. He reprimanded his daughter. "She is a guest in our home," he snarled. "How dare you question me!"

Alexis stepped in, and both sisters accused Martin of having an affair with Jillian.

He told his daughters they were no longer welcome in his home. Martin grabbed his cell phone and called the police, reporting Alexis and Rachel for trespassing.

"I was told I needed to leave the home because I wasn't nice to Gypsy," Rachel recalled. "He wanted to make it known that it was either Gypsy or his children, and he chose 'the nanny.'"

25.

Linda Cluff's investigation of Martin soon collided with that of her nieces. In June, after being thrown out of the house, Alexis and Rachel had hired a private investigator to dig up details of their father's relationship with Jillian, because they believed she was really his mistress, Gypsy.

Alexis and Rachel confided in their aunt their now-shared belief that their father had killed their mother. Linda revealed her own thirty-year suspicions of Martin and her resolute conviction he had murdered Michele.

"I didn't know they thought their dad did it for a while," Linda later explained. "For a while, I was on my own until a few months into it."

The three women joined forces in their crusade against Martin. For more than a year they would document Martin's past in an attempt to get police to investigate.

Linda informed Martin's daughters about his criminal past from 1977 and the psychological evaluations that determined Martin was a "latent schizophrenic." While they knew he was bipolar, Alexis and Rachel had never seen any signs of schizophrenia, and believed he had faked symptoms to commit fraud.

Michele's daughters shared details with Linda about Martin's intimate relationship with the nanny. Alexis also related her conversation with her mother, in which Michele had fretted about her own impending death: "If anything happens to me, make sure it wasn't your dad."

Given what she had learned from Alexis, Linda reached out to Michele's two other sisters, who both lived in California. In June, Terry Pearson and Susan Hare flew into Utah for the weekend to help convince police to investigate.

On June 21, Linda returned to the Pleasant Grove Police Department with Susan and Terry. As soon as Detective Marc Wright and his supervisor stepped into the conference room, Linda said she could sense the skepticism. Before they even began the interview, Wright appeared defensive, she said.

"We have very strong feelings that Martin had something to do with my sister's death," Linda told them. She explained what she had learned since their last meeting, including the fact that Alexis and Rachel also feared foul play, and Martin's apparent affair with the nanny.

"Alexis probably said that because she was mad at her dad for having an affair," the detective scoffed.

Undeterred, Linda mentioned she had heard of cases where bodies were exhumed for more testing after police learned new information.

"I've never heard of such a thing," Wright's supervisor said.

As Linda and her sisters continued to explain their reasoning, Wright's posture straightened. "Are you trying to tell me that I don't know how to do my job?"

"No. Not at all," said Linda. "We have just learned new information that we thought you should be aware of."

After a few minutes, Wright spoke up.

"The case is closed, ladies." The detective rose from his chair. "That is that."

Neither Wright nor his supervisor asked any questions about Michele or took any notes, Linda said. "They were very rude. They made us feel like we were wasting their time and putting them out," she recalled. "They were not interested in anything we had to say at all."

As the sisters exited the station, Linda felt deflated. She would get nowhere with the Pleasant Grove police; the detective had ceased the investigation. The brief report mirrored the investigation.

"The victim had apparently slipped and fell after filling the tub with water," the police report stated. "The case will be closed due to the autopsy results."

Information was later added about the family's suspicions. The final report included a number of errors. Investigators apparently mistook Linda for her deceased sister: her name was transposed with Michele's. "Linda's death was natural," the report stated. "Michele brought in documentation regarding Martin's criminal past."

Alexis also contacted the Pleasant Grove police on a number of occasions, later submitting an official statement outlining her concerns. It too was ignored.

A few days after being kicked out of the home for the second time, for questioning her father's relationship with the nanny, Alexis tried once again to make amends, appearing remorseful, loving, and obedient in a series of phone calls and text messages.

"I was trying to calm things down," Alexis recalled. "I wanted to get back into my home to protect my sisters and fight for custody. My goal was to take my sisters away from them and raise them."

In June, on break from medical school, Alexis went on a scheduled trip with friends to Cancún, Mexico. She spent most of her vacation e-mailing and calling her father, attempting to regain access to the home.

"I went through five or six phone cards trying to talk to him," Alexis later said. "I remember having to try and calm the situation down. I was very apologetic and tried to be sweet."

Martin didn't return her e-mails, and most of her calls went to voice mail. She purchased a few postcards, scribbling her pleas for peace. "Sorry. Please forgive me. I want to come back home. I need to be back home."

On another she wrote: "Hi, Daddy. I hope you're feeling better. Can't wait to see you."

In mid-June, she also sent him a card for Father's Day. "Hi Daddy. I love you and wish I was with you. I know we've had some hard times lately but we can get through anything."

Amid simmering tensions, Alexis eventually returned to the house.

Martin had no desire to spend eternity with his dead wife. But because the marriage had been sealed in the Mormon temple, Martin was spiritually tied to Michele forever in the view of the church. Once he died, his spirit would join hers in heaven, where they would be together for eternity.

Now Martin wanted to spend his life and afterlife with Gypsy.

The couple discussed marriage, and by June Martin was inquiring about "unsealing" his cursed union to Michele so that he could have a celestial marriage with Gypsy in church. Although Gypsy had turned her back on the LDS faith years before, with Martin she suddenly embraced her Mormon roots. Because Gypsy had also been married in the temple, she sought out information on unsealing her own marriage to Jayson Jensen.

Both Martin and Gypsy seemed enthusiastic about getting engaged as soon as possible.

Searching online for rings, on June 26 Martin placed a bid on an online jewelry auction Web site called bids.com, purchasing a four-point-five-carat diamond engagement ring for seven thousand dollars.

Two days later, Gypsy contacted an astrological Web site, comparing her and Martin's respective zodiac signs to determine a potentially fortuitous wedding date.

To celebrate their pending engagement, in early July 2007 Martin and Gypsy took another trip to Wyoming to visit with Vicki and Howard Willis. In nearby Cheyenne, Martin rented a banquet room at a restaurant called Poor Richard's to host a party. Martin paid for the food and purchased bottles of sparkling cider for a toast. On July 3, Martin, Gypsy, her parents, siblings, and family friends gathered for the celebration.

"There was a big party," Vicki remembered. "It was a big deal."

When it came time for the toast, Martin got down on one knee and professed his love for Gypsy. "I've loved you from the moment we first met," Martin said, looking up adoringly at his girlfriend. "Will you marry me?"

Tears filled Gypsy's eyes as she enthusiastically gasped, "Yes."

It seemed Gypsy would finally have her happily ever after.

"They were both very, very happy," Vicki said years later. "He made a speech about his love for her and made a very public show of dropping to one knee and asking her to marry him . . . It was a happy event."

The next day Martin accompanied Vicki into town to run an errand. During the drive, Martin spoke of his adoration of Gypsy.

"I never loved Michele. But I love Gypsy," Martin told Vicki.

Vicki was taken aback. "But Martin, you made a family with Michele!"

Martin then amended his previous statement. "Well, I did love her—I loved her as a sister. But I did not love her the way I love Gypsy."

Following their engagement, Martin and Gypsy no longer tried to conceal their relationship. It soon became obvious even to the neighbors that they were a couple.

"At first we learned she was the nanny," Doug Daniels later said. "But everyone could tell the relationship was more than that. It morphed into 'when are you getting married?'"

Martin sent all his children an e-mail informing them he had fallen in love with Jillian and that they would be wed in the temple.

Alexis and Rachel were disgusted.

On July 20, Martin and Gypsy obtained a marriage license. But the happy new couple would never actually wed.

Still, Gypsy would discover a vile way to become the new Mrs. MacNeill.

26.

The profound grief caused by Michele's death erased the last twisted shred of pretense remaining in the MacNeill family. The house in Pleasant Grove was in turmoil. Martin was preparing to marry his mistress. The younger children hated their new nanny. Alexis was desperate to get custody of her sisters. And Martin's daughters suspected their father of murder.

But not everyone in the family had turned on Martin. Damian stuck firmly by his father, eventually becoming his sole defender. By then Alexis's conviction that her dad was a murderer was absolute. It drove a wedge between the sisters and brother.

"I had talked to him about my concerns, and he didn't want to believe that my father was capable of killing my mom," Alexis later said in an interview.

The constant fighting caused Martin's mood to fluctuate erratically. Even Gypsy found life inside the house insufferable.

"They were fighting all the time," Gypsy recalled. "It was terrible. It was so hard. And then dealing with Martin was very difficult also. Because everything had to be on his terms."

Unaware of how to help him combat the stress, Gypsy wanted him to stop fighting with his daughters and just make peace. The adopted girls *wanted* to be with their older sister—Gypsy told him he should just give up custody to Alexis.

In July, two months after she had been fondled by her father, Alexis called the Pleasant Grove police. But she still wasn't ready to file charges. Instead, she inquired about procedures to report abuse.

By then Martin had lost all desire to fight for the adopted children, but he still wasn't ready to give them to any of his biological daughters.

Late that summer, Martin, Alexis, Rachel, and the younger girls took a trip to California, where they visited with family friends, the Bledsoes—whom Alexis hadn't seen for sixteen years. Martin told the Bledsoes that following his wife's death he was having difficulty caring for his young daughters and discussed the possibility that they adopt the girls. Alexis, who had repeatedly expressed desire to take custody of the children, had no idea what her father was proposing until much later.

Alexis would later report that during their trip she was sleeping in her hotel room when she awoke for a second time to find her father fondling her. Disgusted, Alexis shot out of the bed, screaming.

Once again, Martin apologized, claiming he mistook Alexis for his wife. But by then Alexis had no doubt: her father was a sexual predator.

Still, she did not call the police. Her main priority remained the welfare of her sisters. And she worried that if she pressed charges, the tenuous bond she had with her father would dissolve.

After they returned home, Martin made a request of Alexis. Giselle, then sixteen, had long planned on spending the summer in Ukraine with relatives. Martin asked for Alexis to escort the teenager on the trip. "We'll go get her after the summer," Martin told Alexis.

At first, Alexis rebuffed him. She and her father argued, and Martin once again threatened to keep her from her sisters. "If you don't do this, I won't let you see the girls," he sniped.

Fearful of losing her sisters, Alexis did as her father commanded. In July, Alexis flew with Giselle to Ukraine. Because it was simply a summer visit, Giselle packed only a small bag of clothing.

Martin had also instructed Alexis to keep Giselle's U.S. passport. "Giselle might lose it," he said. "Bring it back so I can keep it safe."

Leaving Giselle with the girl's biological sister in Ukraine, Alexis flew back to Utah with the passport. But instead of turning it over to her father, Alexis kept the passport.

A few weeks later, Martin sent a text message to Rachel, Vanessa, Alexis, and Damian: *I'm turning over custody of the girls to the Bledsoes in California.*

In desperation to get her sisters, Alexis hired an attorney, and, soon after, Martin received legal documents concerning custody. Enraged, Martin called his daughter.

When he once again refused to give up the girls to her, Alexis threatened to report him to the police and child protective services for sexual assault stemming from the two fondling incidents.

Over the next few weeks, Martin waged a furious campaign of intimidation. But Alexis remained firm. "I'll do whatever it takes to protect them."

Martin was willing to let things get ugly. "If you fight me, I'm going to get you thrown out of medical school," Martin screamed over the phone. "I'll destroy you."

But he had no clue of the lengths his children were willing to go to at that moment. Upping the ante, both Alexis and Rachel contacted their father.

"We'll go to the police," Alexis told her dad. "We'll get them to reopen the investigation for Mom's murder."

The very next morning, the girls were dropped off at Alexis's Nevada apartment.

That same day, Rachel packed up and moved to Nevada to assist Alexis with their care. Departing Utah abruptly, Elle, Sabrina, and Ada had packed only a few bags and abandoned most of their toys and possessions. Ada's collection of dolls and her beloved princess bed also remained in the home in Pleasant Grove.

Frightened of their father, Alexis, Rachel, and the girls went into hiding. They lived out of hotels around Nevada, avoiding security cameras in case Martin was searching for them. "We feared for our safety and for the safety of our younger sisters," Alexis later said in an interview. "The stress we felt when we woke up every morning was incredible."

Now that the girls were in her care, Alexis became ruthless in her war against her father. Currently stonewalled by the police in the murder investigation, Alexis pursued other legal avenues. Her attorneys filed a lawsuit to take possession of the family home in Pleasant Grove.

When Michele died, the house had been in her name because of Martin's puzzling plans to prepare for his own death. Also due to his supposed terminal illness, Alexis had been appointed executor of her mother's estate.

The home was paid off, and although the property value had plummeted due to a slump in the housing market, it was currently valued at $363,000— all in equity.

To provide her sisters an inheritance, Alexis wanted to take possession of the house, sell it, and split the assets to pay for the girls' college education. Despite the fact that the will granted the house to Martin, Alexis filed motions stating that her father had killed her mother and should not benefit from his victim's death.

For the next seven years, legal ownership of the home would be entangled in probate court.

On September 11, Alexis also called Pleasant Grove police and child protective services to press charges for the sexual assault. Martin was charged with forcible sex abuse, a second-degree felony.

"Alexis stated there had been two incidents where she had been fondled by her father within three months of her mother's passing," the police report stated.

When Martin learned Alexis was pressing charges, he threatened to take back the girls. Their confrontations grew vicious. To build a case against her dad, Alexis secretly recorded many of their phone conversations.

During one call, Martin admitted he put his hands down Alexis's pants. "I'm still a sexual person," he said in a recorded conversation. "I have desires that need to be met."

In an attempt to extort Alexis, Martin told her if she signed a statement denying he'd ever touched her, he would relinquish all rights to custody of the girls.

Alexis refused and took the recording to police. Martin was then slapped with an additional criminal charge: witness tampering, a third-degree felony.

Now in serious need of legal representation, Martin consulted a former Brigham Young University law school professor, who recommended an attorney. Randall Spencer would become Martin's loyal and trusted advocate for the next seven years.

By 2007, Spencer had already built a formidable reputation in the field of criminal defense. In his midforties, with a toothy grin, narrow face, and wire-rimmed glasses, Spencer was married and had three children, including a son with cerebral palsy.

Born in Illinois and raised as a Mormon, Spencer was a graduate of Brigham Young University law school and had begun his legal career working as a public defender for the state of Utah before entering private practice at a firm known as Fillmore and Spencer.

Spencer had risen to prominence by representing the controversial video store owner Larry Peterman in the infamous "MovieBuff" pornography case. Peterman rented out X-rated material from his stores in American Fork and Lehi, in Utah County—one of the most conservative parts of the country. Police conducted a raid on the stores, uncovering explicit material, and Peterman was brought up on obscenity charges, including fifteen misdemeanors for distributing pornography.

As a Mormon family man, Spencer found pornography morally repugnant, but he also viewed the charges against Peterman as legally unjust.

"I quickly became passionate about the case despite the fact I despise pornography. But this was a case that wasn't about pornography," Spencer recalled. "In my opinion it was a case where the prosecution was seeking to impose moral standards on one person."

The case went to trial, and in 2000, Spencer secured an almost immediate acquittal.

Now, as he got to know his newest client, Dr. Martin MacNeill, Spencer felt MacNeill was also being unfairly persecuted.

"He is obviously a very intelligent and articulate man," Spencer later said. "As I learned his story I believed then as I do now that he's not guilty of the murder."

In his representation of the sexual assault charges against Martin, Spencer's legal strategy mostly involved filing motions to have the charges dismissed based on technicalities.

In a statement about the case, Spencer also argued that Martin should not face criminal charges of sexual assault, because he was asleep when he fondled Alexis.

"A person cannot be accountable for his actions while he's asleep," the statement read.

Waging the latest battle in the war against their father, Alexis and Rachel attacked Martin where he was most vulnerable—his finances.

Rachel contacted management at the Developmental Center and both she and Alexis prepared an official statement. In it they outlined their father's conviction from 1977 and the pending charges of sexual abuse. The Developmental Center investigated, and in September Martin was fired from his prestigious job, partially for concealing his 1977 felony conviction.

Martin was infuriated. And because of his disregard for legal and moral restrictions, he could be much more vindictive than his daughters could ever fathom.

Martin planned to sell the Pleasant Grove home, undercutting Alexis's legal right to the property. But because possession of the house was being challenged in probate court, it could not legally be sold. Meanwhile, Gypsy had her own catalog of troubles stemming from her substantial tax debt, and they were obstructing her future with Martin.

The debt was crippling. With awful credit and no credit cards, Gypsy was unable to even open a bank account without the money being potentially seized by the Internal Revenue Service. If they were to legally marry, Martin feared he would be held responsible for her debts. Even adding Gypsy as a signer on Martin's bank account posed a threat that his assets would be frozen.

To untangle both of their financial snags, Martin employed the same skills he had developed in his early twenties when he committed check fraud. Once again he found a clever way to circumvent the law.

And the latest deception would involve making one of his daughters disappear.

27.

The awful fall and winter of 2007 crept by sluggishly for all those ensnared in Martin's life.

While Alexis was fighting to gain permanent custody of Elle, Sabrina, and Ada, their sister Giselle, in Ukraine, languished in abject poverty. The tiny home in which she resided was dilapidated, the walls covered with mold and rust. The bathroom consisted of little more than a toilet and a small pan on the ground that served as a shower.

For months Giselle tried to reach Martin. She had no money for food or school. He didn't answer her calls and never returned her voice messages.

Throughout her stay she heard no word from anyone in the MacNeill family. Giselle felt discarded and forgotten. She wasn't sure if she would ever see the United States again.

Despite the lack of cooperation from the Pleasant Grove police, Linda, Alexis, and Rachel continued to investigate Martin.

In the months following Michele's death, Linda had been consumed with uncovering Martin's dark secrets. Ultimately she would take a year off from her job in insurance claims, sacrificing her career to get justice for Michele.

"It was a difficult time," Linda recalled. "It took a toll on me."

The Somers family had always felt Martin received money illegally. They knew the timing of his schooling didn't add up. But they dismissed their concerns because everyone seemed to accept Martin—he kept obtaining prominent and well-paying jobs.

"Nothing seemed right with Martin MacNeill from the minute we knew him," Linda later wrote on her Web site. "I guess I find it strange that he could fool so many people, but quite honestly he didn't fool us ever."

Searching public records from each city he'd lived in, Linda collected documents. Eventually she would piece together a timeline of his questionable past, creating an overstuffed three-ring binder of evidence against Martin.

Through her investigation, she developed a theory as to his motives. She believed he was done with Michele and wanted a divorce, but he was unwilling to give up any money, assets, or his status in the church.

"It's in his nature to be finished with people," Linda later said. "He was on to bigger and better things and Michele was in his way and starting to figure him out."

For months Linda sent dozens of e-mails and letters to the Utah County Attorney's Office, many of which she delivered personally to prosecutors. She phoned agencies across the state and repeatedly contacted the Utah governor, Jon Huntsman Jr. Her daughter Jill personally went to the capital to deliver information to the governor's office, marked "urgent."

Alexis and Rachel also urged the police and prosecutors to investigate. When they were repeatedly stifled, the sisters contacted every newspaper in Utah. They received no response.

"I could not understand why no one would listen," Alexis lamented. "My mother was murdered. And no one cared."

Meanwhile, Gypsy was discovering that life with Martin was anything but a fairy tale.

As he had been with Michele, Martin was controlling and domineering in his relationship with Gypsy. After she had moved into the house, she also learned he was bipolar. Suddenly, Gypsy was dealing with his rapid cycles between mania and depression. While he could be fun and exciting, about once every six weeks he would become paranoid, angry, and belligerent.

"When he was manic, he was very lively and would do random things," Gypsy said years later. "After I'd known him for about a year I realized he was bipolar."

To assist with his mood swings, Gypsy employed the same calming tactics she had learned as a nurse working with mentally disturbed patients.

Recognizing these nursing strategies, Martin reprimanded her. "Cut the psych nurse shit."

For Gypsy it was exhausting. Eventually, she even began to empathize with how Michele must have felt throughout her marriage to Martin. "I could see how she was worn out dealing with that," Gypsy later said. "In the space of a year and a half that I was with Martin I broke out in shingles twice."

After Martin was fired, he was furious and grew hostile toward Gypsy. At one point, things became so bad he turned violent. Martin hit her, leaving bruises, which she documented on her cell phone camera. In November, she called the police and filed criminal charges for domestic violence. But soon after, Martin apologized and the couple reunited.

A few weeks after she'd reported the battery, Martin escorted Gypsy to the police station to request the charges be dismissed. Martin controlled the conversation with officials, as if he had scripted the interview. In the notarized documents, Gypsy's last name is even spelled wrong.

Still, Gypsy remained loyal to Martin.

She would later claim that being with someone so successful, accomplished, and educated caused her to settle into a more passive role in the relationship. She relinquished total control of her own life—which in a strange way was freeing for Gypsy. As the eldest child, she had always been the one held responsible for her siblings. Working as a nurse, she was charged with caring for dozens of patients. Allowing Martin to draft their futures was alluring.

"I felt like he was the one in charge. At the time I was happy to some degree to let that happen. Because I had never really felt taken care of," Gypsy later said. "To have someone say 'I'll take care of you. This is how we're going to do things.' I let that go. And that's the number one thing I regret."

Martin's latest scheme was utterly diabolical.

To mask Gypsy's debt and poor credit, she would assume a new name and take on a new Social Security number. Gypsy Jyll Willis would become Jillian Giselle MacNeill, the new wife of Martin MacNeill.

Martin created this new persona for his girlfriend by stealing the identity of his own sixteen-year-old daughter, Giselle Marie MacNeill.

Martin used Giselle's birth certificate and altered it by twenty years. Gypsy's new birth date was March 13, 1971, making her five years older than her actual age. With the fake birth certificate, Martin took Gypsy to apply for a new Social Security card under the name Jillian, essentially creating two separate individuals with the same Social Security number. In the fall of 2007, Gypsy obtained a new Utah ID card. By moving forward with the new identity, they were able to wipe away her tax debts.

Martin then accompanied Gypsy to the U.S. military offices to obtain a military identification card, which she was eligible for as the "wife" of an army veteran. On the application, Gypsy stated her name as Jillian G. MacNeill. The military ID allowed "Jillian" access to military bases and gave her the ability to open bank accounts.

In a deplorable twist, when Martin and "Jillian" filled out the application for the ID, they listed their supposed wedding date as April 14, 2007—the day Michele was buried.

Through each move of the elaborate scheme, Gypsy knew what they were doing was illegal. But she claimed Martin was so persuasive, he convinced her to take part in the scam, telling her it would be mutually beneficial.

"This was Martin's idea. This was Martin's activity. I didn't want to do it. I told him I didn't want to do it," Gypsy later said. "He said this is the best way to do it. It's temporary. It's not going to hurt anybody. No one will notice."

Martin accompanied Gypsy to Zion's First National Bank in Utah to open a checking account, on which they both were signers.

On September 28, Martin obtained and recorded a quit-claim deed on the house in Pleasant Grove. The deed would later be integral for Martin's next phase of the plan—to sell the house out from under Alexis.

That fall Martin also made changes to his will. Alexis was removed as executor of his estate. Instead, Martin willed everything to Gypsy, under the name Jillian MacNeill. When he died, each of his children would receive just one dollar.

Martin had effectively tossed away his adopted daughter Giselle. He thought she wouldn't be missed, that no one would look for her. However, as Linda continued investigating Martin for murder, she discovered that Giselle remained in Ukraine. Both Linda and her daughter, Jill Harper-Smith, were compelled to bring her home.

But they had no contact information for Giselle or her sister—no e-mail and no idea how to find her. Searching on the Internet, Jill discovered comments on Michele's online obituary from a woman named Yulia Shust— the MacNeills' translator from Ukraine. Clicking on the woman's name, Jill found an e-mail contact for Yulia.

Jill wrote to Yulia and asked if she knew how to reach Giselle. Days later, Jill received a response from Yulia with a phone number for Giselle. Jill called the number, eventually making contact with the teenager.

On the call with her cousin, Giselle sobbed about how she had been abandoned with no money. "He just left me here."

Without notifying Martin, Linda secretly purchased a plane ticket and sent Jill to Ukraine to bring Giselle back. Before leaving, Jill also obtained Giselle's passport from Alexis, who still had it in her possession. After arriving in Ukraine, Jill saw the conditions in which Giselle had been living, and was appalled. "I've never seen anything that horrible," Jill later said.

Giselle flew back to Utah with her cousin. Once she had returned, Linda decided to adopt the teenager.

In a bid to obtain guardianship of Giselle, Linda filed a protective order against Martin, paying for an attorney at her own expense. But despite having deserted his adopted daughter, for the next few months Martin peculiarly fought for custody of Giselle. Due to the legal battle, Giselle had to spend months in foster care before returning to Linda's home.

Dejected by her abandonment, Giselle was bitter and wanted no contact with the MacNeill family. She would never speak to her sisters again.

2 8.

The first anniversary of Michele MacNeill's death was agonizing for her loved ones. Adding to their pain, Michele's grave remained unmarked by a tombstone or plaque. For her grieving daughters it was just another sign of disrespect toward their mother.

When they had still been speaking to their father, Rachel, Vanessa, and Alexis had complained that he hadn't yet purchased a gravestone. They offered to put one up themselves, but Martin forbade them.

During a court hearing concerning custody of her sisters, Alexis addressed the issue with the judge. "He doesn't even have a headstone up for my mom," Alexis said.

About a month later, Linda was at her home in Spanish Fork thinking of Michele when she had the sudden urge to visit her grave at the Highland City Cemetery, about forty-five miles away. Linda drove to the cemetery, parked her car, and walked across the graveyard. As she approached Michele's burial site, she stopped in her tracks. Martin and Damian were kneeling by the grave.

Returning to her car, Linda retrieved a pair of binoculars. Conspicuously flipping up the hood on the jacket she was wearing, she scurried across the cemetery, crouched by a gravestone, and pretended to be paying her respects. Using her binoculars, she observed as Martin and Damian poured wet cement into a mold atop Michele's grave, creating their own tombstone.

"I happened to go there the same day that they were there, which is weird . . . I saw them up there," Linda recalled. "And they were up on the lawn pouring cement, pouring their own headstone. It was so bizarre."

After about fifteen minutes, Martin and Damian left, pulling a trailer across the lawn of the cemetery and back to the parking lot. Once they were gone, Linda dashed down to Michele's grave to observe what Martin had constructed. "It was the craziest-looking thing I had ever seen," she later said. "It was like cement scratched with a rock."

When she returned later, she saw that someone had polished the cement to make it appear more finished. Several months later Martin added a plaque with Michele's name and a poem to the slab.

Still, it was an undeniable monstrosity.

The final stone was a crude, six-foot-tall concrete slab that resembled a surfboard. When Alexis went to the cemetery to see it, she was shocked. She wasn't sure of Martin's motive behind it, but she assumed it was to save money.

Many complained to the Highland City Cemetery management about the "eyesore." When the cemetery manager spoke to Martin, the widower threatened to sue: he could pour his own headstone if he wanted, Martin argued.

Linda returned to the cemetery religiously on her sister's birthday and the anniversary of her death to feel closer to her spirit. That year Linda also went to the cemetery on Michele's wedding anniversary—out of curiosity to see what Martin might be doing.

At her sister's grave, Linda peered down and noticed a card with a picture of an angel. Immediately Linda recognized it—it was the same Christmas card she had received the year before from her sister. She picked it up to examine it.

Crudely pasted over the lettering "Merry Christmas" was a yellow Post-it note with Martin's handwriting: *Till we meet at Jesus's feet. Martin.*

Beside it was a plastic flower arrangement covered in a thick layer of dust. Linda took a picture with her cell phone and sent it to Alexis.

OMG! My mom used that for Relief Society, Alexis replied. *He just grabbed something from the garage.*

Linda kept the card and stored it as evidence.

"He just grabbed something out of their garage, sat the . . . flower arrangement on there. And he took an old Christmas card and glued a yellow sticky note over the Merry Christmas and brought it out. That's what he sat on her grave," Linda recalled with disgust. "Like he just had to stick something there because he knew other people would be coming."

In April 2008, Alexis's charges of sexual assault against her father were dismissed, just weeks before the scheduled trial date. The judge ruled that there wasn't enough evidence in the case and said prosecutors did not have a "good faith" basis to proceed.

Martin thought he won. And Alexis worried that her father would never be held accountable for the crime.

But soon prosecutors in that case would have a reason to take a closer look at the life of Martin MacNeill.

Following her mother's death and the implosion of her family, Vanessa's drug addiction had once again spiraled beyond her control. But she never lost her desire to find sobriety.

In June 2008, Vanessa went to her father, hoping he'd pay for her to go through rehab. Instead, he suggested another way of defeating her addiction: ending her life. Martin told her they could go to heaven together.

"Take my hand and leave with me." Martin loomed over Vanessa. "I will end your life and I will end my own."

"What are you talking about?" Vanessa said, her eyes flooding with tears.

"That's the only way you'll feel peace," Martin said calmly.

Vanessa sobbed, suddenly afraid her father would kill her.

"Don't be afraid." He reached out for her. "Take my hand."

Fearful, Vanessa called Alexis for a ride. When she arrived, Vanessa told her sister what had happened.

They were both horrified.

Meanwhile, as Martin feuded with his daughters, Gypsy's own family issues reemerged.

Gypsy owned an Italian greyhound, and that summer she had temporarily placed it in her parents' care while she searched for a rescue organization. She drove to Wyoming to take custody of the dog, but when she arrived, her mother refused to return the animal. They argued, and the squabble turned violent.

Gypsy pounced on Vicki, biting her.

"She lunged forward and she bit me on my upper left bicep—a bad bite. You could see every single tooth mark," Vicki said of the incident. "She doesn't care who gets hurt. She doesn't care what circumstances are ruined."

Gypsy claimed her mom grabbed her from behind and choked her, leaving her injured. "I was bruised from head to toe. I had a sprained knee. I had choke marks around my neck," Gypsy later said.

They tussled for a few moments. Once they'd separated, Vicki told her to leave. "Get out of here. You will never see Heidi again."

Gypsy called Martin, but her mother grabbed the phone, hung up, and dialed the police. Jumping into her car, Gypsy drove away. As she was leaving she saw fire trucks and an ambulance heading to her parents' house. No charges were filed, but police took a report.

Howard Willis would later say Gypsy was the aggressor during the fight. "It was an ugly situation," he remembered.

That day in August would be the last time Howard and Vicki would see or speak to their daughter.

"We feel awful for the choices she has made, and cannot have her around us," Howard later said of his relationship with Gypsy. "She is basically not welcome on our property."

Howard and Vicki felt their oldest daughter had become an ugly and awful person. Eventually the entire family would turn on Gypsy.

"I would consider Gypsy to be a deceptive, malevolent, malicious, calculating person," her sister Julie Willis said years later. "If she sees something she wants, she will rationalize that to the point that she will get that no matter who stands in her way."

After more than a year, Martin had grown weary of battling for custody of the children he never really wanted. That summer, he relinquished parental rights, and Alexis formally adopted Elle, Sabrina, and Ada.

Linda, meanwhile, had been fighting her former brother-in-law for custody of Giselle. But as she navigated through the thorny adoption process, Linda noticed something peculiar. She traveled to Salt Lake City and petitioned the court to have Giselle's original adoption papers unsealed. Once she obtained the documents, she compared them to Giselle's original birth certificate and found the girl's birth date had been altered by twenty years. Giselle's adoption could not continue.

By the summer of 2008, Linda, Alexis, and Rachel had been hounding the prosecutor's office for months, inundating them with letters and packets of information. Finally, their labor paid off.

A few months earlier, the women had received a call from the Utah County Attorney's Office: investigators were looking into the case. But months had passed and no progress had been made.

Then in July, the case was assigned a new investigator—one who would probe deeper into Michele's mysterious death.

His name was Doug Witney.

29.

The slim manila folder landed on investigator Doug Witney's desk with a thwack. Raising an eyebrow, Witney glanced up at his supervisor, who had just flung the case file onto his desk.

"Can you give this a look?" asked Jeff Robinson, supervising investigator of the Utah County Attorney's Office Bureau of Investigations. "See if there is anything we can do."

Witney nodded as he thumbed through the pages of the file. Inside there were just a few sheets of paper: a couple of statements, a letter addressed to county prosecutors, and a court report from 1977.

Witney scanned the documents, assessing the details: fifty-year-old woman found dead in the bathtub after a face-lift—the victim's family believed the husband was the killer.

It wasn't a typical case for the bureau, which primarily investigated financial fraud, corruption, and officer-involved shootings. The bureau's investigators, who serve as fact gatherers for Utah County prosecutors, strictly handled murder cases that involved a legitimate complaint about the agency in charge of the case. But while they received dozens of such complaints each year, they had yet to work any such case that warranted going to trial.

Still, had Michele's family not pushed for the investigation to be re-opened, it would have never made its way to Witney's desk.

The bureau had been brought onto the case seven months prior, as Robinson explained to Witney. Following persistent provocation by Linda, Rachel, and Alexis, prosecutors handed the case to Robinson, who had originally assigned it to a different agent. A few months later that agent had resigned, having not touched the case. So Robinson gave it to Witney to take a look.

Witney was a dogged investigator in his sixties with white hair, a sharp chin, and blue eyes encircled by wrinkles. Witney had originally joined the bureau in 1991, and worked with Robinson for twelve years before moving on to the Utah County Sheriff's Office.

He retired a few years later, but a life of leisure didn't suit him, so when Robinson asked him to reexamine one of his old cases, he didn't hesitate. He was working only twelve hours a week on the other case and had the time to delve into the strange details of the death of Michele MacNeill.

As Witney looked over the file, something caught his attention: a letter written by Helen Somers, attached to a packet of old court records. There was something that struck Witney about a mother holding on to documents for thirty years because she feared her daughter's husband.

Michele's mother must be resolute in her conviction, Witney thought.

Witney looked up at Robinson. "I think there's something we can do."

He couldn't have known then, but he'd soon be entangled in one of the thorniest murder mysteries of his career.

"When I started the case there were a couple of statements in the case file, a couple of letters—not a lot of information," Witney recalled. "So I started collecting information."

Witney contacted Alexis, Rachel, and Linda, who explained their concerns and provided the investigator with the reports and information that they had been compiling about Martin. At first, Witney didn't know what to make of the amateur sleuths. But once he started reviewing their research, he sat up in his chair, intrigued.

"They started to challenge a lot of things about their father," Witney later said. "Who he was. Where he was. What he was doing."

Over the next few years, Linda and Michele's children would work closely with Witney in building a case against Dr. Martin MacNeill.

Witney's supervisor and close friend, Jeff Robinson, would also work on the case throughout the investigation. Robinson was a seasoned investigator with over twenty-five years in law enforcement, including eighteen years at the bureau. He had thinning brown hair and inquisitive eyes that peered through oversized glasses. A graduate of the FBI National Academy, he had previously worked with the Brigham Young University Police Department as a patrol deputy before joining the bureau, which he had led for the last decade.

Over the next few months Witney and Robinson conducted extensive interviews with all of the MacNeill children. As an eyewitness to Michele's pre- and post-surgery appointments as well as her recovery, Alexis was a vital resource. She explained to investigators that on the night Michele was released from the hospital following the plastic surgery, she was drugged with the same cocktail of medication that was found in her blood after her death.

The black notebook where Alexis had written all of Michele's vitals and medications was never found. However, Alexis was able to hand over the Zyrtec notepad, in which she had first recorded the information. Rachel also provided the shirts and bra her mother had been wearing when she died.

Witney and Robinson immediately requested and received reports from the Pleasant Grove police. Aside from demonstrating how lacking the initial investigation was, the documents did little to further the case.

The Pleasant Grove police never investigated Michele's death as a crime—not from the very first day. So investigators Witney and Robinson interviewed witnesses the police never had. They would talk to dozens of police officers, paramedics, nurses, and the MacNeills' neighbors who had seen Michele on the day of her death, honing in on the vast discrepancies between what Martin had told police and the reports from other witnesses at the scene.

While Martin had informed first responders that Michele was taking a lot of medication, he told the ER doctor she was taking only "a Percocet" and an antibiotic.

Several officers said Martin's angry, belligerent attitude was unlike any death scene they had ever worked. Nurses at the hospital said Martin's hysterics were inconsistent with the behavior of a bereaved husband.

"Martin's behavior, including swearing, screaming, pounding his wife on the chest at the home and at the hospital, and cursing her for having an operation he insisted upon, appear to be a façade," Robinson wrote in the report.

Through interviews with neighbors, investigators also learned that Doug Daniels had tried to clean the bathroom but could find no towels. "This would indicate that Martin MacNeill would have to have stopped any lifesaving measure long enough to wipe up blood and water on the floor," Robinson wrote.

Most glaring was the position of Michele's body. Neighbors had first found Michele slumped inside the tub. But Martin told police, paramedics, and his children that she was draped over the tub's edge, her face submerged in the water. The lividity on the back of her legs and buttocks suggested Michele died on her back.

"Upon arrival of police and paramedics, Martin immediately started lying about the events surrounding Michele's death in an effort to hinder, delay, or prevent any police investigation," wrote Robinson.

The more Witney and Robinson probed into the inconsistencies in the first few moments after Michele was discovered, the more they realized the importance of interviewing the very first person at the scene: Ada MacNeill.

30.

Grasping a crayon in her fist, Ada MacNeill scribbled on a piece of paper. She was seated at a desk in a room filled with toys and stuffed teddy bears.

As the female police officer took a seat across from the girl, Ada fidgeted.

"How do you feel about talking to me today?" asked Officer Patty Johnston.

"Mmm." Ada shrugged. "Okay."

It was September 9—almost a year and a half after Michele's death—and Ada, now seven years old, was being formally interviewed for the first time about exactly what she saw on April 11, 2007. The interview was being conducted at the Children's Justice Center in Provo, a homelike facility where children involved in criminal investigations can be interviewed in a comfortable and serene atmosphere.

One day prior, Alexis had driven Ada and her sisters from Nevada to Provo for the interview. They stayed the night with Michele's friend Loreen Thompson.

In a comforting tone, Johnston, a child advocate and investigator with the Utah County Attorney's Office, began the interview by talking about Loreen's dog Otis, Barbie dolls, and SpongeBob.

Johnston explained to Ada the importance of telling the truth. If a subject was too scary, the officer told her just to say that she didn't want to talk about it.

"The reason, Ada, that you came here to talk to me today is we're trying to find out what happened in your house in Utah," Johnston said gently. "Can you tell me who you used to live with?"

"I don't want to talk about it," Ada murmured.

For much of the interview Ada avoided all questions about what happened to her mom and anything related to her father.

"When you lived in your house in Utah, tell me all the people who lived there."

"I don't really want to talk about it," Ada repeated.

"You don't want to talk about your house in Utah? Tell me, how come?"

Ada softly whispered, "I don't know."

"Were there some things that happened in your house in Utah that made you sad?"

"I don't want to talk about it," Ada said.

"I know there were some happy things that happened and I think there were some sad things that happened. Is that true or not true?" Johnston asked.

"That's true," the girl said softly.

"It's important that we talk about some things that happened in your old house. Do you think you can be brave enough and talk about some things?" Johnston asked.

"I don't know." Ada looked down.

"It's hard, isn't it?"

Tenderly, Johnston tried to ask more questions about the girl's father, but the only thing that Ada would say was his name was Martin.

"Why don't you really want to talk about it?"

"I don't know." Ada sighed.

"How does it feel to talk about your dad? Does it make you happy to talk about your dad?"

"No."

"Does it make you sad?"

"I don't really want to talk about it," she whispered.

When asked, Ada spoke fondly of her mom, saying she was happy, nice, and "real pretty," but she said that it made her "sad" to talk about her.

"Do you miss her?" Johnston asked.

"Yeah," she whispered.

"Someone told me that a little over a year ago your mom died," Johnston said. "Do you know what happened?"

Ada nodded and slowly started to reveal the details of what she saw that day.

"Dad came in with me and we walked in the room," Ada said faintly. "The water was like almost brown and stuff and you could hardly see it. So my dad told me to go next door and get somebody."

Ada said she thought her mom was wearing a blue shirt, pants, and a jacket. "She just was wetting her hair. But she was still in her clothes."

Ada then described the position of her mother's body.

"She was just laying down in the bathtub. She was trying to wet her hair," she said. "Then my dad came in and saw the bathtub and he was like trying to pull my mom up, I guess."

"What was your dad doing in the bathroom?" the officer asked.

"He was screaming, 'Quick. Help. Run next door and get somebody.' So I had to run next door."

"How did you feel that day?"

"Sad," Ada said.

Johnston explained that Ada was very brave to get help. She told her to pick out a teddy bear, which all children that come to the Children's Justice Center are allowed to do when interviewed in a criminal case.

"We talked about you missing your mom. Is that right?" Johnston asked. "What about your dad. Do you miss your dad?"

"I don't want to talk about it." Ada glanced down.

At the end of the interview, Johnston asked Ada to draw a picture of how she found her mom that day. In black pen, Ada drew a rudimentary stick figure surrounded by an amorphous shape meant to represent the tub. Next to it were notes about what she remembered.

"Her head was out of the water. Her hair was going down the drain. All the water was red. Her eyes were open."

31.

Michele MacNeill's cause of death was a mystery.

If her husband murdered her, how exactly did he do it? How could prosecutors press murder charges when the medical examiner believed heart disease had killed her?

Those questions looped endlessly through the minds of investigators Doug Witney and Jeff Robinson.

Overcoming the medical examiner's ruling would be a nearly insurmountable task in a homicide investigation. To build a case, investigators needed to convince the pathologist to reconsider the original findings.

To complicate matters, Dr. Maureen Frikke, the medical examiner who had performed Michele's autopsy, had died. On March 22, 2008, Frikke passed away in her home at the age of fifty-nine, following an eight-year battle with breast cancer that had metastasized to her liver.

Witney and Robinson had come to believe Dr. Frikke did not have all the facts when conducting the autopsy and that her conclusion may have been different if she had been privy to all the information. Because the death was never investigated as a crime, it's unclear if Frikke was even aware that Michele expelled several cups of water when the officers performed CPR. And while the autopsy showed she had acute inflammation of the heart, it might not have been what caused her death.

"Unfortunately, because of Dr. Frikke's death, all we have remaining are the notes she made at the time of her conversations with Martin," Witney later said.

Reviewing those notes, Witney noticed that Frikke had placed several question marks by answers Martin had given her during their phone conversation. For the investigators it seemed like an indication that Frikke found his responses questionable—that his explanations didn't match the evidence.

In September, Witney and Robinson consulted Dr. Todd Grey, the chief medical examiner for the state of Utah and Frikke's supervisor, and asked him to review Michele's case.

Grey was an experienced and respected pathologist. He was tall with shaggy hair graying around the temples, rugged facial hair, and round-frame glasses. Grey had worked as a forensic pathologist in Utah since 1986 and as an assistant medical examiner before becoming chief of the department.

Witney and Robinson provided Grey with materials they had gathered through the investigation, trying to get him to consider changing Michele's cause of death.

Autopsy findings are changed only under the rarest of circumstances. In Utah, the medical examiner's office receives only three to four cases a year where they are asked to reconsider the cause of death because of suspicions of a homicide. Of those, less than 5 percent are actually reopened.

Witney and Robinson provided Grey with reasons they were reopening the case, including information about Martin's affair.

But in evaluating the autopsy and toxicology report, Grey found that Frikke's investigation was thorough. The drug levels detected were not sufficient to explain death and were not indicative of an intentional lethal overdose. Further, the weight and condition of Michele's lungs did not make him suspect drowning. Grey sent Witney an e-mail in which he declined to amend both the cause and manner of death.

"While the investigation subsequent to the victim's death raises questions about the possible role of her husband, there's nothing in the autopsy or toxicology that proves her death was from an unnatural cause," Grey wrote. "The autopsy findings certainly provide evidence of natural disease that could explain death."

The investigators were disappointed, but were not ready to give up. Over the next two years they would meet with Dr. Grey numerous times in hopes of getting him to change his opinion.

Witney and Robinson spent months examining the background of Martin MacNeill. The investigation would ultimately unravel years of fabrications, fraud, and unconscionable lies.

"MacNeill's a thespian," Witney later said. "It appears his whole life was scripted and staged."

Using Linda Cluff's amateur sleuthing as a starting point, Witney and Robinson dug deeper. The Somers family had often doubted Martin's educational credentials—specifically how he was in school long enough to earn a medical and law degree. Additionally, they suspected he might have an illicit source of income. With those leads, the investigators began speaking with officials and requesting records, working to piece together a time-line leading back thirty years.

After obtaining Martin's military record, they traced his first deception to when he was seventeen and lied about his age to enlist in the military. Two years later he had been deemed a latent schizophrenic and was discharged from service.

There is no cure for schizophrenia. And although medication can mask symptoms, Martin had no prescriptions for the disorder. His family believed he had fabricated symptoms of schizophrenia during his time in the military to commit fraud. Witney and Robinson would also come to believe Martin's mental illness was feigned to gain an early discharge and collect military benefits. In 1975, Martin applied for and received Veterans Benefits Administration and Social Security benefits.

Despite gaining dual degrees, becoming a successful doctor, and earning a six-figure salary, Martin continued to collect disability benefits illegally from the Veterans Benefits Administration for the next thirty-five years, amassing a total of more than one hundred thousand dollars. By the time

Witney and Robinson uncovered the scam, Martin was receiving three thousand dollars in benefits a month.

Searching through the reports, the investigators kept returning to Martin's college transcripts. How did he get accepted into medical school while on felony probation? Why did he spend so little time in Mexico?

Witney and Robinson obtained Martin's college transcripts from Washington, California, Mexico, and Utah. While living in Washington, it seemed that Martin had graduated from Saint Martin's University. To acquire degrees in psychology and sociology, Martin had transferred sixty-five credits from the army's extension program. But there were no records to show if those military credits were legitimate.

After graduating college he was arrested for the check-forging scheme. Once again he used an apparently fictitious mental illness in an attempt to plead not guilty by reason of insanity.

Later that year, while living in Mission Viejo, Martin met and married Michele. Around that time, Helen Somers had discovered the seal from Saint Martin's University, which Linda provided to investigators.

Comparing the transcripts Martin used to get into medical school with the originals from the colleges, Witney and Robinson discovered he had falsified transcripts with inflated grades, and had lied on applications. It appeared he had obtained another student's school transcripts and changed the name to his own.

"He obviously took somebody else's transcripts," Witney later explained. "There was a different date of entrance, different date of graduation, and all of them were straight As."

With those phony transcripts, Martin had been accepted into medical school in Mexico, where he did not disclose his recent felony conviction.

"Here is a man who went to jail for one hundred and eighty days," Witney later said. "He was on felony parole when he went into medical school."

After just one semester, Martin transferred to Western University of Health Sciences in California, claiming he'd spent a full year in Mexico. Witney tracked down the original application.

"He had actually been there for a semester," Witney explained. "It was very obvious . . . it was totally falsified as well."

The same year, Martin had an interview with the army for a checkup on his disability leave, during which he told the examiner he had not been working or attending school. It made him eligible for 50 percent disability pay from the Veterans Benefits Administration; he later received 100 percent pay. Martin also managed to receive 100 percent pay from Social Security.

In 1983, after three years in school, Martin used his falsified records to obtain a medical degree and get a license as an osteopathic surgeon in California and later in Utah. From there Martin spent two decades as a successful doctor. In 1998, he also used those same bogus transcripts to get into BYU's law school.

"It is an amazing story about how he got from one place to another through lies," Robinson commented. "Whenever you can become a doctor and an attorney based on lies, that is an amazing thing."

In addition, as Witney and Robinson interviewed former colleagues at the various hospitals and clinics in which Martin had worked, they learned of multiple accusations of misdiagnoses and sexual assaults. At each job Martin also failed to disclose his diagnosis of a psychological disorder or his felony conviction.

The investigators were now convinced that Martin MacNeill was anything but the esteemed doctor he claimed to be.

"This was a case that because nothing was known about the individual, nothing was done," Witney stated. "The guy is brilliant. I am not saying that he is not smart . . . he just lies."

Sitting down with Martin's daughters in late 2008, Witney and Robinson revealed the totality of what they had uncovered. Rachel and Alexis were shocked and angry.

"He was able to hide an entire life from us," Rachel said years later. "We basically found out that our entire lives had been based and surrounded on lies. That everything about our experience with our father was a lie."

For days all Rachel could do was cry and erratically scream. "The father that I knew was a fictional character. It was an act the whole time," she said in an interview.

For Alexis it was agonizing to realize that the man she patterned her career after was a fraud. "The father we knew . . . he was just a façade," Alexis later said. "He betrayed us to our very core. I mean, everything that we thought in our life was just all shattered. It was a sham. It really is. It's been a whole sham."

32.

Emboldened by what she had learned about her father, Rachel launched a blog about Martin. On it she made a request pleading for witnesses to come forward with information.

During the next few months she would receive calls from people across the country with disturbing stories of their encounters with Martin. Some women said they had been propositioned by the doctor, one man claimed he witnessed a rape. However, no one ever reported Martin to the police and no charges were brought.

"It's horrifying to hear their stories and how their life has been affected by my dad," Rachel later said. "He really knew who he could take advantage of. I thought I had an idea of who my father was, but I had no idea."

For Rachel, not only was it disturbing to learn of her father's perverse sexual secrets, it was also heart wrenching. Had any of her father's former mistresses approached Michele before she died, perhaps she would have left the marriage.

"To think if my mom would've known, her life would've been saved," Rachel lamented.

Alexis also believed that if Michele had understood the lengths of her father's deception, she would not have stayed in the marriage. "If she would have known who my father was, she would have been gone in a minute," Alexis commented. "She would have wanted to protect her children and she would not have stayed if she would have known what was going on."

The case that had been composed of a single manila folder when the Utah County Bureau of Investigations first took it on soon spilled into boxes of evidence strewn around the investigators' offices.

As Witney and Robinson continued to interview witnesses, the investigators gathered police reports, medical records, and financial documents. Witney subpoenaed cell phone records for Martin, Michele, and Gypsy. The Developmental Center's office phone records were gathered as well.

Mobile phone triangulation—a common tool in police investigations—allows for cell phone signals to be traced by locating the tower origin of the last signal the phone received. In this case, if investigators were able to trace the location of the cell phones, they could show who was at the house on the day of the murder.

Unfortunately, the data needed for such calculations is stored for only sixty to ninety days, depending on the cellular phone provider. By the time the bureau got the case, those records had been purged and could never be recovered. Also lost to time was the content of text messages, which phone providers store for a short period of time. Investigators would be able to review what time a message was sent and to whom, but not the contents.

Still, the phone records provided valuable insight into the relationship between Martin and Gypsy. The two had communicated regularly for more than a year, but in early 2007 the frequency of their communication increased dramatically. Each day the couple exchanged more than a dozen messages, many late at night.

The texting pattern also showed the apparent callousness Martin had toward his wife.

On April 5, the day she was drugged, Martin and Gypsy exchanged twenty-five texts. On April 12—one day after Michele had died—the two sent twelve messages back and forth, including two pictures. The next day they exchanged seventeen messages.

Using Martin's work phone records, investigators were able to trace his activity on April 11. Witney cross-referenced those records with witness statements, creating a timeline of Martin's whereabouts on Michele's final day.

After arriving at work, Martin called Gypsy at 6:48 A.M. About an hour later he returned home to take the girls to school. Ada was dropped off just before 8:20 A.M. From 8:30 to 9:11 A.M., there was a gap in Martin's traceable timeline.

At 9:26 A.M., he called Gypsy again. And at 11 A.M. a call from Martin's phone was placed to an 800 number, lasting six minutes.

"We don't know if Martin made this call," Witney wrote in his notes.

The call Martin made from his office to Alexis was also peculiar—both because he didn't call from his cell phone and because of the odd way he had expressed concern that Michele was not staying in bed.

"I believe Martin's call to Alexis is likely a pretext call, being made from Martin's place of employment, as an attempt at an alibi," Robinson wrote in his report.

Shortly after 11 A.M., Martin arrived at the safety fair to accept his award, where coworkers said he was "nervous and belligerent," so much so that a written complaint was filed against him. He had insisted he be photographed, "so people would know that he was present," furthering his alibi.

By 11:35 A.M. Martin picked up Ada.

Records showed that Martin called 911 twice, at 11:46 A.M. and 11:48 A.M. Witney received a recording of the call. Because Martin was so angry, aggressive, and condescending on the call, it had been saved for training purposes.

And because Martin didn't state his address clearly, nearly fifteen minutes elapsed before paramedics arrived.

There are only two time gaps in Martin's schedule. From about 8:30 to 9:11 A.M., there are no phone records. And from about 9:30 to 11 A.M. Martin's whereabouts were also untraceable.

Widening their investigation, Witney and Robinson delved deeper into Martin's financial activity over the past year. When Linda had been unable to complete the adoption of Giselle because of the discrepancies with the birth certificate, she alerted Witney and Robinson, with suspicions that it could be related to another scam.

Soon they had uncovered Martin's latest deception involving the theft of Giselle's identity. Federal investigators were notified of the fraud, and an investigation was launched against Martin and Gypsy.

A federal agent from the U.S. Postal Inspection Service spent months collecting incriminating documents related to the financial fraud and identity theft. Because the crimes were widespread, the postal agency worked in conjunction with the Social Security office, the Department of Veterans Affairs, and the Department of Professional Licensing.

It became clear to prosecutors that Martin had sent Giselle to Ukraine to fend for herself with the intention of stealing her identity. Prosecutor Karen Fojkt with the U.S. Attorney's Office believed the trip was to be permanent.

"He knew he was plotting and planning to steal her identity," Fojkt commented of the case. "This is the first time that anybody has put a timeline on this guy and has seen everything that has been going on with him for thirty years."

Unaware of the criminal investigation, Martin made plans to flee Utah. The Pleasant Grove property was still entangled in litigation, and although he was the legal resident of the home, it could not be sold. To avoid going through probate or paying taxes, in late 2008 Martin used Gypsy's new identity to devise a scheme to sell the property.

Acting as if his wife were still alive, Martin masqueraded as Michele's attorney. Then he had the property transferred into his own name. The same day the transaction went through, Gypsy filed a one million dollar lien on the house, under the name Jillian MacNeill, in order to discourage Martin's daughters from claiming rights to the property.

It was an illegal transaction—there was no reason to file the lien.

Because federal agents had been monitoring Martin's financial activity, they quickly became aware of the plan. Posing as a potential buyer, a federal agent made an offer to buy the house. Gypsy then went to remove the lien so the property could be sold.

Once the scheme was uncovered, a warrant was issued for the arrest of Martin MacNeill and Gypsy Willis.

If Michele had lived, January 15, 2009, would have been her fifty-second birthday. That day, Martin was returning to Utah after a brief trip to Washington for a job interview. Witney, Robinson, and a slew of federal investigators went to the Salt Lake City airport to await his flight.

Once Martin stepped off the plane, he was arrested on multiple charges stemming from the identity theft and fraud. As he was handcuffed, he looked stunned.

"It was quite a surprise," recalled Robinson. "He had no idea what was going on . . . and that was the beauty of it."

That same day Gypsy was alone in the kitchen of the Pleasant Grove home when a SWAT team dressed in bulletproof vests burst through the front door, shouting commands.

"Get out! You can't be in here!" Gypsy yelled.

The FBI soon swarmed the house. Agents searched the premises and took photos. Detectives pulled Gypsy aside to question her. Exiting the house, she saw police cars lining the block.

"I was shocked, scared, and angry," Gypsy remembered.

Gypsy was arrested and charged with eleven felony counts, including misuse of a Social Security card and aggravated identity theft. Martin was indicted in federal court on nine counts of aiding and abetting in aggravated identity theft, misuse of a Social Security number, and making false statements.

Both Martin and Gypsy would also face state charges for felonies including making inconsistent statements, insurance fraud, and forgery.

In January, Martin was also recharged with sexual abuse and witness tampering for the 2007 assault of Alexis. A new prosecutor took on the case and was determined to pursue charges. The defense filed an immediate appeal, arguing the prosecution hadn't produced any additional evidence and that refiling charges violated Martin's right to a speedy and public trial.

The case crept slowly through the justice system and would remain tied up for the next three years in appeals court.

Following the arrests, the investigators served a search warrant on the Pleasant Grove home. Witney and Robinson took measurements of the bathroom and collected evidence, including computers, cell phones, cameras, and camcorders. Numerous documents were also recovered, such as the report from Martin's visits to the Mayo Clinic.

In addition to medical testing for his genetic condition, Martin had undergone a psychological evaluation, during which he made several statements that the investigators found intriguing.

Martin told the doctors he struggled with "death ideations," and admitted he was bipolar but said he controlled his condition with medication. Martin also claimed he was a psychiatrist who headed up a psychiatric unit of a Utah hospital.

The report also proved Martin wasn't suffering from a terminal illness, despite telling his family, neighbors, and church congregants that he had six months to live. "At the time these statements were made, Martin MacNeill knew he was not dying of cancer or any other ailment," Robinson wrote in his report.

The investigators would come to believe that Martin contrived his illness for months, inventing an excuse for why he would later be unable to lift an unconscious Michele from the tub and to deflect blame from himself for her death.

"These ailments seem to be used as a method of obtaining sympathy from those close to his family and thereby diverting any possible suspicion of complicity in Michele's death," Robinson wrote.

Much of the next few months passed by in court for Linda, Alexis, and Rachel, who attended hearings for both Martin and Gypsy.

Damian, who continued to advocate for his father, was also a regular at court hearings. Sauntering through the courtroom, he brushed past his sisters and sat next to Martin's attorney. He gave his father a supportive glance and then winked at Randall Spencer.

The subsequent trials would be presided over by Judge Samuel McVey, a retired U.S. Marines colonel appointed to Provo's Fourth District Court in 2004. With a law degree from Brigham Young University law school and a former law firm partner, McVey was in his sixties, with thinning white hair and a heavily lined face.

Through the next few months, Martin MacNeill would become a familiar face in McVey's courtroom, where witnesses would testify about his staggeringly deceitful criminal past and how he used his credentials as a doctor and a lawyer to skirt the law.

"It was astounding that someone could have that amount of incidents in the past and avoid additional prosecution," one witness told the judge. "I can tell you he was very articulate, intelligent, well-educated, and he premeditated these criminal acts."

But far from being a brilliant forgery, Martin's identity theft scheme was brazen and sloppy, explained Witney. "You are talking about a state ID card. You are talking about bank accounts that were opened up under false names, false Social Security numbers," Witney later said. "We don't know why these people did what they did, because it was so likely that they would be caught."

Weeks after her arrest, Gypsy was granted pretrial release, and she remained free for the next few months. But since Martin was facing charges of fraud, identify theft, and sexual assault, he was denied bail.

Still, Gypsy and Martin would not see or speak to each other for the next three years. Having been arrested for a scheme she was convinced her boyfriend coerced her to commit, Gypsy was initially livid. She blamed him for ruining her life. While embroiled in the criminal charges, she dated other men, eventually reconnecting with a former lover who lived in Texas.

Meanwhile, when Gypsy's family and many of her friends learned of her part in the scam, they turned on her. Although Howard and Vicki hadn't spoken to their daughter in months, when they found out about the arrest, they were horrified. Soon, the truth was revealed about Gypsy's affair during Martin's marriage and the suspicious details of Michele's death.

It seemed to Howard and Vicki that their daughter was a sick individual.

"When you've got a daughter that loses her morals and her spiritual guidance, she could be led on by a pathological killer," Howard reflected on his daughter's relationship with Martin. "The moment she found out Martin was married, she should have shut that relationship off."

When younger sister Julie Willis learned about the case, she would come to believe that Gypsy had found her match in Martin MacNeill. "In a bad way, they were perfect for each other," Julie Willis said in an interview. "Together, I believe that they are perfectly capable of killing Michele."

This was the Willis family's greatest fear—that Gypsy was somehow involved in Michele's murder. "I hope and pray to God that she did not have anything to do with this thing. I just hope and pray," Howard commented. "But if she did, I can't help her. But I do hope that Gypsy looks at her life and says 'I've got to make some changes.'"

When Michelle Savage learned of her former roommate's arrest, she shuddered. Searching online, she came across Rachel MacNeill's blog and sent her an e-mail. The story she had to tell was chilling.

During Gypsy's affair with Martin, her infatuation with him had spiraled into a dark obsession, according to Savage.

While Savage lived at the house in Bountiful, Gypsy often spoke about the intense sexual chemistry she had with a married doctor she called "Neil." After learning of Michele MacNeill's death, Savage now believed that was an alias for "Martin MacNeill."

Though it seemed most of her boyfriends were married, Gypsy had been particularly obsessed with "Neil." On one occasion Savage escorted her roommate to an event that Gypsy said she knew Neil would be attending.

"That's him." Gypsy nodded in the direction of a handsome older man sitting with his wife at a table across the room.

Later that evening Gypsy disappeared for about half an hour. Rejoining Savage, Gypsy whispered in her friend's ear, "We just had sex." Gypsy explained that she and Neil had slipped into a closet and made love while his wife believed he was using the bathroom, according to Savage.

On another occasion, Neil came by their house in Bountiful. Gypsy gave Savage and another roommate two hundred dollars. "Why don't you get lost for a few hours." Gypsy smiled. "So we can have the place to ourselves." Taking the money, the roommates left the apartment.

Weeks later, Gypsy turned to prescription diet pills to lose weight for her boyfriend, Savage reported. After that she turned dark and violent.

One night a sullen Gypsy told Savage that Neil's wife had grown suspicious and he wanted to take a break from the relationship. "He said we need to cool things off for a while," Gypsy explained.

Furious with her boyfriend's wife, Gypsy began to stalk the woman. She broke into the couple's home to snoop around and steal a photograph of the wife, Savage said. Gypsy hung it in her closet, telling her roommate she needed to "know my enemy."

Gypsy spoke often about poisoning her lover's wife or tampering with her car. "I heard her plot to cut the brake lines of her lover's wife, saying that the woman's children would be in car seats and should survive, as if the children were just an inconsequential annoyance to her as long as her objective was reached," Savage later testified.

Later, Savage and Gypsy were watching a story on CNN about a doctor who poisoned his wife with a drug. The next day, Gypsy demanded Savage reveal the name of the drug, claiming she needed to get rid of the woman keeping her from "her man."

"Gypsy tried to pressure me into telling her about a common ER injectable I had heard about on CNN that would kill people without a trace unless someone specifically looked for it in an autopsy. It made it look like a plain old heart attack," Savage said in court.

Suddenly fearful of the woman she'd once called a friend, Savage and her daughter abruptly moved out of the home. "I was scared. I'm still scared of her," Savage later explained. "I was scared to death of Gypsy when I moved out, that's why I moved."

After hearing the unnerving stories, Rachel MacNeill connected Savage and her daughter with prosecutors and investigators. Both women would later testify in court during a preliminary hearing. The validity of their statements would become a contentious issue.

Gypsy would claim Savage was lying about the entire account and had fabricated the character of "Neil." Gypsy added that by the time she met

Martin, she had no contact with her former roommates and had sold the home in Bountiful.

Suspicious that Gypsy may have been involved in Michele's death, Witney and Robinson would spend months investigating, trying to tie Martin's mistress to the murder. But it appeared she had an alibi and was miles away from Pleasant Grove on the day of Michele's death.

Given the mountain of evidence against Martin, his attorney, Randall Spencer, advised Martin to cut a deal.

Months after the arrest, Martin pled guilty to two counts of aiding and abetting for the aggravated identity theft, one felony charge of making false or inconsistent statements, as well as charges of recording a false or forged instrument and accepting benefits from false or fraudulent insurance claims.

Martin was sentenced to forty-eight months in federal prison on August 8, 2009. He had also pled guilty on state charges, but, as part of the plea, his sentences would run concurrently.

Gypsy also pled guilty to one count of aggravated identity theft and was sentenced to twenty-one months behind bars. A month before she was scheduled to begin her sentence, she flew to Texas to see her new boyfriend. When investigators found out she had left the state, they were convinced she was attempting to flee to Mexico. When her plane landed back in Salt Lake City, she was arrested at the airport and thrown in prison to begin serving her time.

While all this was going on, Linda, Alexis, and Rachel attended their father's final sentencing hearing. As he was handcuffed and led away by officers, Martin sneered at Alexis. "I hope you're happy with what you've done."

33.

Rows of barbed-wire fencing cage the cluster of squat buildings that make up the Texarkana Federal Correctional Institute. A looming white tower overlooks the low-security prison in the northeast corner of the state of Texas, along the Arkansas border. The surrounding landscape visible through the fencing is flat and barren.

More than fifteen hundred inmates are housed at the prison, most of them convicted of drug crimes or robbery. In August 2009, Martin Joseph MacNeill—the doctor, lawyer, and newly convicted felon—became inmate number 16083-081.

On a hot, humid morning in September, Martin, then fifty-three, checked in to the prison. Like all inmates, he went through an orientation and was given a work assignment as a temporary orderly. Turning in his clothes, he was provided a standard-issue khaki uniform to be worn every day.

Martin's new home was a section of the prison known as the G-Unit, one of three semiautonomous living quarters. His new roommate was a wiry, shaggy-haired Hispanic man in his early twenties named George Martinez, who was serving time for his first felony, conspiracy to sell cocaine and marijuana.

Martin and Martinez would share a six-by-eight-foot cell furnished with a set of bunk beds and a stainless steel toilet bolted to the floor.

The doctor got along well with the other inmates, several of whom would come to call him a friend. Word quickly spread that Martin was a doctor "on the outside." He used his medical knowledge to assist other inmates with ailments, and was soon known behind bars as "Doc."

When speaking with the other inmates, he was often elusive about the reason he was imprisoned, insinuating that his conviction was related to writing phony prescriptions. Perhaps behind bars prescription fraud was more noble than stealing the identity of your sixteen-year-old adopted daughter.

Since it was a minimum-security prison, Martin was not confined during the majority of his day, and had the freedom to take part in educational programs, exercise in the rec yard, and watch television. To fill his days, he read, wrote letters, and took classes, including a computer course. Because he had put on weight while in jail and was concerned about his physical appearance, he exercised daily in the prison yard, running four to five miles a day and lifting weights.

Mostly, however, Martin thought of Gypsy.

About 250 miles west of the Texarkana prison, Gypsy was serving her sentence in the FMC Carswell Women's Correctional Institute in Fort Worth, Texas. It had been nine months since Martin and Gypsy last saw each other, but his feelings for her had not diminished. During his prison stay, Martin often talked of Gypsy to other inmates, referring to her as his wife and admitting she was also behind bars.

Soon after they both were confined, Martin began writing to Gypsy. Over the next two years, he would write her lengthy, romantic letters, sometimes sending one each day. In the handwritten letters, Martin described his jailhouse routine, daily workouts, and the books he was reading. In flowery prose, he professed his love and made plans for their future once they were released. Most of the letters were addressed, "Dearest love."

In one dated October 1, 2009, Martin told Gypsy he considered her his common-law wife and attached a document attesting to that fact. "The only reason I do anything is because I want to be as good as I can be when I get out of here so that you will still feel the same way about me," he wrote. "I love you and miss you more than you can imagine."

Behind bars, Gypsy had time to reflect on her relationship with Martin. Letting Martin convince her to steal Giselle's identity had ruined her own life. At her sentencing, Gypsy told the judge she had ended her relationship with Martin. Yet, two days after receiving his letter, she wrote back, reciprocating his feelings and signing her correspondences, "your girl."

Because it is against prison policy for convicted felons to communicate with one another, they sent letters through a third party, a friend of Gypsy's named Carol Smith, who acted as a go-between, forwarding their communications to the prisons.

Out of concern the letters could end up in police custody, Gypsy warned Martin to be wary. "Babe, be very careful about what you send in your mail," she wrote.

Gypsy later contended that her time behind bars was bleak, lonely, and depressing. Desperate for contact with the outside world, she said she wrote Martin back simply so he would continue sending her letters. "At the time I had lost most of my friends and all of my family. I wanted to be in contact with anyone I could be," she said years later. "I was so lonely. I was thrilled out of my mind to get a letter."

Her letters, however, seemed to reveal an undying love for the man she'd once planned to marry. While she had many regrets, being with Martin didn't appear to be one of them. "I would not change the fact that you and I were together but certainly regret all else," Gypsy wrote to Martin.

At Texarkana, Martin was elated to receive a letter from Gypsy in early October and quickly wrote her back. "Dearest love," he penned on November 3. "I wish I could sleep for the next twenty months and do nothing but dream of being with you. I love you with all of my heart and think of nothing but a future with the two of us, never to be separated again."

Weeks later he reaffirmed that he had loved her from their first meeting in 2005. "It really is a combination of small things that makes me realize how much I miss you and how much I love you," he wrote on November 9. "Know that I love you and have loved you from the day we met. I will work hard to keep your love for me."

Gypsy's correspondence was equally amorous: "I hope you know that I love you and I think about you all the time."

Despite what their relationship had cost them, Gypsy was still concerned about losing Martin. In her letters she wrote about her worries that he would leave her. Martin tried to ease her fears.

"Stop worrying about anything to do with me abandoning you. It is not going to happen," Martin wrote on November 12. "As far as giving up on you, how silly. I thought that you had given up on me. Remember I love you more than you love me. As far as common-law marriage, why don't we just get married for real?"

In another letter, he sent her a marriage agreement. "I have enclosed a common-law statement that I have created. Hopefully it will do the trick. But if not let's get married and shut these people up once and for all," Martin penned on November 17.

Gypsy responded with her own commitments of love. "Do not fear my loss, not ever. I have always loved you and always will."

In prison, money can buy better food and toiletries from the commissary. While incarcerated, Martin helped improve Gypsy's locked-up lifestyle by putting money on her books, allowing her to purchase various sundries, including stamps, deodorant, toothbrushes, clothing, and snacks.

"You are so sweet to send me money," she wrote.

In a November letter, Martin also told Gypsy she could take ownership of his BMW: "The car is yours."

"Whatever I have is yours," he wrote amid professions of his love on November 24. "I can think of nothing but how wonderful you are."

The letters continued during the two years of Gypsy's incarceration. During that entire time their passion didn't diminish.

"I love you and miss you every minute," Martin wrote. "You are worth everything I go through to get you back in my life."

With their father locked away, Martin's daughters no longer had to live in fear. But they knew he would be released from jail in just a few short years. It was terrifying to think he might never be held accountable for Michele's murder.

Following her mother's death, Alexis was plagued by panic and had difficulty sleeping. But each day she remained strong for the sake of the girls she was now raising. Elle, Sabrina, and Ada were thriving under her care. Meanwhile, Martin's youngest but most persistent daughter continued fighting in court for ownership of the Pleasant Grove home.

In 2009 a judge ordered that Michele's estate go to Martin. Alexis appealed, asking Witney and Robinson to write a letter on her behalf to submit to the court. She had no intention of giving up.

Shortly after her father's incarceration, Vanessa showed up on her aunt Linda's doorstep.

When Linda saw Vanessa she was stunned. The twenty-seven-year-old was gaunt, with sunken cheeks, gray skin, thinning hair, and red-rimmed eyes.

"I have nowhere else to go, Aunt Linda," Vanessa told her.

At the time, Giselle was living in Linda's house, and the adoption process was pending. Because Vanessa needed help, Linda let her live in the basement. With both Vanessa and Giselle living under her roof, the house was chaotic. Linda often came home to find her basement filled with heroin needles.

But Vanessa refused to abandon hope, and expressed a continual desire to find sobriety. Having located a rehab program online that promised patients no withdrawal symptoms, due to a method known as "rapid detox," Vanessa pleaded with her aunt to help send her to the clinic.

"That's the only thing that's going to help me," she told Linda.

To aid her in her sobriety, Linda found a volunteer from church to donate the money to pay for the program. Her daughter Jill agreed to accompany her cousin to the detox center in North Dakota. Vanessa completed the program and returned to Utah a few weeks later with a new lease on life.

"Thank you so much," Vanessa cried when Linda picked her up from the airport.

For Vanessa, sobriety was a daily struggle. After detoxing, she stayed clean for about a year before relapsing.

Following Martin's arrest, Damian briefly lived alone in the Pleasant Grove home. The relationship with longtime girlfriend Eileen Heng had ended. That fall he moved to New York to attend law school at New York University. He kept close to his imprisoned father, exchanging letters and speaking with him periodically by phone. Damian remained distant from his sisters, which was disheartening to Alexis.

"Once my dad was sentenced, he kind of didn't want anything to do with us," Alexis recalled.

In December, the Utah Division of Occupational and Professional Licensing began the process of revoking Martin's medical license based on his "unlawful or unprofessional conduct and the crimes of moral turpitude." Martin agreed to voluntarily surrender his license to practice, acknowledging his guilt in the charges against him. He forfeited all rights to practice as a physician in Utah and agreed he would not reapply for another license for ten years.

His attorney, Randall Spencer, considered at the time that his imprisoned client's medical license surrender would be temporary. "He hoped after he got out of prison that he could prove himself worthy of getting his medical license back sometime in the future, after he did his time," Spencer remembered. "Ultimately that didn't end up being the case . . ."

Once it was discovered his license was based on false credentials, Martin lost all rights to ever work as a doctor again. Gypsy would also surrender her practical and registered nursing licenses and would never again work in health care.

Meanwhile, while Martin was locked up, Spencer managed his finances, paying to maintain the Pleasant Grove home while withdrawing his own legal fees. In addition, the attorney negotiated a settlement with the United States Veterans Benefits Administration for the fraud.

By the time he was released, Martin would be a penniless, unlicensed former doctor.

While Martin and Gypsy were both behind bars, Doug Witney continued to collect evidence to try and link them to Michele's death.

In 2009, Witney's investigative team—along with Alexis, Rachel, and

Linda—made the collective decision to go to the media for help generating leads. They released part of the investigative report to the press and spoke with reporters.

"We were still at that point trying to find out what we had and were kind of at a stalemate," Jeff Robinson later said. "We needed more to move forward and knew it couldn't hurt."

The case received coverage in Utah's oldest daily paper, the *Deseret News,* when a reporter named Sara Lenz took interest in the story. Alexis, Rachel, and Linda gave extensive interviews, and soon the incredible tale of the demonic doctor regularly appeared on the paper's front page.

Worried about their father's eventual release, Alexis and Rachel used the media coverage to spur public interest in their mother's death. "I'm afraid for my little sisters' safety," Rachel said in an interview. "And for anyone he comes into contact with for the rest of his life. He is a predator."

In defiance of his sisters, Damian spoke to reporters in support of Martin. "Some people are quick to infer that because of my father's actions following my mother's death, he had to also be involved somehow in the death itself," Damian wrote in an e-mail to the *Deseret News.* "This seems ludicrous to me."

Meanwhile, as Witney and Robinson continued building their case, they reviewed the evidence with county attorneys. Soon prosecutor Chad Grunander became intrigued with the complicated criminal life of Martin MacNeill. Grunander was assigned as the lead attorney on the case and would work closely with investigators to bring it to trial.

In his early forties, Grunander was brawny with a bald head, prominent jaw, and deliberate manner of speaking. A Utah native who grew up in a small town ten miles south of Provo, Grunander was Mormon and served on a mission in Argentina in the early nineties.

After attending BYU, where he earned a degree in political science, he went on to graduate from law school at California's Western School of Law in 2003. Grunander then worked for eight months as a clerk for a judge in Provo before joining the Utah County Attorney's Office in 2004. As a prosecutor, he said he truly found his calling. "I really just fell in love with prosecution, primarily the courtroom," Grunander explained.

Throughout his career Grunander had tried a variety of cases including misdemeanor drug possession, robbery, sexual assault, and murder. He was well liked among his colleagues and had a reputation for turning down unfavorable plea bargains. Grunander was also a married father of four, with three boys and a girl.

As Grunander worked on the MacNeill case, he was concerned that the evidence was all circumstantial.

"When I started to learn more about the case, I thought it was a very compelling story," Grunander recalled. "But like most people, I didn't know where the case was going to go. It was a tough case, nowhere near a slam dunk."

Over the next few years, investigators would take the case to Grunander many times, urging him to press charges. But the prosecutor wanted more—something he could take to court. "Show me how she died," Grunander told Witney. "The jury will want to know how she was murdered."

"I believe I know," Witney replied. "I just can't prove it yet."

While working the case, Witney developed a theory: he believed Michele was drugged and then drowned in the bathtub. To Witney, one particular detail kept jumping out. Through interviews with Pleasant Grove police officers Joshua Motsinger and Ray Ormond, they learned that Michele had expelled a significant amount of water. So much so, in fact, that both officers had to change their uniforms after performing revival efforts. It was a fact that assistant pathologist Maureen Frikke hadn't known when she declared Michele's death natural.

If Michele had expelled water when the paramedics did CPR, that meant Martin—a supposed doctor—hadn't done CPR properly or at all. If it had been performed correctly, the water should have been regurgitated within the first few breaths he delivered.

On the phone with 911, Martin had claimed he performed CPR, but at that point Michele was still in the tub, making the resuscitation efforts unlikely. "It would be virtually impossible to give chest compressions to someone in that position," Witney wrote in his report.

Further, while performing CPR alongside Martin, neighbor Doug Daniels never saw Michele's chest rise or fall. Doug had also reported seeing a significant amount of mucus on Michele's face, although none had transferred onto Martin.

Even though Frikke didn't find water in Michele's lungs, it was still possible she had drowned, as investigators learned through interviews with pathologists. If Michele inhaled water, most of it could have been expelled during the CPR. Regurgitating water during resuscitation can be an aftereffect of "dry drowning," in which the airway spasms shut, preventing both oxygen and liquid from traveling to the lungs.

While it was a solid theory, Grunander was still reluctant.

"You see the medical examiner's report," the prosecutor told Witney. "It says natural cause of death."

Prison can be a lonely and unsettling place. The lack of privacy, loss of freedom, and unappetizing food can erode an individual's self-worth. But it's the boredom that will gradually consume a prisoner's soul.

To keep busy in December 2009, Martin enrolled in an A-Plus Computer Technician course. He attended classes every day from 7:30 A.M. to 2:30 P.M., learning skills including computer support fundamentals, Web page design, and information systems basics.

In the classroom a few seats from Martin sat a tall black man in his midthirties named Michael Buchanan who had been locked up since 2007, serving a nine-year sentence for possession of cocaine with intention to distribute.

When they first met, Buchanan learned Martin was a doctor and asked about the cause of his conviction.

"Well, Doc," he said. "You must be in here for writing bogus scripts."

Nodding in affirmation, Martin made a reference to the prescription pain pills Percocet and Oxycontin. Weeks later, Martin advised Buchanan about treatment for a foot injury the inmate had suffered.

Although they were housed in separate units on different sides of the prison, during the following six months, Martin and Buchanan got to know each other in class, becoming unlikely friends.

Weeks later, Martin was resting against the exterior of an eighteen-person prison dormitory nicknamed the "Chicken Coop" when he was approached by a burly black man with a shaved head and gravelly voice named Von Harper who was serving twenty-seven years on drug charges.

Leaning against the building, Harper addressed Martin. "What are you locked up for?"

"They think I killed a few bitches," Martin replied flippantly.

The two continued talking and soon became workout buddies, running on a large track in the prison yard. Martin's exercise routine also included bench lifts, curls, dips, and sprints, and about fifty push-ups a day.

"I work out a lot. And Doc started asking me questions about working out," Harper recalled. "And sooner or later we started working out together." .

As Harper got to know "Doc," he learned of Martin's nasty temper.

"He can be mean—most of the time mean," Harper later said. "If you got on the wrong subject with him . . . Just whenever I asked him questions or something it's just like you see another side to him. He'd get mad or not want to talk about it."

When not working out with Harper, Martin trained with two other inmates, including Frank Davis, a muscular man with a chiseled jaw and sloping forehead who had a twenty-year history of felonies. When Davis was suffering from a hurt shoulder, another inmate referred him to Dr. Mac-Neill. "That's Doc. He really is a doctor. He's pretty good too."

Soon Davis joined Martin and Harper in their daily workouts.

"That's basically why I was talking to him, to get in the idea of how I could get in that kind of shape," Davis later said.

The media coverage of the MacNeill case resulted in a number of promising leads for investigators.

Anna Osborne Walthall had long believed her former lover was a serial killer. And in 2009, when she learned of Michele's death, she contacted investigators. Through a series of interviews, Anna related to Witney and Robinson the dark stories of murder Martin had told her during their six-month affair.

According to what Witney and Robinson learned from Anna, Martin could have been responsible for attempting to kill his mother, successfully murdering his brother, and euthanizing patients throughout his career as a doctor.

Anna also seemed to provide a plausible explanation for Michele's mysterious death. During the autopsy, the medical examiner had found elevated levels of potassium in Michele's system. Perhaps Martin had injected his wife with an overdose of the chemical.

Anna was willing to testify in court, and enthusiastic about putting Martin behind bars. "I want him convicted for killing Michele," Anna told investigators. "I'm very excited about the prospect of Martin being off the streets for a very long time."

In her zeal to help convict Martin, Anna would keep in regular contact with Witney and Robinson through phone calls and e-mails in the ensuing months. She also divulged further suspicions, saying she now believed Martin and her ex-husband had conspired to kill her. She also suspected he had made plans to fly to Ukraine to kill Giselle and possibly one of Anna's former lovers.

While investigators were thrilled that Anna had come forward, there was also a problem with their potential witness. Anna suffered from dissociative identity disorder, a severe mental illness formerly known as multiple personality disorder, in which a person experiences two or more distinct personality states. Anna also believed she could somehow communicate telepathically with the beyond and that she had a sixth sense that enabled her to experience a person's sins while they engaged in sexual intercourse.

As Witney and Robinson later learned, Anna also had a macabre fixation with murderers and wrote letters to David Berkowitz, the notorious "Son of Sam" serial killer, convicted for a string of shootings in 1976 that left six dead. Berkowitz was serving six life sentences at New York's Attica Correctional Facility.

In a rambling letter to Berkowitz, Anna discussed at length her assertions that Martin was a serial killer with an unusual motive for murder. "I believe with my whole heart that MacNeill's victims were occult blood sacrifices," she wrote. She further stated she had "adopted Martin" and was attaching herself to him so "Satan could not take him."

Anna was candid with investigators about her mental illness and assured Witney and Robinson that it didn't cause her to confuse reality with fantasy. Using Anna's leads, Witney and Robinson began investigating whether Martin had committed other murders. Yet decades had passed since most of the deaths Martin had discussed. Proving murder in these cases would be almost impossible.

Although Martin had told Anna he tried to kill his mother as a child, she was still alive and currently living in California. When Martin's sister Mary was contacted, she said she had no memory of calling 911 to resuscitate her apparently inebriated mother.

As for the death of Rufus Roy MacNeill—the details Anna described were eerily close to those of Michele's death. Yet, during Michele's funeral, Martin said Rufus Roy had died of an apparent overdose: "Ten nickel bags were his ticket out."

Witney and Robinson contacted New Jersey police and learned that Martin's brother had indeed been found dead in his mother's bathroom in 1986. But he had been discovered on the toilet, not in the bathtub, with a heroin needle sticking out of his arm. His death was ruled an overdose.

Still, investigators suspected Martin may have killed before. And when they learned of the strange circumstances surrounding the 1977 death of Martin's father and the mysterious premonition he had shared with Michele, they also questioned if the doctor may have played a part in Albert MacNeill Sr.'s demise. But because so much time had passed, it would be nearly impossible to prove.

Investigators would spend months trying to link Martin to other crimes, but no evidence was uncovered to connect him to those cases. Beyond the death of his wife and molestation of his daughter, Martin would not be charged in connection with any additional murders or sexual assaults.

Still, as Linda and Michele's daughters learned of Anna's allegations, they too began to wonder whether Martin was a serial killer.

34.

amian MacNeill had become obsessed with death following his mother's passing.

Three years after Michele's demise, he struggled with the loss. "My mother's death destroyed him," Alexis recalled.

In late 2009, the twenty-four-year-old was living in New York City and had just completed his first semester of law school. Alone and estranged from his sisters, dark and disturbing thoughts churned through Damian's mind. Under the Twitter handle @damianmacneill, he used the social networking site as a forum to express his reflections, which involved the "joys of killing."

"I want to know what it's like to kill without remorse," Damian wrote on Twitter.

Continuing her investigation against Martin, Linda discovered Damian's Internet postings. Concerned, she printed out the Twitter feed and showed it to Witney and Robinson.

"I was scared. I thought it was my duty to do something about it," Linda recalled. "What if he goes off killing people?"

The investigators also were disturbed and thought they needed to inform Damian's school about the posts. In September 2009, Witney sent an e-mail to New York University officials to express his apprehensions about Damian. "To be perfectly clear, Damian MacNeill is not a suspect in the death of his mother. However, at the insistence of MacNeill family members, we entered 'damianmacneill' into Google search and were shocked at the postings found on his Twitter site, which suggests a propensity to commit indiscriminate violent crimes," Witney wrote. "The comments by Damian MacNeill are very troubling wherein he speaks of killing others and the joy of such."

Witney's e-mail went on to say the Utah County Attorney's Office considered Damian MacNeill a "ticking time bomb, someone who has been through a lot in his life and apparently it is coming to a head." Witney explained that NYU officials should take whatever action deemed necessary and that the attorney's office didn't want to ignore what could be warning signs of violence to come.

While it was unclear if Damian was reprimanded, his postings on Twitter vanished and he completed classes that semester with passing grades. But during the school's winter break in January 2010, Damian sank into a cavernous pit of misery. He spent the hiatus from school watching depressing films, many dealing with the subject of death.

On January 7, Damian uploaded to his Facebook page clips from one of his favorite movies, the 2009 Danish art film by Lars von Trier, *Antichrist*. He posted the movie's prologue, a gloomy black-and-white scene in which the protagonist couple has sex, neglecting their son as he falls out the window of their apartment, his blood splattering upon the sidewalk. "Love and death come hand in hand," Damian wrote in a Facebook message accompanying the clip.

A few days later Damian uploaded another scene from what he said was his favorite movie, *The Fountain*, a 2006 film by Darren Aronofsky about a man dealing with the death of his wife.

On what would have been Michele's fifty-third birthday, Damian reposted Rachel's tribute video for Michele. In his posting, Damian quoted the song the video had been set to, by Ladysmith Black Mambazo: "Do not cry. Mother is absent. Mother shall come back."

During the last few days of winter break, Damian was fixated on one particular movie: *The Hours,* the 2002 film based on the Pulitzer Prize–

winning novel about three women whose lives are interconnected by the Virginia Woolf novel *Mrs. Dalloway*. The film focuses on suicide, with the opening and final scenes depicting the 1941 drowning of Virginia Woolf, played in the movie by Nicole Kidman. Each of the movie's three main characters consistently contemplates suicide as a way of evading her own problems.

On his Facebook page, Damian posted several clips from the film, including one in which the character of Virginia Woolf speaks to her husband about killing one of her novel's fictional characters.

"Why does someone have to die?" Woolf's husband asked.

"Someone has to die in order that the rest of us should value life more. It's contrast," Virginia replied dryly.

"And who will die? Tell me."

"The poet will die. The visionary."

In his posting on the video, Damian wrote, "I still have to face *The Hours*."

In *The Hours,* one of the characters mirrors Virginia Woolf's protagonist in *Mrs. Dalloway.* As in the book, the woman named Clarissa Vaughan spends her final day hosting a party. Damian referenced Clarissa's quotes in his last two Facebook posts.

"They're all here, aren't they? All the ghosts . . . all the ghosts are assembling for the party!" Damian typed on January 15, his mom's birthday.

His chilling, cryptic final update: "I don't think I can make it to the party."

The next day was January 16—a Saturday. By that point Damian had plunged into a deep depression. It seemed he no longer cared if there was an afterlife, or if following death there was nothing but oblivion. Either was more promising than the bleakness of life.

Alone in his dorm room, Damian took a handful of prescription pills, placed a plastic bag over his head, and killed himself.

Following his suicide, Damian's siblings were haunted with blistering pain. Rachel wrote his obituary. In it she didn't reference her father or her sister

Giselle. Survivors were listed as sisters Rachel, Vanessa, Alexis, Elle, Sabrina, and Ada.

"Damian returned to his loving Mother's arms," the obituary read. "Damian was blessed with a mother who taught him the true meaning of love. The true meaning of life. The truth . . . Together we will live forever."

As she had done for her mother, Rachel created a Web site and video tribute in honor of his memory.

Damian's funeral was held on Saturday, January 30—one day before what would have been his twenty-fifth birthday. It was attended by hundreds of heartbroken friends, family, and former classmates. Damian was laid in his final resting place at Highland City Cemetery, beside his mother.

Losing her only brother nearly broke Alexis. She would come to believe that although Damian chose to end his own life, it was still a result of her father's influence. "No matter what, my dad was involved, even if it was a suicide," Alexis later said.

Linda knew that growing up under Martin's influence had left Damian troubled. She also considered that Martin's actions had led Damian toward his own self-destruction.

"I think he just got so messed up from his dad," Linda commented. "And he knew things about his dad. I think he really knew that his dad killed Michele and he just couldn't deal with it. And he was messed up himself."

35.

How Michele died was puzzling—even to the medical examiners.

While the original autopsy listed her death as natural, the result of "chronic hypertension and myocarditis," the investigators believed there was more. Yet, in the absence of a finding of homicide, it was difficult to develop a case against Martin. Investigators wanted a second opinion about the effect of the prescriptions in Michele's system in hopes of finally convincing the Utah medical examiner to change the cause of death. "The reason we have a homicide investigation is that we believe that there is probable cause . . . there is foul play involved here and we believe we are on the right track," Witney said in an interview.

In early 2010, Witney and Robinson contacted two toxicology experts: Dr. Doug Rollins and Dr. Gary Dawson. Both doctors indicated that Michele had taken a potentially lethal dose of medication and were concerned about why she would have taken a sleep aid at 10 A.M.

Dr. Dawson, a forensic toxicology expert from Boise, Idaho, noted in his report, dated March 31, that the drugs would have created a "potent cocktail" causing sedation. "Such a condition would likely render the victim unable to respond appropriately to her environment including potential threats to her safety," Dawson noted.

The heart condition of myocarditis could also have been exacerbated by certain drugs. "This drug/disease interaction cannot be ruled out as a possible contributing factor in the victim's death," Dawson added.

University of Utah professor of pharmacology Dr. Douglas Rollins similarly concluded that the drugs alone could have been lethal.

Armed with these two expert opinions, the investigators and the prosecutor, Grunander, went directly to the office of Chief Medical Examiner Dr. Todd Grey and asked him to reevaluate the findings of Dr. Frikke.

"Have you read all the reports?" Witney asked.

"I've scanned them," the pathologist said.

"You cannot scan this report," Witney said, flipping through the pages. "Just read this much while we're here."

After a few minutes of reading, Dr. Grey seemed intrigued. "I think I'm going to look at this deeper."

Weeks later, Witney and Robinson gave Grey an extensive and in-depth presentation of the reasons they felt the case was a homicide. For the first time, Grey took notice and amended Michele's manner of death to include potential drug toxicity. Yet it was only a small change, and Grey refused to call it homicide. In an addendum dated October 6, he certified the manner of death as undetermined.

"I came to that conclusion because of what I thought about the possible role of drugs in her death. Meaning that if drugs were a factor, this was not a natural death," he explained years later. "They certainly were another series of pieces of information that raised a question of whether this was a straightforward natural death."

In early 2010, Alexis completed medical school and moved back to Utah with her adopted sisters. She had since married her longtime boyfriend, Brett Doxie, also a physician. The family purchased a house in South Jordan, just a few miles from the Pleasant Grove property where Michele had died.

Alexis was now a working doctor, treating patients as a primary care physician at Utah Valley Regional Medical Center. She had achieved her dream of following in her father's footsteps, although she no longer wanted anything to do with the man who raised her. Because she found the idea of being known as "Dr. MacNeill" repugnant, she changed her last name. But instead of taking her husband's surname, she became Dr. Alexis Somers to honor her mother.

Rachel, meanwhile, moved to Los Angeles, where she worked as a waitress. Despite her ongoing anguish, she hoped someday to make peace with the loss of her mother.

By 2010 Giselle was nineteen. She had dropped out of high school and moved out of Linda's home into an apartment. The theft of her identity continued to plague her. She had trouble opening a bank account and getting her driver's permit, and later was evicted from her apartment for bad credit.

"The nightmare continues for her," Linda later said. "It's an ongoing struggle. She is being challenged constantly to prove she is who she is."

In her never-ending war against her former brother-in-law, in the fall of 2010 Linda launched the Web site www.martinmacneill.info to generate leads.

"This site is dedicated to providing the public domain with information concerning Martin MacNeill," Linda wrote on the Web site's homepage. "The site is also a method to obtain new information from people who know Martin and have been affected by him or have information that could be useful in legal pursuit."

By 2010, the national and local media had gravitated to the strange case of the Mormon doctor who allegedly murdered his wife using plastic surgery and a bathtub.

The investigators, along with Alexis, Rachel, and Linda, were interviewed on programs including *20/20* and *Dateline*. *People* magazine also wrote lengthy articles. And the *Deseret News* covered every development.

The Willis family, now completely estranged from Gypsy, also spoke to media. "She belongs in a controlled facility where she can't hurt anybody," Julie Willis told reporters. "I'm sorry to say, but she does hurt people, and she will continue to hurt people to get what she wants."

The well-known crime-show host Nancy Grace frequently aired segments on the case, calling for Martin to be brought to justice. In an episode that aired on December 7, Grace featured a prominent medical examiner who gave a unique opinion on Michele's death.

"I want to go out to special guest Dr. Joshua Perper, the chief medical examiner out of Broward County," Grace introduced the doctor. "Thank you for being with us."

On-screen appeared a bald eighty-year-old pathologist with sunken eyes and an angular head—the result of a blood clot when he was a child that had thickened his skull. A noted forensic pathologist and toxicologist, he has conducted autopsies on a number of celebrities, including Anna Nicole Smith. Dr. Perper is a Romanian immigrant who escaped the Nazis during World War II, and he speaks with a heavy accent.

"I need to understand something," Grace continued. "Apparently water came out of not only her lungs, but her stomach when the EMTs got there. What does that say to you?"

"She ingested the water when she was under the water, because when people are asphyxiated or drowned, they try to breathe, and then in their attempts, water enters both in the airway and in the stomach," Perper said. "And that's one of the signs in the syndrome or the process of drowning. So this would be consistent with ingesting water from the—from the tub."

"Why would all that have still been in her if he had performed CPR? Doctor?" Grace asked.

"Well, the CPR would be performed, most of the water which would come out, but on the second attempt, so-called second attempt, there would not be any more water to be expelled from the stomach because whatever could have been expelled was expelled, assuming that over several minutes he tried to resuscitate her."

That evening, viewers around the country tuned to Grace to hear the "stunning twists" and "bombshell developments," in the "Utah Face-Lift Murder," with Grace asking viewers, "Will a prominent doctor and lawyer get away with murder?"

One of those viewers was Chad Grunander, who later recommended investigators contact Dr. Perper. Other viewers that night included a horde of inmates gathered in the TV room of the Texarkana federal prison—including Martin's workout buddy Frank Davis.

Davis saw Martin's face flash on-screen, along with pictures of his wife and girlfriend, and was stunned. He had been under the assumption that Martin's wife was in prison, not dead.

Another inmate, recognizing Martin, darted down the hallways to grab Michael Buchanan, who was in the housing unit studying his textbooks on his bed. "Hey. Come look at the TV real quick," the inmate told Buchanan.

Once he reached the television room, the inmate asked, "Do you recognize the guy right there?"

"Yeah! That's Doc!" Buchanan said.

By the next morning, word had spread through the prison, and all the inmates seemed to be talking about the newly notorious doctor.

At first Martin was unaware he was the subject of the prison gossip. In the cafeteria, Buchanan had just finished eating and was getting ready for his computer class when he saw Martin coming through the breakfast line.

Buchanan approached him. "Hey, Doc. Did you see the TV last night?"

"No," said Martin.

"Well, they had you on TV last night."

"About what? I had no idea," Martin said.

"It was something about you may have killed your wife," he said.

Martin's voice became hushed. "Don't say anything about it. I'll talk to you later."

Hours later they met in the prison rec yard, where Martin scoffed at the reports. "They're just running that because my girlfriend is about to get out soon," he said.

But the coverage continued. The next day another program on the case aired, and Buchanan again approached Martin. "Doc, did you catch it this time?"

"No," Martin said, adding that he'd heard it was on. "They can't prove anything so I don't know why they keep running it on TV."

But over time Martin began opening up to Buchanan. And what he had to say about the death of his wife was so cold-blooded it caused the inmate to cringe.

A year after being separated by their crimes, Gypsy and Martin continued to communicate through secret jailhouse correspondence.

In one letter, Gypsy quoted the deceased British politician Charles James Fox, who had written to his mistress, Elizabeth Armistead, "I have examined myself and know that I can better abandon friends, country and everything than live without you. I could change my name and live with you in the remotest part of Europe in poverty and obscurity. I could bear that very well, but to be parted I can not bear."

In Martin's messages, he mentioned their intention to live together and marry once they were both released. "Do you think you want to settle here? I don't mind settling in Texas or anywhere you might want. If Texas, what city?" he wrote.

In 2010, the letters were uncovered by guards during a search of Martin's jail cell and were provided to Witney and Robinson. Martin refused to speak with investigators, but in October, Witney and Robinson traveled to the women's correctional institute to interview Gypsy. In the interview Gypsy was guarded, not admitting her contact with Martin until she was confronted with the letters.

"Have you been in contact with Martin since your arrest?" Witney asked.

"No," Gypsy lied. "The last time we spoke was in January 2009."

"You haven't been writing him letters?"

"Nope," she said. "I haven't heard from him."

The investigators pressed her on her plans following release.

"I can't see myself being with this guy anymore," she said. "The idea of it terrifies me."

Once they showed her the letters, Gypsy smiled nervously, knowing she had been caught. She admitted the lie, saying she didn't want to get in trouble for violating prison policy, and claimed she was only communicating with him because she was lonely.

"I've learned my lesson," Gypsy said. "He's out of my life."

It became apparent to investigators that Gypsy knew more than she was saying.

In the interview she admitted that her affair with Martin began in 2005 and that he paid for her to live in the duplex in Lehi. But she denied that her relationship with Martin had intensified in the months prior to Michele's death.

Gypsy also confirmed that the seemingly chance meeting with Martin outside the temple had actually been a ruse to get her into the house after Michele died.

"So you staged and scripted that meeting?" Witney asked. "When did you script it? Was it at the funeral? Was it before the death?"

Although Martin hadn't mentioned plastic surgery to Michele until March 11, 2007, Gypsy said she had been told of the surgery in February, suggesting to investigators that Martin had planned the killing for months.

During the investigation, Witney had watched a home video filmed by the MacNeills during Ada's sixth birthday. In one scene they noticed a silver Volkswagen Beetle parked in front of the Pleasant Grove home. When they showed Gypsy a picture of the vehicle, she told the investigators it looked like her car. She said she didn't remember if she was at the house that day, but if she was, it was at Martin's behest.

Throughout the interview, Gypsy repeatedly denied having any knowledge about the murder and said she didn't believe Martin killed his wife to be with her. Still, the information she provided helped prove Martin's motives.

While Martin had been sentenced concurrently on state and federal charges, Gypsy still potentially faced several more years in jail. After consulting with her attorney, John Easton, Gypsy said she would be willing to testify truthfully against Martin in exchange for a plea on the state charges of identity theft.

After the interrogation, Gypsy returned to her prison dormitory. Seven days later she mailed Martin another letter. Despite having claimed to be done with Martin, she continued to discuss their plans for the future.

As Gypsy's release date on the federal charges approached, the news coverage swelled. In prison, Martin was asked frequently about his dead wife by other inmates.

In April 2011, *People* magazine ran a lengthy article on Martin Mac-Neill entitled "Utah Scandal: A Family's Web of Lies," featuring photographs of Martin, Michele, and Gypsy.

"As he counts down the days to his scheduled release in July 2012, the three women are hoping that an ongoing investigation will soon result in charges of a far more nefarious crime: the murder of his wife," the article read.

That spring, while working in the prison's leisure library, Von Harper came across the magazine article. Flipping the pages, he found that most of the article had been ripped out, although there was still enough remaining to understand Martin was being investigated for his wife's death.

Harper mentioned the piece to Martin.

"Hey Doc," he said. "They said you murdered your wife."

Martin's eyes narrowed. "No. I didn't murder my wife. I'm fixing to go home. And even if I did they don't have any evidence." Martin turned and walked away.

Weeks later Martin was talking with inmate Frank Davis at the lunch table.

"Do you get any visitors?" Davis asked.

"No," Martin said. "My wife is also in prison."

"Man, they told me you killed your wife."

"If they could prove that do you think I'd be sitting here talking to you?" Martin shrugged.

"Did you do it?" Davis asked.

"The bitch drowned," Martin said coldly.

"The talk in the room was that Doc killed his wife," Davis said years later. "When he told me his wife was in prison, I was relieved. I was thinking, *Hey man, this is a decent fella.*"

As the publicity continued, Martin grew irritated. After another episode of *Nancy Grace* aired, Martin stormed out of the TV room and back into his cell.

His cellmate, George Martinez, was sitting in his bunk when he saw the nervous, scared look on Martin's face. Martinez, who had also heard the rumors, sat up in his bunk and curiously asked, "Is it true? What they're saying on TV, that you killed your wife?"

"They can't prove it." Martin flicked his hand dismissively. "That medication was prescribed."

Later Martin told Martinez that his wife had surgery, suffered a heart attack, and passed away.

In January 2011, Doug Witney resigned from the Utah County Attorney's Office after being elected the new Utah County commissioner. Jeff Robinson took over as the case officer in the murder of Michele MacNeill.

By March, Robinson was beginning to close in on Martin. A search warrant was served to obtain all of Martin's and Gypsy's e-mails since 2005. Robinson spent the next few weeks poring through a slog of e-mail.

While Robinson was able to find proof of the couple's relationship, there was no mention of Gypsy having any knowledge of Michele's death.

In the fall, Robinson reenacted the route Martin had traveled on April 11, timing how long the drive would take under various conditions. The fastest he was able to drive from the Developmental Center to the MacNeill house was three minutes and seven seconds. The longest took him five minutes and thirty-nine seconds.

Robinson also tested how long it took to drive from the Developmental Center to Ada's elementary school and found that it took an average of one minute and twenty-four seconds. American Heritage School to the MacNeill home was approximately four minutes and thirty-nine seconds.

Robinson concluded there would have been more than enough time for Martin to sneak off from the Developmental Center, return home, and kill Michele.

By early 2011, Gypsy had served the entire twenty-one months of her sentence and was about to be released from federal prison. While anxious to be free, she also knew the life she was returning to would be difficult.

At thirty-four, she was now a convicted felon. She had no money, home, or job prospects. Martin had told her she could continue to live in the Pleasant Grove house, but her attorney advised against it, especially as he negotiated a plea for her to testify against the former doctor.

In February 2011, Gypsy was transferred to Utah County Jail, where she would serve the last few weeks of her federal sentence before returning to court in Provo to answer for the state charges.

In March, Alexis, Rachel, and Linda attended Gypsy's plea hearings at Provo's Fourth District Court.

Wearing a red and white jumpsuit, her hands cuffed and chained around her waist, Gypsy nodded as she quietly spoke with her attorney. She glanced at the gallery, locking eyes with Martin's daughters, and smiled.

Standing in front of the judge, Gypsy pleaded guilty to one count of identity fraud, two counts of making false and inconsistent material statements, and one count of filing a wrongful lien.

As part of the plea, she agreed to testify against Martin and avoid more jail time. Instead, she was sentenced to thirty-six months of probation. The judge noted that she should not have contact with Martin or his extended family or go near the Pleasant Grove home. To help her realize the impact of her decision on others, she also was ordered to go through a cognitive restructuring course to assist her with changing her manipulative behavior.

While the plea would require her to potentially implicate the man she had professed her undying love for in letters, both Gypsy and her attorney doubted Martin would ever actually be charged with murder.

Days later, on March 12, Gypsy was released.

Meanwhile, Alexis and Rachel were terrified that Gypsy was now out of prison. Linda was also disturbed to see the woman who wronged her sister and stole Giselle's identity appear so smug in court.

"It was really hard," Linda told the *Deseret News*. "The fact that she just glares at you and then smiles—it's just hard to see someone who destroyed our family's lives."

On May 17, Gypsy returned to court, a free woman, for another hearing. Alexis and Rachel sat toward the front of the courtroom. Gypsy stepped in, glanced around, and took a seat in the back. She wore a blue blazer with a gold crest on the front pocket, and her hair was swept into a bun. Alexis and Rachel recognized the jacket.

It had once belonged to Michele.

"We are completely horrified she's out on the streets now," Rachel told reporters outside the courtroom. "I'm very fearful for our family and our sisters. I'm afraid she will hurt and destroy other people as well."

Gypsy spent the next few months attempting to rebuild her life. She took possession of the 2005 Silver BMW Z4 convertible Martin told her she could keep and stayed with friends while she searched for a job. Because she had lost her nursing licenses, she could no longer work in health care and had few career opportunities.

"I've had a really, really difficult time finding a job," Gypsy later explained. "I'm recognized all the time. I'll be in the store and people will start talking to each other and looking at me."

Her life was in shambles—a fact for which she took little accountability. She still blamed Martin for her plight. "I loved Martin. I care for him on a very, very deep soul level," Gypsy later said. "I can't say I'm sorry I loved him but I think everyone's lives would have been better if I had not met him."

The day she was released from jail, Gypsy ceased all contact with Martin. She took all the love letters from her time in jail, placed them in a box in the garage, and buried her feelings for her former fiancé.

After going through rapid detox, Vanessa had stayed clean for about a year. But by 2011, dealing with the grief of her mother's and brother's deaths, coupled with her father's arrest, she returned to heroin. At the time she was dating a man named Jeff Grange, who was tall with light blond hair, a sloping forehead, and a neck tattoo.

Vanessa and Jeff were living together in a basement belonging to a friend, Derek Clay, a burly twenty-seven-year-old with a shaved head who was on probation for drug charges. At the time Vanessa wasn't working, and to raise cash she and her boyfriend resorted to stealing and selling copper piping and wire from construction sites.

In March, on a tip in an investigation of one such theft, the police arrived at Clay's doorstep. While questioning the man, the officers searched through Clay's basement, discovering Vanessa and her boyfriend surrounded by stolen copper wiring and a stash of drugs.

All three were arrested for stealing about two hundred pounds of copper from businesses around Orem. Vanessa and Jeff were also charged with possession of heroin and drug paraphernalia.

Vanessa and her boyfriend initially denied stealing the wiring, but Clay confessed to driving them to two businesses to commit the crimes. Officers also matched Vanessa's shoes to prints left at a crime scene. Clay and Grange were held on $10,000 bail; Vanessa was bailed on $7,500.

In her mug shot Vanessa appeared frightened. Her hair was thinning, her skin dull, gray, and covered with blemishes.

Vanessa eventually took a plea, and while serving a jail stint, she finally found sobriety. She went through rehab and turned her life around.

Once she was off drugs, Alexis and Rachel embraced her, and Vanessa was finally able to build a relationship with her biological daughter, Ada. Later, Vanessa reunited with Jeff Grange and the couple had a son.

In 2011, Martin petitioned for early release into a halfway house. Alexis and Rachel wrote letters to the prison, asking for him to remain confined due to the fact that they thought he was guilty of murder. Based partially on his daughters' pleas, Martin was ordered to remain jailed to serve the rest of his sentence.

When Martin learned an early release was denied, he was furious with his children. He stomped down the jail hallways, passing by inmate Von Harper.

"He came down the hallway and he had this mad look on his face," said Harper later. "I was like 'Doc. What's wrong?'"

Martin rolled his eyes. "My fucking daughter and my bitch wife!"

"Whoa, Doc," Harper replied. "You're talking ill of the dead, you know what I'm saying?"

Martin shook his head and walked away.

Frank Davis also ran into Martin that day. "He was talking about the halfway house. He was mad," Davis later said in court. "He said he was tired of being around all these child molesters and everything."

Martin would spend another year behind bars. As his release date grew closer, he became increasingly stressed. He was angry and short-tempered, fellow inmates reported. Something appeared to be weighing on him heavily.

By the summer of 2011, Utah County investigators resubmitted the homicide investigation to prosecutor Chad Grunander. Because the pathologist, Todd Grey, was unwilling to declare the death a homicide, Grunander authorized a forensic review of the medical examiner's report.

Remembering Dr. Perper's appearance on *Nancy Grace,* Grunander suggested Robinson hire him to review the findings. Robinson subsequently provided Perper with the autopsy, photographs, and the police and medical reports.

Perper was unable to state with reasonable certainty the manner in which Michele died, although he specifically ruled out natural causes, accident, or suicide. He also found there was no evidence of acute or active myocarditis.

The cause of death he determined: drowning.

On Friday, July 6, 2012, Martin was released after three years in federal prison. At fifty-six, he was still under federal and state probation, requiring him to remain in Utah for the next three years.

He returned to the house where his family once lived and where his wife had died.

Dandelion weeds sprouted from the unkempt front yard of the house at 3058 Millcreek Road. Overgrown hedges masked the brick façade. Cobwebs hung in the entryway.

The house had been vacant for nearly four years.

On Sunday, July 8, Martin took a bus from northeast Texas to Utah and was picked up at the station by his attorney. Randall Spencer pulled up to the house, and Martin got out of the car. Neighbors peeked through the window blinds to get a glimpse of the man whose face had dominated the front pages of the newspapers left on their porches.

Word of his return spread quickly throughout Creekside through text messages and phone calls. Martin MacNeill was out of jail and back in Pleasant Grove.

No one knew how long he'd stay, and opinions on his presence were mixed. Those who knew him from church had difficulty reconciling the Martin they knew with the crimes for which he had been accused. Others were nervous about what he might do next.

Just thirty-five miles north of the Pleasant Grove home, Alexis Somers was living with her husband and raising Sabrina and Ada, then eleven years old. Elle, nineteen, was attending a trade school called Bridgerland Applied

Technology College and living on her own in Logan, a college town about one hundred miles from Pleasant Grove.

In the fall, eighteen-year-old Sabrina would also move to Logan to attend Utah State University.

With Martin living so close by, Alexis was fearful. "It's really sickening to me," she later said. "I am back into this panic feeling, just really nervous knowing what he is capable of doing."

Upon Martin's release, Alexis cautioned the girls that their father was now free. Sabrina and Ada were scared and confused. Ada often woke in the middle of the night and crawled into Alexis's bed, complaining of nightmares. Ada confided in Sabrina, sharing her fears. "What do I do if he shows up at school?" Ada asked her sister.

Alexis would do whatever it took to protect the girls. But she was also unwilling to back down. For Martin's entire life, he had gotten away with crimes using coercion and scare tactics, but for the last five years she had tried to stand up and show the world what he had done. She was not going to be intimidated. She was not going to run.

"He's lived his whole life getting away with things," Alexis later said. "I don't want him to get away with murder."

While Martin was free, Gypsy had actually returned to Utah County Jail.

She had been arrested on July 6—the same day Martin was freed—for a probation violation, stemming from a failure to keep her address current with probation officers and a lie about driving the silver BMW Martin gave her, claiming she had no vehicle and was getting rides from friends.

When confronted by her probation officer about the lie, Gypsy reluctantly admitted to driving the vehicle. The car had remained registered to Martin due to her back taxes.

Gypsy was jailed for more than a week before she could see the judge. In court her attorney argued the violations were minor. "This probation violation report has some of the most benign allegations I've seen," John Easton told the judge.

Gypsy believed she was locked up to ensure she wouldn't run away with Martin.

"I was so scared," she said in an interview. "I didn't even know when Martin was being released, and wasn't allowed to have contact."

Ten days after she was arrested, Gypsy was granted bail at five thousand dollars and released. Now she and Martin were both free, for the first time in four years.

In July, Grunander said he soon planned to file homicide charges against Martin. For assistance on the case, Grunander teamed with two other attorneys at the Utah County Attorney's Office: Samuel Pead and Jared Perkins.

Pead was a Mormon and 2007 graduate of the Brigham Young University school of law, and had practiced as a lawyer in Utah since 2008. Slim and balding, Pead was known to be tenacious and aggressive in court.

Perkins was also a Mormon, and had graduated from BYU law in 2003. Raised in Upstate New York, he moved to Utah with his family in 1991 and served a mission in Brazil two years later. He attended Cambridge in England, graduating with a master's degree in philosophy before going to law school. Broad-shouldered with coiffed brown hair and strong, handsome features, Perkins was a skillful and confident attorney.

The three lawyers negotiated their legal strategy. Expecting that Martin would call Gypsy and discuss the case now that he was free, they went to a judge and got a warrant to place a wiretap on Martin's phone line, which was put in place on July 17. Martin did attempt to call Gypsy, but having just been released from jail, she was fearful of revoking her probation and avoided all contact.

After his phone calls had been monitored for just ten days, the wiretap was suspended because of a lack of relevant information.

Martin spent the next few weeks holed up inside his home. He left only to run errands, report to his probation officer, and meet with his attorney. When Martin spoke to Spencer, the attorney continued to express hope that he would not face charges for murder.

After four years behind bars, Martin was broke. His last remaining thirty thousand dollars in the bank was earmarked through his attorney for paying back the Veterans Benefits Administration. At the same time, he informed his probation officer in July that he was in the process of obtaining financial assistance from Social Security.

In August, Grunander and the investigators decided the case was as good as it would get. If they were going to file charges for murder, the time to do it was now.

Because Martin had tossed Michele's medication following her death, Grunander decided he would also seek charges for obstruction of justice.

Investigator Jeff Robinson put together an extensive fifty-seven-page motion for the arrest of Martin MacNeill. In it, all the circumstantial pieces seemed to align in support of the idea that Martin killed his wife. "The investigation shows Martin MacNeill led a life filled with contradictions, deception, and manipulation. I believe it was his intention to rid himself of his family and wife, and that he set into action a series of events leading to Michele's death," the report read.

Robinson outlined the facts of the case. "In reviewing in totality the known events of Martin MacNeill's life and the events leading up to the death of Michele MacNeill, Martin clearly had the motive, the intent, and the opportunity to kill his wife," the report stated. "Martin's attitude and actions show he wanted to be with Gypsy and Michele was keeping him from his new life. The consequences of divorce, including paying for two homes, spousal support, child support, and dealing with a social fallout, were not a viable option."

The motion was filed on August 24, 2012.

Later that afternoon, Martin was checking in with his parole officer. When he stepped out of his car, he found himself surrounded by officers.

"Martin MacNeill"—an officer slapped handcuffs on his wrists—"you are under arrest for the first-degree murder of Michele MacNeill."

After being fingerprinted and photographed, Martin was held in the Utah County Jail on one-million-dollar, cash-only bail, which he could not pay.

At Martin's initial court appearance on August 27, Michele's loved ones made a powerful statement, intending to remind him of the woman he stole from their lives. Alexis, Rachel, Linda, and two of Michele's nieces sat in the second row of the courtroom, holding pictures of Michele on their laps. The women kept their eyes trained on Martin as he lumbered into the courtroom in handcuffs and prison garb.

Martin refused to acknowledge them. He waived reading of the charges. Other than quietly conferring with his attorney, he said nothing in court.

"He saw us. He did," Alexis told reporters. "We want people to remember our mother. And we want people to know that she lived and that she deserves justice."

Following her father's arrest for murder, an already troubled Rachel disintegrated. Days after his hearing, on August 31, she had a mental breakdown and was briefly hospitalized.

That evening she was anxious and animated, rambling and rapidly shifting to unrelated subjects and topics. Her brother-in-law drove her to Intermountain Medical Center, where she was diagnosed with having delusions and psychosis. Rachel made a quick recovery. But Martin's attorneys would later use her breakdown against her.

For Martin MacNeill, facing a potential life sentence, the stakes could not have been higher.

He had no money to hire an attorney. He called Randall Spencer and asked if he would represent him on the murder. At that point, Spencer had been managing Martin's finances and knew his client was broke. Because he was a private attorney, not a public defender, he wouldn't get paid if he took on the case.

"I knew he was out of money. After Martin was arrested, he called and asked if I would represent him. I originally told him no," Spencer later explained. "I made the wrong decision and I called him back and told him I would do it."

Spencer expected it would take months of pro bono work. He had no idea he'd spend the next two years devoted to the case. He believed in Martin's innocence and felt he was being crucified in the media.

"Martin was an adulterer," Spencer later said. "He was very egotistical, perhaps a narcissist. But I do not believe he is a murderer." Because of Spencer's resolute conviction of Martin's innocence, his courtroom fight against prosecutors would grow viciously contentious.

To assist with what was expected to be a complex defense, Spencer called his friend Susanne Gustin, an experienced criminal defense attorney with more than seventeen years of trial experience, to be the defense's second chair. Intelligent and adept, Gustin was accustomed to representing high-profile cases. "I have a reputation for handling major crimes," she later said. As one of the few women in a male-dominated field of criminal defense, her motto on her Web site is: "A woman on your side."

Gustin was in her early forties, with long blond hair that framed her round, tanned face. She is a fourth-generation lawyer and attended law school at the University of Utah, where she also studied political science and Middle East studies as an undergrad. After a short stint in civil work, she joined the public defense office—a fast-paced environment, where she tried up to three cases a week.

She soon found her niche and the calling that would dominate the rest of her career—trying cases related to rape and child sex. "Child and sex abuse cases are difficult," Gustin later explained. "In the public defender's office, when you win one, you can return to the office the next day and find five new sex cases sitting on your chair."

After five years as a public defender, Gustin left to open her own firm in Salt Lake City, where she was known primarily for representing sex criminals. Her Web site includes a lengthy list of recent victories, which included charges for child rape, sodomy of a child, aggravated sexual abuse of a child, and kidnapping.

Gustin also happened to be the mother of a nine-year-old son at the time.

With Gustin's experience and persuasive delivery, combined with Spencer's intelligence, Martin had a capable defense team. Spencer and Gustin immediately got to work, filing a slew of motions that would congest the case in court.

They spent thousands of hours interviewing sources and sorting through evidence. Although they were privately retained, neither was paid.

Martin settled into Utah County Jail, which would be his home for the next year. Estranged from his kids and with Gypsy out of his life, he had no one to write. Besides his attorneys, he had no visitors.

Martin occupied his time writing poetry and working on his autobiography while studying his case file in order to assist with his defense. He also volunteered to be a jail trustee, an inmate who performs menial tasks like taking out trash, mopping, or distributing uniforms.

In December, Martin met an inmate named Jason Poirier, a twenty-year-old misdemeanor shoplifter and married father of a daughter. Poirier was in jail on a probation violation and facing up to a year in prison.

His criminal record had begun when he was eighteen, with a charge of misdemeanor sexual battery for sleeping with a girl who was fourteen. He had a track record of petty crimes: selling prescription pills, using steroids, and selling fake Rolex watches.

In early 2012, he was arrested for stealing a laptop from Walmart. Months later, while on probation, he was busted again for stealing ammunition from Cabella's, a hunting and fishing store. When his house was subsequently searched, guns and weapons were found—another probation violation.

While he was in jail, Poirier's wrist began bothering him and he complained to the nursing staff. Martin overheard and examined his wrist, telling Poirier he had carpal tunnel syndrome.

"What, are you a doctor or something?" Poirier asked.

"Yes, I am," Martin replied.

Poirier followed Martin's advice and the pain went away.

They spoke again when Martin was handing out uniforms from the commissary and Poirier made a comment about the type of special shoes Martin wore due to his toe condition. The two became friendly. They wrote poetry together, and Martin allowed him to read parts of his autobiography.

Before Martin MacNeill could stand trial for murder, there would be a preliminary hearing to determine whether there was enough evidence to warrant a trial. At the end it would be up to Judge Samuel McVey to decide if there was probable cause to proceed.

Given that the case was largely circumstantial, Grunander, the prosecutor, was worried it would not get past the judge's review and make it to trial.

In October 2012, for six days, nearly two dozen witnesses took the stand.

Martin's former coworkers spoke about his demeanor on April 11, 2007. The neighbors testified about finding Michele in the bathtub. Police and first responders also took the stand to tell accounts of Martin's frenzied and hysterical demeanor as they tried to revive his wife. Anna Osborne Walthall told the judge about Martin's murderous claims during their affair.

And on the fifth day, Gypsy took the stand. It was the first time she and Martin had seen each other in four years, and they both looked quite different. Martin, then fifty-six, appeared elderly and thin, barely resembling his once handsome self. And in prison Gypsy had gained a significant amount of weight.

Yet there still seemed to be an attraction. At one point, Gypsy and Martin exchanged a glance and smiled at each other. Gypsy would later say that seeing Martin stirred up strong feelings.

"I would look at him and remember our life together. I don't think anyone could do that and not feel something. Most of it is just sorrow that it didn't work," Gypsy said in one interview. "But I loved Martin, and I don't think that was a bad thing."

During her testimony, she detailed her clandestine relationship with her married lover. "I thought he was wonderful," she said. "It was just for fun, just exciting."

As she left the courtroom, Gypsy locked eyes with Martin, then reached out slightly and ran her fingers along the defense table.

Following Gypsy's testimony, Michelle Savage and her daughter Brandi Smith both answered questions concerning their former roommate's alleged desire to murder her lover's wife. Later, Rachel, Vanessa, and Sabrina gave accounts of how it slowly became evident that the new nanny was really their father's mistress. Perhaps most heartbreaking, Ada bravely testified about finding her dead mother and running to get help. "I kind of pulled him along to the bathroom," Ada said.

Then, the daughter who had led the fight against her father took the stand. "I loved my father," Alexis testified. "I thought he loved us."

Through it all, Martin was stoic, showing no hint of emotion, as Michele's sister Linda Cluff observed from her seat in the gallery.

"He sat there stone-faced and cold. I would have expected nothing different from Martin," Linda wrote on her Web site. "This was not a surprise. This is precisely the Martin I have always known."

As the tragic details of her sister's final days unraveled, Linda ached inside. She found her mind drifting back to fonder memories. "I would hear the proceedings, but would have to, at times, take my mind back to our innocent childhood days as sisters," Linda wrote. "I would reflect back upon some good memories."

At the end of the six-day hearing, Judge Samuel McVey ruled that Martin would stand trial, stating to the court that his actions showed "evidence of a guilty mind."

Shackled and wearing a jumpsuit, Martin cocked his head slightly but otherwise showed no emotion.

Elated by the judge's decision, Alexis left the courtroom in tears. "My mother deserves to be fought for," she told reporters. "It's just a big relief because this has been such a fight."

Martin pleaded not guilty to murder and obstruction of justice, his defense being that Michele's death was natural. The trial was originally scheduled for March 2013, but would be delayed multiple times.

During the next twelve months, the defense filed a series of formidable pretrial motions, the majority of which they won. Witnesses were barred from making several statements and presenting key facts, including that Martin kicked his adult daughters out of the house. Because the judge ruled the comment hearsay, Alexis would not be able to tell the jury that her mom stated, "If anything happens to me, make sure it wasn't your dad."

Prosecutors could not refer to Michele as a "victim," except in opening and closing statements. Anna Osborne Walthall wasn't allowed to tell the jury about any of the murders she said Martin claimed to have committed and could speak only of their affair and his comment about injecting a person with potassium to cause a heart attack. And, ultimately, prosecutors dropped their fight to call Michelle Savage and Brandi Smith to testify,

THE STRANGER SHE LOVED   243

after evidence seemed to prove that the women didn't live with Gypsy during her affair with Martin.

Many of the defense's motions would be aimed directly at the MacNeill children. The defense tried to prevent Rachel from testifying because of her bipolar disorder and keep Vanessa off the stand due to her drug addiction. They would lose both of those fights. But during the trial the defense would successfully bar Ada's testimony, by arguing that her recollection had been tainted by her sisters.

Perhaps most unsettling, in a December 2012 motion, the defense seemed to suggest Damian might have been involved in his mother's murder. "Investigators in the Utah County Attorney's Office deemed Damian MacNeill to be a very dangerous individual who possessed homicidal impulses and discussed the 'joys of killing,'" defense attorneys wrote in a motion.

However, the defense also claimed that Michele's death was natural and not homicide.

Meanwhile, the case concerning Martin's 2007 forcible sexual abuse of Alexis was also moving forward. In October, three years after the charges were refiled, the Utah Court of Appeals returned with its decision, siding with prosecutors that there was enough evidence to proceed to trial. But while the felony sexual abuse charges were allowed to stand, the judge dismissed the witness-tampering complaint.

In that case Martin also pleaded not guilty.

While prosecutors clashed with Martin's defense team in court, the investigator Jeff Robinson continued to seek out witnesses. That mission led him to Texas.

In January 2013, Robinson visited Texarkana federal prison to interview three inmates with whom Martin had served time. Unbeknownst to Martin, his workout buddy during his prison stay had a long history as a federal informant. While he was serving time in an Oklahoma prison, Von Harper's testimony had led to the arrest and conviction of twenty-six people.

Speaking with Robinson, Harper said he was willing to testify but that Martin had never admitted to killing his wife. "The only thing he said is that she had drowned," Harper told Robinson.

Inmate Frank Davis told Robinson a similar story but added that Martin called his wife a bitch. Former cellmate George Martinez also recounted Martin's statements that "they can't prove it was me."

While Martin never revealed to these fellow inmates how he may have killed Michele, Robinson considered the statements suspicious. All three inmates told similar tales: Martin claimed his wife drowned, called her a bitch, and said police had no evidence.

Harper, Davis, and Martinez would all testify against Martin. While each angled for a deal to get leniency in their sentences, Robinson informed them that as a state investigator he had little authority or influence on their federal charges.

Robinson returned to Utah, slightly disheartened. A few weeks later, however, he heard from an attorney who was representing an inmate currently serving time with Martin in Utah County lockup—Jason Poirier.

On January 31, Robinson interviewed Poirier. When the investigator learned what he had to say, his ears perked up. Describing one of their first encounters, while Poirier collected his uniform, Poirier related a joke Martin made about getting away with things in jail. "For instance, I killed my wife. That should say a lot."

"I sat back and kind of chuckled, thinking he was lying," Poirier later testified. "I got the clothes from him and went back to my cell."

Soon after, when Poirier learned Martin's wife was really dead, he offered sympathy.

"Hey man," Poirier told Martin. "I apologize about your wife."

"I'm glad the bitch is dead," Martin responded gruffly.

Poirier said that while swapping poetry, Martin told the younger inmate that he killed his wife because the marriage was going downhill and she would not allow him to continue to cheat.

Robinson found the information valuable—no one else claimed Martin had actually admitted to murder. In exchange for his testimony, Robinson told Poirier and his attorney he would support a plea deal. During a subsequent recorded phone call with his wife, the inmate was cocky. "Listen carefully. I can tell you right now they need me," Poirier said.

Then in May, Robinson would receive an e-mail message possibly uncovering the final piece of the puzzle: how Michele died.

March 5 should have been the beginning of the trial. Instead, the attorneys were continuing to plow through motions while hurling insults and allegations of misconduct.

The defense claimed the prosecution intentionally withheld one thousand pages of documents—some of which they said included information supporting Martin's innocence. Due to this, Spencer tried to get prosecutors disqualified or the charges dismissed.

At one point things became so heated that Judge McVey reprimanded the attorneys for finger-pointing, calling it a distraction. In court, the war between the prosecution and defense became ugly, Grunander admitted. "You can never expect a case like this to be completely amicable," he explained. "But I think it did get personal . . . Inflammatory remarks were made—allegations that have never before been leveled against our offices. It was a hard-fought battle."

After the judge rejected the motion to dismiss prosecutors, the defense successfully got McVey tossed from the case—just weeks before the trial date. The motion to remove the judge was sealed, so the exact details were unknown, but according to Utah code, a judge can be disqualified based on bias, prejudice, or a conflict of interest. McVey would remain the judge on the sexual assault trial scheduled for December.

The murder case was reassigned to Judge Derek Pullan. Described by attorneys as knowledgeable, attentive, and considerate, Pullan was wiry and balding, with narrow eyes and a measured tone of voice. In 1993, Pullan had received his law degree from Brigham Young University. After college he worked as a clerk for the Utah Supreme Court before serving as a deputy county attorney in Washington and Utah in the 1990s. In 2003, he was appointed to Utah's Fourth District Court. In addition he was an adjunct professor at BYU.

Pullan quickly got up to speed on the case and sorted through the remaining pretrial motions.

———

After being locked up in Texarkana, Martin's former computer classmate Michael Buchanan had been transferred to Louisiana to serve the remainder of his nine-year sentence. During the last few months, Buchanan had thought little of Martin, but in April a fellow former inmate from Texarkana approached him.

"You know Doc got out, right?" the prisoner said. "Did you hear what happened?"

"No," said Buchanan.

"He got arrested for the murder of his wife!"

Suddenly Buchanan's mind raced back to those disturbing conversations with the doctor in the rec yard. What Martin had told him was so heinous, he hadn't known whether to believe him.

Over the next few weeks, Buchanan spoke with prison counselors and family members, debating whether to come forward to speak with prosecutors. Maybe if he agreed to testify, he could get a reduction in his sentence, he pondered. On May 19, he e-mailed his niece, Raven.

"One of the guys I met here mentioned Dr. MacNeill," Buchanan wrote. "He said Doc got out and was out for two months and got arrested again. If his case is not over I could tell them what I know and testify and maybe come home."

Raven contacted police at her uncle's request, and the tip eventually reached Robinson. Weeks later Robinson flew to Louisiana to meet with Buchanan.

"He told me how he did it," Buchanan told the investigator.

When the news reports had first reached the prison, Buchanan said, Martin was dismissive and denied the murder. But slowly, he began to reveal details, claiming he'd dosed his wife with prescription pain relievers and sleeping pills.

"He gave her bigger and bigger doses but she didn't die, so he convinced her to take a bath, hoping she would pass out and drown, but she didn't on her own," Buchanan told Robinson. He said that Martin then explained what he did next.

"I had to help her out," Martin had said.

"What do you mean?" Buchanan had asked.

"I had to hold her under the water for a little while," Martin had replied.

Martin also alluded to administering the drugs rectally, by crushing the pills and delivering them through an enema. And Martin had explained his motive.

"He said that she was in the way," Buchanan told Robinson. "That she wanted the house and the kids."

This new information was enticing for Robinson. It seemed to answer the question on everyone's mind: How?

In a last-ditch attempt to change the Utah State pathologist's mind about the cause of death, Robinson contacted Dr. Todd Grey, providing him with a report on the upcoming testimony of all the inmates. He asked Grey to reconsider drowning as a cause of death.

But Grey remained firm in his opinion. "I have reviewed the materials you sent," Grey wrote in an e-mail to Robinson in August. "While the different interviews certainly add to the suspicions that Dr. MacNeill caused or played a significant role in his wife's death, I don't find anything in the materials so compelling that it overcomes the lack of physical evidence from the autopsy that would prove Michele was the victim of homicide."

Fearful that a jury would be unable to convict Martin with no decisive finding of murder, Robinson would continue investigating the case up until six weeks before trial.

Jury selection finally began on October 15, 2013. While most states require twelve jurors to try a case, Utah is one of a handful of states that requires only eight. Five men and three women were selected.

In Utah, the proceedings would be historic—the first criminal trial in the state's history to be broadcast live on TV. A rule banning the use of cameras in the courtroom had been overturned in appeals the previous year, and Utah joined nineteen other states in allowing civil and criminal proceedings to be recorded and broadcast.

Although the prosecution fought the motion, the judge ruled the coverage was warranted. "There is significant public interest in this case," the judge said. Cameras positioned in the courtroom would capture every moment in the case that had grabbed headlines for years.

Court would be held four days a week, with no proceedings on Mondays. In order to be in court every day, Linda Cluff worked graveyard shifts and weekends at her hospital job, while also caring for her mother, Helen, who was in her nineties and in need of full-time care. Her sisters, Susan and Terry, and Michele's nieces would also be regulars in court. Because they were witnesses in the trial, Alexis and Rachel could attend proceedings only after testifying.

The MacNeill family drama would now play out in court for the world to see. Everyone prepared for a battle that had been six years in the making.

37.

The trial of the *State of Utah v. Martin Joseph MacNeill* began on October 17, 2013. The complex, circumstantial case would unfold over nearly a month, the testimony plagued with emotional recollections and shocking accusations.

Perched at the center of the vast oak-paneled courtroom was Judge Derek Pullan. To the judge's left, the prosecutors, Chad Grunander, Jared Perkins, and Sam Pead, were clustered behind a long wooden desk.

On the opposite side of the courtroom, the defense attorney, Randall Spencer, made notes on an open laptop. Next to him, Susanne Gustin occasionally whispered into their client's ear. For the first day of the trial, Martin MacNeill was dressed in a dark suit, blue tie, and sleek, square-framed glasses.

Pead rose from his seat and walked to a podium facing the jury. In a solemn voice—as if he were delivering a eulogy—he began his opening statement by describing the discovery of Michele's body.

"On April 11, 2007, the defendant picked up his daughter Ada from school," Pead said, "and the two of them went back to the MacNeill family home in Pleasant Grove, Utah. Like many young children, Ada went to look for her mom, Michele MacNeill, who was also the defendant's wife."

The courtroom darkened and a picture of Michele's beautiful, smiling face flashed on a projection screen behind the prosecutor.

"Ada found her mom unresponsive in the bathtub and ran to get the defendant," said Pead. "Ada ran to the neighbor's house to get help. And the defendant called nine-one-one."

But this case, as the prosecutor explained, actually began brewing a year and a half earlier, when Martin first met Gypsy Willis. On the projection screen, Gypsy's face appeared.

Pead walked the jury through the events of 2006 and early 2007—the affair, Martin's apparent waning health, and his sudden fixation on his wife's appearance. "The defendant began to look into surgery for Michele Mac-Neill."

At the defense table, Martin's eyes narrowed as Pead described how the disgraced doctor hastily booked a surgeon and requested additional prescriptions. "Dr. Thompson did agree to prescribe all five of these drugs to Michele, but did so because her husband was a doctor and was her primary care physician and would know how these drugs should be properly administered."

Pead told the jury that following the surgery, while left in her husband's care, Michele was found peculiarly overmedicated in her rented hospital bed. A few days later, Michele was dead.

In court, the two 911 calls were played. Martin's gaze was cast downward as his own frantic voice filled the courtroom. "I need an ambulance. I need help, please. My wife has fallen in the bathtub!"

Pead spoke of Ada's pleas for help, and how neighbors rushed to the house to find Michele, her head under the faucet, face covered in mucus. "During this initial attempt at CPR, no witness saw any mucus transfer from Michele's face to the defendant's face or saw Michele's chest rise." Minutes later, paramedics had arrived.

At the defense table, Martin glared at the prosecutor, the muscles in his throat contracting as Pead described the former doctor's belligerent behavior as paramedics attempted to save his wife.

"While all these procedures were being employed, the defendant was acting extremely peculiar. He was yelling. He was screaming and shouting. He would not stay still," Pead said. "These professionals, despite many of them having years and years of experience, will tell you they were extremely taken aback by the defendant's behavior."

Pead documented Martin's various contradictory statements about the position of his wife's body, what medication she took, and the length of time she had been left alone. Martin instructed Eileen Heng to toss out Michele's medication, which Pead told the jurors constituted obstruction of justice.

Following his wife's death, Pead said, Martin did not appear like a grieving spouse. "After the funeral the defendant was jovial, laughing and smiling and again remarking that he was going to have to get used to the life of a bachelor."

Then, a week after the funeral, Martin introduced Rachel to "Jillian" at the temple, "holding out this fabricated but seemingly happenstance meeting as an answer to prayer."

Amid his daughters' growing suspicions, the new nanny moved into the house. Their affair continued as the lovers shopped for wedding rings and traveled to Wyoming, where Martin proposed.

Throughout the prosecution's case, Pead conceded to the jury, they would hear about contradictory opinions from the medical examiners. He told jurors that the original pathologist determined the cause of death as myocarditis and that the death certificate was later amended to include drug toxicity in addition to heart disease. Pead also explained that an expert witness would testify that Michele drowned.

During their case, Pead said, they would not only hear from pathologists and toxicologists, but also Martin's former mistresses and jailhouse informants.

"This case is a puzzle with many pieces. Pieces that are required to show you a complete picture of what happened to Michele MacNeill on April 11, 2007," Pead said as a photograph of a bathtub sliced into puzzle pieces flashed on the projector. "At the conclusion of all the evidence, and the instructions, and the arguments, we—the state's attorneys—will come back up here and ask you to find the defendant guilty of murder and of obstructing justice. Thank you."

"Ladies and gentlemen of the jury, what you just heard from the prosecution reminds me of an Aesop's fable that I first learned about in high school," Susanne Gustin said as she began her opening statements.

Strolling in front of the jury box, Gustin was dressed in a dark suit, her wavy, blond hair hanging loosely. She spoke with a theatrical flair, punctuating her sentences with dramatic pauses, as she compared the murder trial to a classic children's tale.

"And that fable goes like this: A farmer who had gone into his field to mend a gap in one of his fences found on his return the cradle in which he had left his only child asleep, turned upside down—the clothes all torn and bloody. And his dog lying near it was smeared with blood," Gustin said. "Thinking that the animal had destroyed his child, he instantly dashed out his brains with the hatchet in his hand. When turning up the cradle, he found his child unhurt and an enormous serpent lying dead on the floor, killed by that faithful dog, whose courage and fidelity in preserving the life of his son deserved another reward."

Gustin paced back and forth, making eye contact with each of the jurors. "Now what were the morals of this story?" she asked rhetorically.

"Number one is that we should not jump to conclusions. And the other is that we probably shouldn't let emotions cloud our judgment." Gustin paused. "And I'm not here to tell you ladies and gentlemen that Martin MacNeill deserves a reward like the faithful dog in Aesop's fable. Martin has made poor choices in his life."

Gustin admitted her client's actions were morally reprehensible—he had affairs and moved his mistress into the home within days of his wife's death. "We may think he's a total jerk and that's absolutely disgusting. And that's natural, but it's very critical that during this trial you set aside your emotion and you evaluate this case based upon the facts of the case rather than emotion."

The attorney also conceded that Martin was loud, obnoxious, and quite eccentric. The prosecution would use his odd personality, unfairly painting Martin as someone who was capable of killing his wife, Gustin said. "Which is akin to the evidence that the farmer misinterpreted as being proof of the dog's guilt. As in Aesop's fable, the prosecution's perception in this case is wrong, ladies and gentlemen."

Gustin explained that the defense's entire case was based on the original autopsy findings of heart disease. While all the experts would offer different opinions on the cause of death, they agreed on one thing: Michele's heart disease contributed to her death.

"Let's look at the actual facts in this case and the science in this case. The real culprit in Michele's death, the serpent, if you will, was heart disease."

Gustin presented an enlarged poster board of a Venn diagram, the colored circles showing the various opinions of the medical examiners. The circles each overlapped in the center of the chart, in an area labeled "heart disease."

Michele's heart problems were significant, Gustin said, because Martin could not have caused or known about the damage to her heart. "What is very important in this case is that none of the medical examiners believe that Michele's death was due to a homicide, because there is a reasonable and natural explanation for Michele's passing."

Gustin explained it was irrelevant if Michele died from heart arrhythmia or drowned, because either scenario was consistent with a natural death: she could have had a heart attack, fallen in the tub, and drowned.

Further, Gustin said, there was no evidence to indicate a struggle—no unexplained needle marks or bruising not related to the surgery. But the prosecution—convinced Martin had murdered his wife—dismissed any facts that disproved their theory, said Gustin.

"The investigators in this case conducted their investigation backwards. They started with the premise that Martin killed Michele," she said. "And that's why in the medical and scientific part of this case they went to great lengths to change the autopsy report."

In the nonmedical portion of the case, the prosecutors "cherry-picked" certain parts of Martin's life that they perceived to be indicative of guilt, argued Gustin. And in their zeal to prove Martin's guilt, the investigators engaged in deceptive practices not aimed at finding the truth.

As for Martin's health issues, Gustin stated they could all be explained by the genuine genetic condition in his toe. "The prosecution is going to suggest that Martin was limping and using a cane to stage that as a ruse that he wouldn't be able to lift Michele out of the bathtub . . . But the investigators ignored the medical and scientific evidence on this matter as well."

Most important, she said, Martin had an alibi, and the timing would not allow him to kill Michele. He was in his office at 11 A.M., at the safety fair at 11:15 A.M., and picked his daughter up from school at 11:35 A.M., which simply left no time to murder Michele.

"Finally, ladies and gentlemen, the prosecution—like the farmer in the fable—jumped to conclusions about Martin's guilt. But unlike the farmer, who was willing to surrender his faulty perceptions in the face of the facts of the case, the prosecution has continued to cling to its faulty belief despite evidence in the case, including the medical evidence in this case, which shows Michele died of natural causes." Gustin ended her statement emphatically. "Martin MacNeill is innocent, ladies and gentlemen. And, after you hear the evidence in this case, we will ask that you return a verdict of not guilty."

38.

f Martin had planned to shoot his wife, the man who handed him the
bullets was the plastic surgeon who operated on Michele.

Although Dr. Scott Thompson could not possibly know Martin's nefarious intentions when he prescribed the requested narcotics, he had
inadvertently provided him the tools to commit murder. It was no surprise, then, that the prosecution's first witness in their case was none other
than Dr. Thompson, who took the stand with a dreary expression.

Prosecutor Jared Perkins confidently questioned the surgeon about how
Martin had located his services. "I had an ad in the paper, I think it was
for Botox or something like that, and the MacNeills responded to that ad
and called the office," Thompson said.

Thompson explained how Michele deferred to her husband on medical
issues during each of their appointments.

"Did Michele express any hesitations about the surgery?" Perkins asked.

"Yes," Thompson replied. "She was concerned about the recovery and
the downtime and the risks."

The surgeon also testified about Martin's requests for additional medication. "Martin was really the one who directed this discussion," Thompson

said. "He said 'I'm really concerned about my wife. She gets nauseated easily. She gets anxious. And I just really want to make sure I have every thing I might need in the postoperative period for these issues.'"

"Did you prescribe any additional medications?" the attorney asked.

"Yes." Thompson sighed.

Thompson said he warned both Martin and Michele that these drugs would be dangerous when consumed together.

"What would be the effect if someone took Ambien, Phenergan, Percocet, and Valium around the same time?" Perkins asked.

"Those could all interact together to create a combined central nervous system depression."

"Is it safe to say this combination could be dangerous?"

"Yes."

"Why did you prescribe it here?"

"Because Martin was a physician and he asked me for these things. And he mentioned all the concerns," Thompson said. "I felt like because he was a physician I was willing to do that."

"What were your instructions to Michele about these drugs?"

"I told her this was more medication than I usually prescribe, and I told her to be very careful and only take what you feel you need. And they can have overlapping effects and you just need to be careful about taking these medications."

"Would there be any reason for her to take Ambien in the morning?" Perkins asked.

"No." Thompson shook his head.

Thompson spoke about seeing Michele in his office during post-op follow-ups, where she seemed in good spirits. Then, on the afternoon of April 11, Thompson learned of Michele's passing.

"It was an urgent call from Martin that Michele had been found unresponsive in the bathtub," Thompson said.

"What was your reaction?"

"I was very upset." Thompson winced, glancing at the floor. "It was just very upsetting. I've never had anything like this before or since."

Throughout the trial, Randall Spencer's cross-examination style was aggressive as he attempted to discredit witnesses.

"You didn't get any indication that Martin was being overbearing and pushing the surgery?" Spencer asked.

"I didn't," Thompson said.

"You wouldn't have offered the surgery if you felt that way, would you?"

"That's correct."

Utah is one of just three states that allows jurors to pose questions to witnesses. During the process, each question is vetted by the judge before being read to the witness. When Thompson was on the stand, the jury asked two questions.

"Did it concern you that Martin was acting as the primary care physician for Michele?" the judge asked.

"Yeah," Thompson said. "I thought that was a little unusual."

"Did you raise any objections or concerns with Martin and Michele about that?"

"No. And also he consulted with another physician, so that made me feel better."

Prosecutor Sam Pead called the next witness: Dr. Von Welch, the physician who performed the preoperative physical exam on Michele.

"The defendant was anxious that we complete the evaluation so they could proceed with the surgery without a delay," Welch told the jury. "He was a little bit animated, a little bit excited to get things going."

As in Dr. Thompson's testimony, Welch stated that Martin did most of the talking during the examination. After he asked Martin to leave, however, Michele explained she was depressed, Welch said.

"What was your assessment of her health?" Pead asked.

"She was in excellent health, with two exceptions," the doctor explained. "She had elevated blood pressure and she had depression . . . We talked about the fact that she had high blood pressure and it would be ideal to get that under control before surgery."

"What was his attitude about postponing the surgery?" Pead asked.

"He seemed disappointed but seemed to agree with it," Welch stated.

Later, Welch said, he learned Michele had died, and was shocked to hear she had gone through with the surgery.

Spencer then questioned Welch about his previous interactions with Martin. "Is it fair to say that Martin was frequently animated in your associations with him?"

"Yeah," Welch said.

"When you asked to speak to Michele alone, Mr. MacNeill didn't object or throw a fit or anything?" Spencer asked.

"No."

Next, Pleasant Grove police 911 dispatch manager Heidi Peterson was called to the stand, and the two 911 calls were replayed for the jury.

Peterson explained how when Martin first called 911 on his cell phone, he was transferred to the county dispatch in Spanish Fork. When he called back, Martin was connected with Peterson.

"We spoke briefly and he hung up on me," she said. "Then I called back and we spoke again before he disconnected again."

Spencer tried to show that Martin hung up because he was attempting to revive his wife.

"In both of the calls you understand that Mr. MacNeill was attempting to do CPR, right?"

"Yeah. He said he was," Peterson said.

"And you continued to ask him lots of different questions?"

"Yes," she said.

"I assume that that's pursuant to your training?" Spencer asked. "To keep a nine-one-one caller on the line?"

"Absolutely."

3 9 .

A white ceramic bathtub—an exact replica of the one in which Michele had died—was eerily on display at the center of the courtroom on the second day of the trial.

The prosecution had been granted permission to bring the tub to court so witnesses could demonstrate for the jury the position in which Michele's body had been discovered.

Peering down at the tub, the trial's next witness, Kristi Daniels, described how she found Michele inside the basin, knees bent. Kristi pointed to a blue piece of tape, meant to represent the faucet, to explain where Michele's head rested.

Stepping up to the witness stand, Kristi detailed how her ordinary afternoon became chaotic, beginning with a knock on her front door and ending in the MacNeills' bathroom.

"When I first went in I saw that Michele was in the tub and Martin was over the tub. So I saw that something obviously needed to happen," she said. "I went back to get my phone from my house to call Doug."

After Doug took over chest compressions, Kristi waited outside for the ambulance. "It seemed like it took a long time for the ambulance to come," she stated. "In my mind there was a hospital close to our neighborhood and it shouldn't have taken as long as it did."

Kristi also told jurors of her encounter with Martin in their shared driveway days later, and how he explained to her and Doug that Michele had died of heart problems.

"Did Martin ever offer any other explanation for what caused Michele's death?" Perkins asked.

"No," she said.

On cross, Spencer tried to get Kristi to admit that Martin was trying to save Michele.

"When you first ran into the bathroom, it appeared to you that Martin was trying to give Michele CPR?" Spencer asked.

"Yes. I assumed that." Kristi nodded.

Following Kristi's testimony, neighbor Angie Aguilar recounted her own recollections from the tragic day. "I could see stitches in her face that were bleeding just a little bit and she had mucus under her nose," she said. "She was gray."

As Martin performed CPR, Angie said, she never saw any mucus on his face.

After so many years, several of the neighbors and first responders gave conflicting accounts of what Michele wore on the day of her death. Some of the paramedics would recall her in pink sweat pants. Others disagreed about the color of the shirt she was wearing.

On cross, Susanne Gustin questioned Angie about discrepancies she had identified in the preliminary hearing.

"You stated that Michele was wearing a white T-shirt and that T-shirt was wet," Gustin said. "And you're positive she was wearing a T-shirt?"

"I am," she said.

"She was not wearing garments?" Gustin asked.

"The T-shirt was transparent," Angie said. "She was not wearing a bra."

Doug Daniels next told the jury he knew something was wrong with Michele the moment he entered the bathroom that afternoon.

"She just looked lifeless and collapsed, kind of slumped down in the bottom of the tub," Doug said. "The perception was we needed to get her out of the tub."

Perkins asked about the mucus on Michele's face.

"There was quite a bit of mucus around her nose and mouth, running down and mixing with the blood running down her face," Doug said.

"Did you see any transfer of mucus to Martin's face?"

"No," Doug said.

"Were you able to observe Martin's part of the CPR process?" Perkins asked.

"It appeared he was doing CPR," Doug said. "He would go toward her mouth then he would stop and listen and instruct us on when to do her chest compressions."

"Did you ever see Michele's chest rise as he was doing mouth-to-mouth?" the attorney asked.

"I did not," he said.

"How was his demeanor while he was doing this?"

"At times he was very analytical and very in control and very calm, and other times it was a little bit frustrated when he would holler out."

Doug also explained that he thought Martin should have been able to lift Michele from the tub by himself and was surprised that he waited for assistance.

After the ambulance had taken Michele away, Doug told the jury, he returned to the MacNeill home to clean up but found no towels or the pants Michele must have been wearing.

"After Michele's death, did Martin ever talk about his failing health?" the prosecutor asked Doug.

"Yes. We had discussions about his health," Doug said. "I had seen him with a cane or limping a little bit . . . He stopped using the cane . . . Sometimes he would use it and sometimes he wouldn't. It was kind of an off and on thing."

On cross, Spencer attempted to confuse Doug, leaving the witness irritated.

"Michele was kind of large to get out of the tub," Spencer stated. "How would you have done that?"

"I would have gotten ahold of her and lifted her out of the tub," Doug exclaimed.

"You think you could have gotten ahold of her from the top and lifted up one hundred and eighty pounds?" Spencer said smugly.

"Absolutely." Doug nodded his head.

At the defense table, Martin removed his glasses, rubbed his eyes, and shook his head.

Spencer asked how closely Doug was watching Martin during the CPR.

"He could have easily been doing nothing, that's how little attention I was paying to that," Doug said, adding that he was focused on pumping on Michele's chest.

"Did you see the chest rise?" the attorney asked.

"No, I did not," he said.

"At all?" Spencer's tone was inquisitive.

"Never."

Following Doug Daniels, the prosecution called a parade of police, firefighters, and first responders who had encountered Martin on the afternoon of April 11.

Pleasant Grove police officer Ray Ormond told Sam Pead how once he and his partner began performing compressions and stimulating her circulatory system, Michele's appearance seemed to improve.

"I also noticed that her color was going from the bluish condition, pale blue, to more of a pink fleshy color, and a weeping of blood from the incisions around her hairline and eyes."

Meanwhile, the gurgling in Michele's lungs grew louder. "Fluid actually came out of Michele's mouth," he said. "There was quite a lot of fluid that came out . . . If I had to estimate I would say about three cups."

A few minutes later it happened again, Ormond said. "We turned her head to the side, so that it wouldn't go back into her. At that point more fluid came out," he testified. "That fluid was more frothy, cloudy, and it had a little tint of blood."

Ormond also detailed how Martin scolded his unconscious wife as she lay dying. "He was moving back and forth in the bedroom and the bathroom. He appeared to be agitated. He would sporadically yell," Ormond said. "It was distracting because of the volume at which it was yelled at us, and yelled at Michele."

Standing at the defense table, Gustin questioned Ormond about his perceptions of Martin's conduct.

"You didn't know Martin MacNeill before this day?" Gustin asked.

"No," Ormond said.

"You don't know what his normal personality was like?"

"No."

"You don't know if he was an over-the-top personality, or pushy or animated?"

"No," Ormond said. "That was my first time seeing him, to my knowledge."

Ormond's former partner, Pleasant Grove patrol officer Joshua Motsinger, was next to take the stand.

Pead asked about the CPR Martin claimed he had performed on his wife prior to the neighbor's arrival to help lift her from the tub.

"He said he found her slumped over into the tub," Pead said. "Can CPR be done while someone is slumped over in a tub?"

"No," Motsinger said.

On cross, Spencer criticized the method Utah County Attorney's Office investigators used to interview, implying that Motsinger was parroting what others had reported.

"Do you believe that your testimony about what he said is what you heard or what you had been told by other people who responded with you?" Spencer asked.

"It's what I heard," Motsinger said.

Fire Chief Marc Sanderson next detailed Martin's erratic behavior on the afternoon of Michele's death.

"He was very excited, very loud," said Sanderson. "He was moving about quickly. Up and down the hall, into the living room, out onto the front porch. It was very hard to keep him in one place."

Sanderson also explained that Martin refused to speak to the emergency room doctor. "He wanted to talk to another doctor he'd previously worked with. He asked to talk with someone different."

"How were the resuscitation efforts working on Michele?" Pead asked.

"They weren't working at all," Sanderson said somberly. "We did everything that we could possibly have done . . . with no positive effects."

Sanderson testified that although Martin had told officials at the scene that he had last seen Michele approximately ten to fifteen minutes before, he later told the emergency room doctors and medical examiner that it had been one or two hours since he had last seen his wife alive.

"I specifically recall that it was a short enough time that I felt like we had an opportunity to resuscitate Michele," Sanderson testified.

In a seemingly misguided series of questions, on cross Spencer attempted to diminish the importance of the length of time Michele was left alone.

"Whether he had been away for two hours or fifteen minutes, that wouldn't tell you how long Michele would have been down, correct?" the attorney said.

"Oh yeah." Sanderson seemed incredulous. "Ten to fifteen minutes, he returns home and finds her that way, that's a significant difference than if he had been gone from the residence for two hours."

"If he had been gone from the residence for two hours, Michele could have gone down right before he got back as well, correct?" Spencer huffed.

"Yes," Sanderson said.

"So whether he's been gone for two hours or fifteen minutes, it doesn't really tell you how long Michele has been down, correct?"

"Well, it does. It tells us that it's only been ten to fifteen minutes. If that's all he's been gone."

"Okay," Spencer seemed to acknowledge. In what seemed like an attempt to discredit Sanderson's memory, he then reminded the witness of a previous interview with investigator Jeff Robinson in which Sanderson had incorrectly stated that Michele was wearing pink sweat pants, when she actually had a pink towel draped over her lower half.

"You just remember it being a short time period . . . You also said you recall Martin being emotionally upset and frantic," Spencer stated.

"Yes," Sanderson said.

"Is it fair to say that perhaps all of your observations aren't correct?"

"No, I don't think that's fair to say." Sanderson smirked.

The following three witnesses were fire and police officials, who further detailed Martin's erratic behavior on the scene the day of Michele's death.

"He was kind of darting in and out of the room. He would be there for a minute or so then he'd be gone again and then he'd be back again," said Pleasant Grove fire captain Steven Brande. "He was very agitated, very angry."

Deputy fire chief David Thomas recalled how Martin directed the first responders about which medications to give Michele.

"It was disruptive because he was loud and moving about," Thomas said. "He didn't physically come and impede the resuscitation. He would come in and look over the resuscitation and leave again."

Patrol officer Dan Beckstrom described Martin as in "complete random hysteria."

"He was hysterical. He was blurting out things," he said. "And he was pacing about, in and out of the home and just hysterical."

Since conducting the original investigation, former detective Marc Wright had left the Pleasant Grove Police Department and was working as a patrol officer for another city in Utah.

When Wright took the stand, the photos he had taken at the crime scene were displayed for the jury—the puddle of water on the tile floor, close-ups of blood on the tub's ledge, and the wet shirts piled on the carpet.

On cross, Spencer pried into the lack of investigation. "After you took the pictures and left the home, you never came back to the house for a follow-up investigation?" Spencer asked.

"Not in that case, no," Wright said.

"And at the time, while you thought Mr. MacNeill's behavior was strange, you didn't find it suspicious?" he said.

"Not at the time, no."

"No further questions." Spencer turned away from the podium.

Before Spencer could take his seat, Pead rose from the prosecutor's table for redirect.

"At the time you left, you were not suspicious of any foul play, that's what defense council just asked you?" Pead said.

"That's correct," Wright acknowledged. "I was not."

"Were you aware at the time of any evidence that the defendant was having an affair?"

"No, I was not," Wright replied.

"Not aware that the defendant told someone there was blood everywhere?"

"I was not."

"Not aware that she was only taking one or two Percocet a day?"

"No."

"Were you aware the defendant was the one pushing the surgery and not Michele?"

"Just based on the statement that the defendant had made that Michele had to have the surgery led me to believe that she was the one who wanted the surgery."

After making his point, Pead took a seat.

American Fork Hospital emergency room doctor Leo Van Wagoner, as well as one of the hospital's nurses, also spoke about Martin's demeanor that afternoon. When Michele arrived at the hospital, Van Wagoner said, she already had mottled skin, a sign that her heart stopped about an hour prior.

"She didn't have a pulse, she didn't have a blood pressure," Van Wagoner said. "I think she was dead by the time she arrived at our door."

After working on Michele for thirty-eight minutes with no signs of life, Van Wagoner said, he officially announced the time of death. Afterward, he contacted the medical examiner to conduct an investigation because he felt the case was unusual.

"Michele was young—age fifty—relatively healthy, and she presents in cardiac arrest with no known heart history." Van Wagoner crossed his arms and leaned back in the witness seat. "For her to die that way without a certain cause, it became a medical examiner's case."

Van Wagoner also told the jury about the statement Martin made after he declared time of death. "He made an odd request from me, which I still find in fifteen years of practice to be completely unusual and really kind of off the wall."

"What was that request?" Grunander asked.

"He offered me ten thousand dollars to continue my resuscitation and not quit. I'm not sure where that came from." Van Wagoner shifted in his chair. "I think as a physician he probably knew that his wife was already dead, considering we had no signs of life, no blood pressure, no pulse, no breathing on her own. I'm not sure why he made that comment. It struck me as very odd and still remains odd when I think about it."

To explain away Martin's strange behavior, Randall Spencer asked the doctor about his previous encounters with Martin.

"You described him as odd and eccentric?" Spencer asked.

"I always thought he was a little odd, a little eccentric, yes," Van Wagoner said.

"That was before you had any association with him on April 11?" Spencer asked.

"Correct."

A string of Martin's former colleagues from the Developmental Center next testified about the former doctor's hurried manner on April 11, his attitude following his wife's death, and his varied explanations concerning his failing health.

Nurse practitioner Steven Nickelson described his arrival at the MacNeill home and Martin's insistence he tell Alexis that Michele was "coding."

Defense attorneys then questioned Nickelson about Martin's toe pain.

"At first when his foot bothered him it wasn't bad," Nickelson said. "By the time he left he needed a cane."

Martin seemed to have trouble getting a proper diagnosis, and one doctor even recommended amputation. Still, no one at the Developmental Center was under the impression the condition was fatal.

Human resources manager John David Laycock told jurors he saw Martin's swollen toe, and it appeared he had a real condition. "He actually came into my office and showed me his toe," Laycock said. "He actually took his sock off and his shoe and put it up on my desk and showed it to me."

Laycock recalled that Martin seemed peculiar when arriving at the safety fair and insisting he be photographed. "He was adamant," Laycock said. "It was different. He seemed determined."

Administrator Roma Henrie said that she was so put off by Martin's repeated demands to be photographed, she later filed a complaint with human resources. The next time she saw the doctor was after the funeral. "Within a week he was wearing a different wedding band," Henrie said.

The Developmental Center's liability prevention specialist, Melissa Frost, spoke about how Martin's involvement in that year's safety fair was atypical. "Usually he would attend for a brief time, very shortly, and he would create a list of people from the department who would be manning his booth," she said. That year, however, Frost's entire award ceremony was disrupted by Martin's rescheduling.

Gustin, however, attempted to diminish the significance of Martin's actions. "It wasn't unusual for Martin to change the time because he was demanding?" Gustin asked.

"Nobody did anything in his department without his direction," Frost admitted.

40.

Rachel MacNeill stepped into the courtroom wearing a simple taupe dress, her hair pulled back in a loose bun, and heavy black makeup lining her eyes.

Her testimony would be one of the more emotional aspects of the trial. After just a few minutes on the stand, her face was twisted in agony.

Watching his oldest daughter dab tears from her eyes, Martin took off his glasses, his face sagging. Still, he showed no overt emotion.

"Do you recognize the man over here?" Chad Grunander pointed toward Martin.

"He's my father." Rachel sniffed, a look of revulsion passing across her face.

In a shaky voice, she recounted the moment she'd discovered her mother was dead. "When I did get ahold of my father I said, 'What's happening? Is everything okay?' He just said, 'Rachel, come home.' And he hung up on me."

Days after her mother's funeral, Rachel had the strange meeting with "Jillian," who, she later learned, was actually Gypsy—her father's mistress.

Grunander presented a picture to Rachel.

"That's Gypsy Jillian Willis." Rachel made a retching noise.

"Did you see her function as the nanny?" Grunander asked.

"As a nanny, I didn't see her do anything related to the children," she said.

"At some point did you become aware that your father's relationship with Gypsy was more than just a nanny?" Grunander asked.

"Yes." Rachel squinted her eyes. "It was very apparent just shortly after my mother's death . . . And she wasn't doing anything a nanny would do."

At the prosecutor's request, Rachel stepped down from the stand to demonstrate on the tub exactly how Martin said he found Michele. Clutching a tissue, Rachel put her hand on her stomach as if she was going to be sick.

"And just even showing me. And talking about the autopsy." Her hands were shaking as she touched her face. She began to stammer. "It was just—It was so—I was—It was so horrible. I didn't want to know my mom was dead."

Grunander then handed Rachel an exhibit: the clothes her mom was wearing on the day she was found. Wearing gloves, Rachel examined each article.

"Do you recognize those?" Grunander asked.

"My mother's," she whispered.

"Did you find that on April 11, 2007?"

"In the big bloody mess of everything that was thrown in the garage," Rachel said.

As Gustin stood for the cross-examination, Rachel shot her a look of disdain.

"Is it true there wasn't a lot of blood?" Gustin said, her tone condescending, as she addressed Rachel's recollection of finding Michele's bloody clothes.

"I'm not good at seeing blood." Rachel took a slow, ragged breath. "Blood is not something I like to see, especially my mother's blood."

In the most searing part of cross-examination, Gustin attempted to discredit Rachel based on her bipolar disorder.

"Your father didn't want you to be the nanny because of your mental state, isn't that right, Rachel?" Gustin asked.

Openmouthed, Rachel looked toward the judge. "I don't remember."

"You have been diagnosed with a mental illness?" Gustin pressed.

Rachel paused. "Have I been diagnosed in my life with a mental illness?"

Gustin brought up the 2012 emergency room visit, where Rachel was diagnosed with delusions and psychosis.

"You have had delusions and psychosis in your life?" Gustin asked.

"No. Okay." Rachel recoiled in her seat.

"You have been diagnosed bipolar?" Gustin continued.

"Have I in my lifetime been diagnosed as bipolar?" Rachel cocked her head. "Yes."

Rachel leaned back and shook her head, rolling her eyes slightly. Moments later she left the courthouse in tears, surrounded by family.

Vanessa's testimony was equally heartbreaking. Visibly shaking, tears streaming down her cheeks, she told Grunander how after her mother's death, she threw her phone against the wall, breaking it. Martin later gave her Michele's phone, which still had two voice mail messages from Martin.

"He was worried about her. He said he needed her to stay in bed." Vanessa described Martin's message. "He said, 'Take it easy, I'm going to come home and make you a sandwich, we'll have a lovely lunch together.'"

Grunander gently asked about her past, including her felony arrest for drugs.

"Are you a drug addict?" he asked.

"I am." She wiped tears from her face.

"Are you currently clean?"

"I am."

Vanessa also spoke about her involvement in Martin's "nanny hiring committee," where the only candidate interviewed was "Jillian." Finally, she recalled for the jury the sad comment she made to her sister Alexis.

"I told her there is nothing to worry about. Because I was convinced that she wasn't somebody to worry about that my dad might be involved with."

"Why did you say there was nothing to worry about?" Grunander asked.

"Because she was nothing like my mom." Vanessa cried.

At nineteen, Sabrina MacNeill had grown into a gorgeous young woman with long, shiny brown hair. She was currently in college, living in Logan, near her sister Elle.

Sabrina described for the court the last time she saw her mother—on the day of her death. "There was nothing odd about her behavior at all. She was tired because she had just woken up, but we had a perfectly normal conversation."

When the girls returned home from school, Sabrina said, Martin walked into their room to tell them that their mom was dead. It was April 11. The next day, Sabrina turned thirteen.

Gustin asked about Martin's emotional reaction.

"Your dad was upset when he told you about your mom?" Gustin asked. "He was crying?"

"I guess he was crying. He had a towel over his face. He took it down and said our mom had died and that's all I remember."

Five years after her relationship with Damian MacNeill had ended, Eileen Heng's life had dramatically changed. Having since graduated with a law degree from Brigham Young University, she was now a practicing attorney in Lehi and was in a long-term relationship with a man she would later marry.

On October 23, Eileen was forced to reminisce about "one of the worst days" of her life.

"That morning when I was in class I received a lot of missed calls and voice mails," she told Jared Perkins. "When I got out of class I checked and Damian had left me a few messages."

She explained how she rushed to the MacNeill home and later granted Martin's request to flush his wife's prescriptions down the toilet. "At the time it seemed strange," Eileen said.

"Why did you comply with that request?" Perkins asked.

"Because he asked me to and he just lost his wife and I wanted to help," she testified.

Later, Eileen said, Martin asked her to help interview a nanny candidate. But when she learned the only applicant was Martin's suspected mistress, she recommended he not hire her.

"Was Martin and Jillian's relationship limited to that of employer and nanny?" Perkins asked.

"No," she said. "A couple of months later we found out they were in an intimate relationship."

"How did you find out? Did Martin ever tell you he was in an intimate relationship with Gypsy?" Perkins asked.

"Yes," Eileen said. "Everyone found out."

41.

Strutting into the courtroom, Gypsy Willis glanced briefly at her former lover as she took the stand. The beige pantsuit she wore hugged her full frame, stretching across her midsection. Her dark hair framed her plump cheeks.

It was the afternoon of October 25, and Gypsy would spend the next two days reluctantly testifying for the prosecution against the man she had once planned to marry. She was unrepentant and unapologetic as she spoke about her affair with the married doctor. At times she grinned and smirked, appearing flippant.

Having been subpoenaed as part of her plea deal in the identity fraud conviction, her testimony was adversarial. Gypsy still believed Martin did not kill his wife, and seemed determined to protect him. She answered most questions with a "yes," "no," or "I don't recall." By the second day, the judge would declare her a hostile witness after determining "her interests are somewhat aligned with the defense."

While the prosecution tried to paint Martin's relationship with her as a motive for murder, she repeatedly denied their relationship was heating up in the months prior to Michele's death. "This was a very informal thing.

This was a very discreet thing. We were not interested in other people knowing. I think he was trying to keep it quiet. I respected that."

Under questioning, Gypsy admitted that in the spring of 2007 she and Martin were speaking more frequently and that he was paying for her duplex and living expenses.

"This sounds like a commitment," Sam Pead said.

"Yeah. He's helping." Gypsy shook her head nonchalantly.

To further try to prove Gypsy's relationship with Martin, Pead presented the phone records showing the numerous texts and phone calls between the two, including twenty-two texts exchanged on the day of the funeral.

Pead also entered into evidence the racy photographs Gypsy had sent Martin from her cell phone. "In a number of these pictures it's your exposed back," Pead said. "You're showing your buttocks."

"There's one picture where it's a little suggestive," Gypsy admitted unabashedly.

As for the introduction to Rachel outside the temple, she conceded it was a ruse but downplayed the significance.

"So he staged and directed this encounter?" Pead asked.

"I don't understand the terminology there." Gypsy's voice was defiant. "He wanted me to meet his family on the best possible terms."

And although she was eventually hired as the family nanny, she said, the job was not guaranteed prior to her interview. "I don't believe that Martin would have had me come and help if his children would have objected strongly to me."

Looking away from Gypsy, Martin took off his glasses, leaned over, and put his hands on his face. There was no denying that Martin had done just that—hired Gypsy over the objections of his children.

"And the two of you were hiding the fact that you were sexually involved from the children?" Pead asked.

"Yes."

"If I told you that others have testified that you were not much of a nanny in terms of cooking and cleaning and taking care of the children, and were just staring goo-goo-eyed at the defendant, what would be your response?" Pead asked.

Gypsy smiled wide. "My response is that when the adult children were home I deferred to them and went back to studying my nursing. I did actually help with the children."

Gypsy returned to court a second day, and the prosecutor continued to press her on her relationship with Martin. She continued to give calm, direct, matter-of-fact answers.

Pead asked about the seven-thousand-dollar diamond ring Martin gave her during their Wyoming trip.

"I know there was a ring. I know I was given a ring," she said. "I truthfully don't recall the details."

"Have you been proposed to since the defendant proposed to you?" Pead asked.

"Yes." She smirked.

"Despite never being officially married, you still held yourself out as Jillian MacNeill?" Pead said. "The wife of the defendant?"

"Yes," she said.

Finally, Pead added up the details of Martin's relationship with Gypsy just prior to Michele's passing.

"Are you telling us you don't know more about Michele's death?"

"That is correct," she said, her expression impassive.

On cross, Gustin clarified again for the jury the plea deal under which Gypsy was testifying.

"You got a deal from the prosecution to testify here today," Gustin said. "And the deal was that if you testified, you wouldn't have to spend three years in prison?"

"That's correct," Gypsy said.

"And if you didn't testify truthfully, you will have breached that deal," Gustin said.

"Yes," she agreed.

Vicki Willis hadn't seen her daughter in almost five years. And even though they were both in the same city—and would sit at the same seat on the seventh day of the trial—they declined to speak to each other.

Vicki testified that the last time she had seen Gypsy was in 2008—when they got into a physical altercation in Wyoming. On a previous visit in May 2007, when Vicki first met Martin, she had been proud of Gypsy and pleased to welcome her new boyfriend into the family.

Vicki said that later she'd had a chance to speak privately to Martin about his deceased wife. "He said to me that he had never loved Michele. And then he amended that to say, 'Well, I did. I loved her as a sister. But I did not love her the way I love Gypsy,'" Vicki testified.

Earlier in the week, outside the presence of the jury, the defense continued the fight to keep Ada off the stand.

"Ada has been influenced to the point where she believes it true," Spencer told the judge.

Investigators Witney and Robinson, as well as Alexis, all swore that Ada had not been coaxed.

But the following morning the judge ruled that Ada would not be allowed to testify. Instead, her 2008 interview at the Children's Justice Center was played for the jury. The light in the courtroom dimmed, and on the projection screen appeared the then seven-year-old as she described finding her dead mother.

"What did you see when you walked into the bathroom?" the investigator asked.

"It was just like water—just a different color. She was just laying down in the bathtub," Ada said.

"Had you ever seen your mom wet her hair like that before?" she asked.

"I don't want to talk about it."

4 2 .

Linda Cluff rose from her seat in the first row of the gallery, behind the prosecution, and walked directly to the witness stand.

Testifying for the prosecution, she could have talked for days about her beloved sister. Linda would have been pleased to explain to the jurors something that was impossible to truly understand: Michele meant everything to her.

Instead, Linda was questioned for mere minutes.

She was barred from telling jurors about Martin's criminal past, his false education credentials, his history with her family, or even the fact that he banned most of the Somers clan from the funeral. The judge ruled that none of those facts could be presented in court because they were too prejudicial against Martin.

Instead, she testified only about her interactions with Martin on the day of the funeral as he ran back and forth from the parking lot. After just a few questions from the prosecutor, Linda somberly stepped off the stand and returned to her seat.

———

Later, Michele's friends Cheryl Radmall, Loreen Thompson, and Lani Swallow spoke about the shock of learning of their dear friend's death.

"Michele was in great health," Cheryl said.

She also discussed going to the MacNeill family home on the afternoon of Michele's death to offer condolences.

"Did Martin appear emotional?" the prosecutor asked.

"No," Cheryl said definitively.

Loreen agreed that Martin acted odd that evening and also at the funeral when he delivered his eulogy. "It was very different. I just remember the first comment he made was something about the fact that he stood there looking at his wife who was in a pine box," Loreen said.

Lani testified that on the day of the funeral she approached Martin and offered to be the nanny but he refused. "He said that he had already hired a nanny," Lani said. "That it was a nurse that he worked with."

Michele's close friend and the children's ballet teacher, Jacqueline Colledge, also testified about Martin's eulogy. "He talked more about himself than he did Michele," she said.

"What did he say about Michele?" the prosecutor asked.

"I can't remember a lot, actually," she said. "I do remember him talking about how he would survive and the children would survive this terrible thing that had happened to him."

Later in the trial, Martin's former mistress, Anna Osborne Walthall, testified about her affair with the doctor. After sex, she said, they engaged in deep conversations.

"When did conversations like that usually occur?"

"Pillow talk." She glanced around the courtroom. "After you have sex and you're laying there and you feel close so you're a little more open."

"Did Martin ever describe the process of making someone have a heart attack?"

"Yes. There's something you can give someone that's natural . . . that's not detectable after they have a heart attack."

Randall Spencer tried to discredit Anna's testimony.

"You've shared dreams you've had about the case," he said, "that you thought were of evidentiary value."

"Possibly." She shrugged.

"You've been diagnosed with dissociative identity disorder?" Spencer asked. "What used to be called multiple personality disorder?"

"I have."

"You also wrote in an e-mail that you're very excited about the prospect of Martin being off the streets for a very long time, right?" Spencer asked.

"Probably."

43.

The state's star witness, Alexis Somers, took the stand next.

Having just given birth to twins, and on maternity leave from her job as a general practitioner, she wore a loose black blouse with a beige sweater, her hair partially pulled back in a barrette.

Unlike Rachel and Vanessa, who could not hold back their torrent of emotions, on the stand Alexis was subdued, repressing her anger and anguish. But there was a great sadness in her eyes, her voice, and demeanor.

No one wanted this for the family.

"I always wanted my dad to be proud of me." Alexis stared vacantly at the floor for a moment.

Because she had been present for each step of her mother's surgery and aftercare, Alexis was able to paint for the jury exactly what occurred in the days leading up to Michele's death.

She spoke about her mom's desires to delay the surgery, to give herself a chance to lose weight and lower her blood pressure. "My mom was hesitant to get the surgery. She was talking to my dad, saying that maybe we should delay the surgery," Alexis testified. "He got really angry and said, 'No, you cannot do that. If you don't have the surgery now, you're not doing it.'"

She discussed finding her mom extremely sedated following the one night Michele was left in Martin's care. "I went over there to try to wake her up and she wasn't waking up," Alexis said. "I went to my father and I said, 'What happened? Obviously Mom is overmedicated.'"

She also told the jury how Michele wanted to feel each pill in her hands so she knew what she was being given. Because the judge had deemed the statement hearsay, the jury was not allowed to hear the statement that Alexis said Michele had told her: "If anything happens to me, make sure it wasn't your dad."

Alexis explained that she took over as primary caregiver, keeping a meticulous log of what Michele ate and what medications she took.

"Do you recall ever giving your mom any Valium during the week you were caring for her?" Grunander asked.

"No. I never did." She shook her head. "She wasn't having any issues with anxiety."

"Did you ever administer Ambien?"

"No. She never had any issue sleeping," she said. "She didn't like narcotics."

Alexis returned to school the evening of April 10 and spoke with her mother the next day. "She was upbeat and happy, I could hear it in her voice," she said, her own voice breaking from emotion.

Three hours later, a brusque Martin told his daughter her mom wasn't breathing. "I screamed. I dropped my bags. And just ran. Ran to get in my car to drive to the airport to fly home," Alexis testified.

The prosecutor also asked about Michele's bath routine.

"She'd start the water up. Then she'd get in it. Then turn it up as hot as it could go. She liked it really, really hot. Then once it was full she'd turn off the water," Alexis said.

On cross-examination, Spencer attacked Alexis personally and professionally—going so far as to imply that she lied on her medical school application by claiming she worked as a nanny because she cared for her siblings.

For hours over two days of questioning, Spencer played clips from Alexis's appearances on *20/20* and *Nancy Grace* and compared her testimony to that from the preliminary hearing. For ten minutes they debated what defined the word "lucid," when describing how long it took for Michele to recover from being overmedicated.

Throughout it all, Alexis remained unflustered.

"You sued your dad to try and get the family home, claiming that your dad can't inherit from your mother because the house was in her name," Spencer pressed.

"I was appointed the executor of my mom's estate before her death. It's my duty as the executor for my siblings . . ." She paused.

"To sue your dad."

"No. Not to sue my dad, but to make sure the estate is processed like it should be," she said.

Spencer juxtaposed statements Alexis made on the stand, attempting to catch inconsistencies with her testimony from the preliminary hearing and interviews with investigators.

"You've recently been made aware of an inconsistency with your previous statement," he accused her. "And you've modified your testimony here at trial today, right?"

"No, that's incorrect," she said.

As for Alexis's testimony about her mother's bath routine, Spencer suggested she was making it up. "You never told anyone until today that it was your mother's habit to start the tub and then get in?"

"That's not true. I e-mailed Doug Witney," she said.

"You weren't with your mother all the time when she took a bath?"

"Every single time she took a bath?" She wryly smirked and shook her head. "Yeah. I couldn't be."

Contention grew as the hours passed.

As she was speaking about the last time she'd talked to her mother, Spencer attempted to trip Alexis up on timing.

"It took me a while to put it all together," Alexis said.

"So what you're saying is it took you a little while to put together your story." Spencer's voice rose.

"No. That's not what I was saying," she replied calmly.

"You've made up this story that you've told today," he berated her.

"No, I have not," she said, her voice low and steady.

On redirect, Grunander addressed two important issues.

"Do you stand to gain anything financially if your father is convicted of killing your mother?" he asked.

"Not at all. I've already spent so much more money than I'd ever receive. I don't stand to gain anything," she said.

"Why were you seeking information about your mother's death?" he asked.

"Because I believe my father killed her."

44.

The experts next squabbled over the amount of drugs in Michele's system, the severity of her heart disease, and how much water was in her lungs.

Utah Chief Medical Examiner Dr. Todd Grey explained how the late Dr. Maureen Frikke originally ruled that the death was due to natural causes related to heart disease.

"How frequent in your experience is it that the cause of death is changed?" Grunander asked.

"Changing cause of death is pretty rare, particularly if you have done a complete examination originally," the pathologist said.

Grunander's voice was unwavering as he tried to get Grey to concede that Michele's death may have been a murder.

"Dr. Grey, if you were to learn that the defendant told somebody or others that he had drugged up Michele MacNeill and convinced her to get into the tub and held her down a little bit and it caused her death, would that scenario be consistent with how Michele MacNeill may have died here?" Grunander asked.

"Yeah. Certainly," Grey said. "It's possible."

Spencer cross-examined Grey about his decision not to rule Michele's death a homicide.

"If drugs were a factor, it was not necessarily a homicide either, correct?" Spencer asked, turning toward the jury.

"I did not feel that I could reach a conclusion of homicide," Grey said.

Next on the stand, Utah heart specialist Dr. David Cragun told jurors that after reading Michele's medical reports and EKG readings, he came to the conclusion that her myocarditis was not severe.

"The lack of symptoms and the mild histology both suggest that her course would be benign generally. That the chance of a serious or life-threatening complication would be very rare," Cragun testified.

Forensic toxicologist and clinical pharmacologist Dr. Gary Dawson—an expert witness for the prosecution—delivered detailed testimony about the drugs found in Michele's system.

The combination of drugs at the levels in Michele's blood would not have been lethal, Dawson said. However, he testified, the mix would have had a dramatic effect on her central nervous system, leaving Michele unable to think properly, focus, or multitask.

"It would cause sedation and cognitive impairment. It would be likely that that person would be obtunded or unable to respond constructively to their environment," he said. "They may be difficult to arouse and may not understand the circumstances surrounding them at that time."

On cross, Spencer confronted Dawson with an e-mail sent to the investigators, Witney and Robinson, in which the pharmacologist seemed to imply the toxicology report did not support the theory of murder.

"There's not a smoking gun in here, that I see," Dawson had written. "There are a lot of empty casings on the ground, but there's not a smoking gun."

Dawson attempted to clarify that his "smoking gun" reference was meant to imply there was not one drug that could be identified as a lethal dose.

"In those five drugs there's not one combination that's lethal—that's the smoking gun," he said on the stand. "There is other evidence there that says there is contributing factors from all five drugs but not one that you can point to and say that's the one that did the damage. That's the fatal dose."

Forensic pathologist Joshua Perper next gave his opinion—one that was most beneficial to the prosecution.

"My opinion was that Michele died as a result of drowning; in addition to that she had some drugs on board which were not in toxicology lethal levels but in my opinion could have contributed to her death," Perper told the jury.

Randall Spencer paced back and forth in front of the witness stand as he questioned how Perper became involved in the case.

"Prior to being hired by the Utah County Attorney's Office, you had appeared as a guest expert on the *Nancy Grace* show?" Spencer asked.

"Yes." Perper nodded. "What I said on *Nancy Grace* was based on the information I had at the time."

Later, Grunander questioned sheriff's sergeant Spencer Cannon, who worked with the Utah State medical examiner and was the one to pick up Michele's body from the hospital. At the time, he did not deem her death suspicious.

"If you had learned the defendant had thrown out a number of narcotics, and then told another person that the police had taken them, would that have raised suspicion in your mind?" Grunander asked.

"That would have, yes," Cannon replied.

The next four witnesses shuffled into the courtroom shackled and dressed in prison garb. The names and faces of four inmates who had served time with Martin at Texarkana Federal Correctional Institute were not shown on camera, to avoid any of them being labeled a "snitch," and facing violent repercussions from other prisoners.

Each inmate spoke of their interactions with the man they knew as "Doc," and the comments Martin had made about his wife's death.

On the stand, Von Harper identified Gypsy as the woman Martin referred to as his wife. In an amusing part of his testimony, Harper misspoke her name. "He said her name was Dipsy or Gypsy or something like that."

On cross, Spencer aggressively confronted Harper about his criminal record, accusing him of making up allegations against Martin to get a reduction in his sentence.

"So as an inmate you understood that by providing information to law enforcement you could potentially get a reduction in your sentence?" Spencer said.

"I understand that if I help out with a federal investigation I can. But this is not a federal investigation. This is a state investigation, right?"

Spencer smiled smugly. "I'm asking the questions here."

Frank Davis next told jurors of working out with "Doc" in the prison yard, and Martin's comments that "the bitch drowned," in reference to Michele's death. During cross-examination, Spencer strangely got the inmate to admit he did not seek any benefit for his testimony, in a series of questions that seemed more beneficial to the prosecution.

"I never contacted any of these people. They contacted me," Davis said.

Martin took off his glasses, rubbed his eyes, and sighed.

Seeing his former cellmate, George Martinez, approach the witness stand, Martin's jaw tightened and teeth clenched.

"Did the defendant ever talk to you about having cancer? MS? Notice he have a limp?" the prosecutor asked.

"No," he responded.

When word got out on TV about Martin's case, Martinez said, he asked Martin if the allegations were true. "He said his wife had had plastic surgery and that she had a heart attack and passed away."

Michael Buchanan, Martin's former friend from computer class, provided the most valuable testimony, documenting how TV host Nancy Grace ignited gossip throughout the prison.

Buchanan was the only one of the four Texarkana inmates to provide jurors with an explanation of how Martin killed Michele.

"He said he gave her some Oxys and some sleeping pills and got her to get in the bathtub," the inmate said. "Later on he said he had to 'help her out.' I asked him what that meant. He said he had to hold her head under the water for a little while."

Spencer grilled Buchanan, again attempting to get him to admit he was testifying against Martin to get a deal. Because it was not a federal case, he wasn't eligible for a deal, Buchanan countered.

"Part of my rehabilitation coming back into society. I made some wrong decisions and I'm just trying to do right," Buchanan said.

Spencer seemed annoyed as they went back and forth, trying to prove no inmate would testify without a deal.

This time, however, Randall Spencer may have got it right.

45.

Did Martin talk about the relationship he had with his wife before she died?" the prosecutor asked Jason Poirier, Martin's writing partner from Utah County Jail.

"That it was going downhill. That she's trying to get his money. And that she was not going to let him keep cheating on her," Poirier said.

Poirier later asked if he was "serious" about murdering his wife, to which Martin had remarked: "Look where I'm at."

"At that point I believed what he was saying," Poirier testified. "And I immediately told the guards I needed to switch sections. I didn't want to be around him."

The roughly fifteen minutes of directed testimony was countered with nearly an hour and a half of grueling cross-examination that seemed to confirm little more than Poirier's extensive criminal record and poor financial state.

"Truthfulness isn't your strong suit, though, is it?" Spencer asked.

"Yes it is," Poirier insisted.

———

The man so integral to the criminal investigation against Martin MacNeill—investigator Jeff Robinson—was on the stand for mere minutes.

Robinson provided the only direct evidence he could: timing of the trips between the MacNeill home, Ada's elementary school, and the Developmental Center.

Spencer pointed out that the trip did not include the time it would take to walk from the Developmental Center building to the parking lot.

Finally, Gypsy Willis was called back to the stand, on the twelfth day of trial.

Sam Pead questioned Gypsy extensively about her continuing relationship with Martin while they were both incarcerated.

On the stand, Gypsy claimed she wanted nothing to do with Martin. "I found myself in prison for two years as a result of being with this guy. That was terrifying to me," Gypsy said. "The relationship was over after prison. I needed his support during that time. I had never had even so much as a speeding ticket up to that point, and I was terrified."

But Pead pointed out that in her letters, Gypsy wrote of her love for Martin.

"You did reciprocate his feelings?" Pead asked.

"I did. I wanted him to write back to me," she said.

At one point Gypsy scoffed at the idea the letters somehow proved she was devoted to Martin. "You know this was two years after she passed away. I don't . . ." She let the thought trail off.

In many of the letters, Gypsy and Martin had discussed resuming their lives together once they were both released.

"Again alluding to future plans?" Pead thrust the letter toward Gypsy.

"Yes," she admitted.

"Did you ever tell him the relationship was over in any of those letters?" Pead asked.

"I was so lonely. I was thrilled out of my mind to get a letter."

"Ms. Willis, isn't it fair to say you appear to be minimizing your relationship with the defendant?"

"I don't believe so."

Looming over her on the witness stand, Pead had Gypsy read dozens of jailhouse letters out loud.

" 'The only reason I do anything is because I want to be as good as I can be when I get out of here so that you will still feel the same way about me,' " Gypsy spoke Martin's words. " 'I love you and miss you more than you can imagine.' "

As he heard his professions of love, Martin became emotional. He looked down and dabbed tears from his eyes.

They were the first tears he had shed during the trial.

4 6 .

After Gypsy left the courtroom, prosecutor Grunander stood and calmly said: "The state is resting at this point."

The defense would call just four witnesses.

Jim Van Zant, a nurse practitioner who worked with Martin, told jurors he had noticed nothing unusual about Martin's demeanor on April 11.

Ada's kindergarten teacher, Linda Strong, confirmed it was Martin who picked the girl up from school that day.

Jason Poirier's probation officer, Tammy Black, was called to speak about the misdemeanor offender's character.

The defense's only expert witness was an industrial hygienist for the Department of Labor, Brett William Besser, who testified there would be no way that Martin could lift his wife's body from a tub. Based on his calculations, in fact, there would be no way for two people to lift Michele from the tub.

On cross, Sam Pead pointed out that two people had, in fact, gotten Michele out of the tub.

Although the defense had lined up other expert witnesses who had reviewed the autopsies, Spencer decided to rest his case.

"We made that decision because we thought the state's expert witnesses were so inconsistent with their testimony that there was still reasonable doubt," Spencer recalled. "In hindsight I wish I had made the decision in trial to call the expert witnesses."

At the conclusion, the defense asked the judge for a directed verdict, saying there had been no evidence presented to warrant a charge of obstruction of justice, much less murder.

The judge denied the motion.

47.

"On April 11, almost seven years ago, Martin MacNeill murdered his wife, Michele." Chad Grunander's voice was outraged and impassioned as he pointed at Martin. "The defendant carried out a cold and calculated plan to murder his wife. Make no mistake. The defendant's fingerprints, if you will, are all over Michele's death."

In the gallery, Michele's daughters listened to Grunander's closing arguments on November 8. Rachel sat still, at times closing her eyes. In the second row Alexis and Linda stared straight ahead.

Grunander stood at the podium, wearing a blue suit and striped tie. On an easel in front of the jury he placed an enlarged picture of Michele sitting in a chair wearing a white blazer and pearls, her hair pulled back. Michele looked elegant and beautiful, her expression serene.

"A trial like this is about the truth. It's not about games. It's not about gotcha moments among the attorneys or the witnesses. It's about getting to the bottom of what happened to Michele MacNeill," Grunander continued. "And that is that she was murdered by her husband."

The motive, Grunander said, was Gypsy.

"The defendant had a beautiful wife—a lovely family. But things had changed because he and Gypsy were together," Grunander said. "Martin's secret life with Gypsy Willis was beginning to intersect with his life with Michele. He was going to have to make a choice between Michele and Gypsy."

In his speech, Grunander saved one of the most biting remarks for Gypsy.

"At trial, Gypsy Willis testified her relationship was casual. She took the stand and talked about the death of Michele MacNeill on April 11, 2007, like it was any other day . . . It was offensive." Grunander's voice rose. "It was transparent. Her desire to protect the defendant and her minimizing of the relationship. Don't be fooled by her act. Let's call a spade a spade. She minimized just about every opportunity she could get when talking about the relationship and her knowledge."

Grunander reminded jurors of what he called the most significant evidence of motive: the falsified military ID application in which Gypsy and Martin claimed to be married, listing a wedding date of April 14, 2007— the day Michele was buried. "Ladies and gentlemen, that is nothing short of an admission of guilt. That screams to you what happened on April 11, 2007," he said. "The defendant may as well have said in his application that 'I murdered Michele.'"

The evidence of the planning was overwhelming, Grunander continued. He referred to the drugs prescribed to Michele as the vehicle Martin used to kill. Martin had tried to use those drugs to overdose Michele at the first opportunity he was alone with her, Grunander said.

"They were also his cover to hide from the almost perfect murder. And I say almost perfect murder because along the way he left a number of clues. A number of clues that all point to him as the murderer."

Grunander's words dripped with disdain as he spoke of the testimony from the defense's health and safety expert who had claimed a single person could not possibly lift Michele alone.

"Ladies and gentlemen, how about getting inside the tub and straddling her?" Grunander said as he himself stepped inside the tub and mimed lifting a body. "Grabbing her by the shoulders . . . Why not do anything you could to try and save your wife's life?

"But he couldn't do anything. Because he had a hurt toe," Grunander said sarcastically. "Or maybe he has cancer? He was using that cane off and on."

The prosecutor was assertive as he pled with the jury not to have mercy on Martin. "It's time for the truth to have its day," he said. "It's been almost seven years since Michele's death. It's time for the truth to come out. Do the right thing and convict Martin MacNeill of murder and obstruction of justice. Thank you."

Grimacing, Martin scowled at the prosecutor. The defendant took off his glasses and dropped his head in his hands.

"Ladies and gentlemen of the jury, it's a pleasure to be with you, participating in our justice system," Randall Spencer began his closing argument. "I hope I haven't done anything offensive. It certainly wasn't my intent. I hope that . . . that both our efforts . . . we've endeavored to represent both our positions in as effective a manner as possible."

Dressed in a gray suit, Spencer recounted the Aesop's fable that Susanne Gustin had used in opening arguments. "My mother also taught me idioms like don't judge a book by its cover. This is a case where those principles are applicable. My client, Martin MacNeill, was living an alternative lifestyle. There's no dispute to that."

The defense had to concede Martin was a cad and a cheat. But the prosecution hadn't proved there was a murder, let alone that Martin committed it, according to Spencer.

"These are all circumstances. Not all circumstances are circumstantial evidence," he told jurors. "There are reasonable interpretations of all the circumstances consistent with an odd and eccentric man, generally."

Reviewing the opinions of the medical examiners, the defense attorney pointed out that no one could agree it was a homicide—aside from the medical examiner he called "Nancy Grace's expert."

"There were many inconsistencies and problems and variations and evolutions. There might also be fabrications," Spencer said.

If the medical examiners could review all of the information and fail to conclude it was a homicide, then a jury couldn't either, Spencer claimed. Surprisingly, the attorney then gave the jury permission to do just that.

"It's certainly your prerogative to do so. I don't mean to be suggesting that it's not. You are the ultimate finders of fact in this case." Spencer laced his fingers. "But you do have an obligation to consider the evidence."

Spencer dismissed the importance of Martin's mistakes. "Michele arrives at the hospital, Martin continues to be hysterical. He says some things that are certainly odd. The ten thousand dollars comment is odd. I have no explanation for that other than it's odd," Spencer said. "Certainly it's not necessarily indicative of homicide—much more consistent with a very hysterical man who just lost his wife. He may have been living an alternative lifestyle. But he was clearly hysterical at the loss of his wife."

Finally, Spencer implored the jury to examine the evidence closely. "There is an abundance of reasonable doubt. When you get back to the jury room I certainly hope you will evaluate the evidence. And as you review it and consider everything you've learned in this case you will return with a verdict of not guilty on both counts."

As Spencer returned to the defense table, Martin sagged in his chair. Almost imperceptibly, his eye twitched.

48.

Jurors had sat through thirteen days of testimony with more than five dozen witnesses in a nearly monthlong trial. At 1:57 P.M. on Friday, November 8, the five men and three women entered the jury room to decide Martin's fate.

Michele's loved ones were nervous but confident as they stepped out of the courtroom, surrounded by news media.

"We're anxious but hoping for the best," Linda Cluff said as she left the courtroom.

Alexis publicly thanked the prosecutors. "We're just very grateful that my mom had a voice."

Martin returned to his holding cell optimistic, according to his attorneys. "Mr. MacNeill has been very anxious for this day to come," Spencer told reporters.

The minutes crept by slowly in Provo as both sides waited for the verdict. Day turned to night and still there was no word from the jury room.

Television and newspaper reporters crowded the corridors outside the courtroom. Around the world thousands who had followed every moment of the trial periodically checked their cell phones, iPads, and laptops, excitedly waiting for the final act of the real-life reality drama.

At 9:30 P.M., the bailiff was handed a note: a jury question. Proceedings briefly resumed as the judge and attorneys heard the query: "Is it Utah law the surviving spouse inherits the estate regardless of what a will says?"

Both sides considered the answer before the judge decided he felt less information was better. The judge sent his reply: "The law relevant to the case is in the instructions."

An hour later the jurors requested to listen again to the 911 call. An attempt was made to make a copy of the call, but this was prevented due to technical difficulties.

Hours passed. Midnight came and went. The jury still debated.

Then, after eleven hours, word spread—a verdict had been reached.

It was 1 A.M. on Saturday, November 9.

Exhausted and bleary-eyed, the attorneys, Michele's family, and reporters filed back into the courtroom. In the front row, Alexis sat beside Linda and Michele's other sisters, holding hands. Sitting nearby, Rachel glanced up at the ceiling, her lips trembling.

Martin smiled and winked at his attorney, who joined him at the defense table. As the jurors funneled back into the jury box, he placed both hands on the wooden defense table in front of him, literally bracing himself for the verdict.

At 1:10 A.M., Martin stood beside his attorneys for the reading of the verdict.

"We are on the record with the *State of Utah v. Martin Joseph MacNeill*." Judge Pullan crossed his arms. "Has the jury reached a verdict?"

"Yes, Your Honor," the foreperson replied.

The bailiff passed the decision to the judge, who scanned it, his expression unchanged, and asked for it to be read by the clerk.

"We, the jury, having reviewed the evidence and the testimony in the case, find the defendant, to count one, murder"—the clerk paused—"guilty."

Martin remained motionless, his eyes widening ever so slightly.

Gasps came from the gallery. Michele's family yelped with joy, before dissolving into tears.

Shoulders shaking with agonized sobs, Rachel released the breath she had been holding. Linda embraced Alexis, her eyes closed tightly as she cried.

The verdict for count two, obstruction of justice: also guilty.

With a resigned frown, Martin took his seat.

Sentencing was scheduled for January 7, 2014. Martin faced fifteen years to life, with an additional one to fifteen years for the obstruction of justice. He essentially faced a lifetime behind bars.

The convicted murderer hugged Randall Spencer. With his hand on the lawyer's shoulders, Martin smiled slightly and said, "It's okay, really."

Until that moment Spencer believed, perhaps more than Martin himself, his client would be acquitted. "I think Martin took it better than we did," Spencer recalled. "I was thinking 'I'm not okay.'"

Relief washed over the family as they left the courtroom, surrounded by flashing cameras and reporters holding microphones and recorders in their outstretched arms.

"We are just so happy he can't hurt anyone else," Alexis told reporters, tears streaming down her face. "I can't believe this has finally happened."

The attorneys also addressed the media.

"We're absolutely thrilled," prosecutor Grunander said, smiling. "It was amazing to meet with this family. This has been so long in coming for them."

A weary Spencer darted from the courtroom. "Of course I'm disappointed, but I don't have any comments right now," he told the media throng.

At her home, Gypsy learned of the verdict through the Internet. She felt sick to her stomach.

"I was shocked. It took me a little while to pull myself together," she recalled. "I never, ever, ever thought that it would—it would come to such a thing."

And just like that, the case seemed finished. The more than six-year crusade to get justice for Michele was complete.

The morning after the verdict, Alexis awoke and a relieved smile came across her face as the memory of the previous night flooded back into her consciousness. She reminded herself it was over.

"And now I can move on, and my mother would want us to move on and focus on the good things that we have to come," Alexis said on *Nancy Grace* the Monday after the verdict. "I'm just so grateful that this is over and justice was served."

But the saga of Martin MacNeill was far from over.

49.

With a steady hand, Martin gripped the blade he had pried out of his disposable razor. Removing the prison jumpsuit he wore from his bottom half, Martin drew the blade across his upper thigh. Digging deeper into the flesh, he pierced the femoral artery. Blood gushed rapidly from the wound.

Glancing around his jail cell, his eyes passed by the handwritten suicide note he had placed on the bed bolted to the floor.

It was the evening of December 5—less than a month after the verdict—and Martin was prepared to die.

Just weeks earlier, on November 18, Martin had been back in court, looking ragged and deflated. Shoulders sagging forward, he shambled into the courtroom wearing a red-and-white-striped prison garb, his hands cuffed to the chain around his waist.

He remained in the jury box, shackled alongside other inmates waiting to see the judge, for a routine pretrial hearing for the sexual assault trial scheduled for December.

Randall Spencer approached the podium, addressing Judge Samuel McVey, the original judge on the murder case.

Spencer asked for a delay, telling the judge he was exhausted from the murder trial and he didn't feel he could adequately represent Martin. "I'm not in a state where I could possibly try this case in December," he said.

Spencer also requested permission to withdraw as counsel on the case. The request to withdraw was denied, but the trial date was moved to February 4, 2014.

"Weighing the rights of the victim against those of the accused, a two-month continuance would not be excessively long," McVey said.

The judge added that the date was firm and would only change if "somebody is in the hospital."

When Spencer left the courtroom, he was ambushed by reporters. They asked how Martin was handling the verdict.

"He is not doing well," Spencer said. "It is very tough on him to be convicted of something he always professed he didn't do."

Seventeen days later, on the afternoon of Thursday, December 5, Spencer stopped by the jail to visit with Martin.

While Martin had been dejected following the verdict, that afternoon he was content and even a bit upbeat. After discussing a possible appeal with his client, Spencer left the jail.

At 5:30 P.M., a corrections officer passed by Martin's cell and handed him a disposable razor to shave his face, as part of the jail's hygiene protocol. The officer would return to collect it about fifteen minutes later. By then, Martin had dismantled the razor and slashed his artery. The blood poured from Martin's leg, dripping onto the jail floor.

Minutes later, during a routine check of his cell, officers found Martin bleeding and quickly radioed for help. The guard unlocked the cell, rushing to Martin's side. Glowering, Martin turned away from the deputy and attempted to hasten the blood flow.

"Martin was unhappy he was interrupted in his suicide attempt and not cooperative with treatment efforts," sheriff's sergeant Spencer Cannon later said.

Paramedics soon arrived and treated Martin's wound. He was taken by ambulance to Utah Valley Regional Medical Center in Provo. At the hospital, Martin's wounds were stitched. He was listed in stable condition and informed he'd make a full recovery.

"He was discovered early enough by guards so his injuries were not life-threatening," Cannon commented.

When Martin's defense attorneys heard of the suicide attempt, they rushed to the hospital. Spencer and Gustin tried to visit their client but were not permitted to see him. Gustin later spoke to the media.

"Randy and I are really shocked and saddened by this . . . He seemed kind of upbeat. So it came as quite a surprise," she told reporters. "Obviously in any case like this, it's always in the back of your mind, in a big murder case like this, that someone may kill themselves. We weren't concerned about any overt signs or anything that would trigger us to let the jail know he would [try to] take his life."

News of the suicide attempt also reached Michele's loved ones. Linda Cluff said she believed her former brother-in-law finally realized he would spend the rest of his life in prison and was looking for an easy way out.

"The first thing I thought when I heard about the suicide attempt was 'He can't stand this,'" Linda said in an interview. "I'm glad that he survived. I want him to see what it's like in prison . . . I would like to see him face life behind bars because that's more justice to me, because he'll have to face what goes on behind the prison walls, which to me is a harsher penalty."

She also didn't believe Martin felt any remorse—just pity for himself.

"I believe that it is not about remorse for any actions that Martin did. I believe that he is incapable of feeling remorse," she told the press. "This is not a shock. It's just another portrayal of who Martin really is."

Given Martin's history of suicide threats, the MacNeill daughters also were not surprised. The day after the suicide attempt, Alexis issued a statement.

"My family continues to struggle to heal and move forward with our lives after the murder of our beloved mother. Our lives have already been torn apart," the statement read. "We do not pretend to understand the senseless, distressful, and hurtful actions of our father."

––––––––

After a brief stay in the hospital, Martin returned to jail, where he spent three weeks in a medical bay. He was then classified under suicide watch, where he would remain for the rest of his stay in the Utah County Jail.

Housed alone in an isolated cell, a light shone on him twenty-four hours a day. He was devoid of any human interactions and monitored constantly by guards. When he moved outside of his cell to the shower room, he remained cuffed. His only attire was a suicide robe, a heavy, tear-resistant, single-piece garment.

The conditions in isolation slowly ate away at Martin mentally and physically, Randall Spencer said. He had been unable to sleep and had lost weight. Martin grew increasingly depressed, slipping deeper into the recesses of his dark mind.

"The manner in which he is being housed at the jail is slowly killing him, and having a significant effect on his mental health to the point that I seriously question his competency to reasonably assist me in preparing for the trial," Spencer wrote in a motion filed in January 2014.

Spencer had filed the petition to request a competency hearing or a trial delay to restore his client to a "reasonable degree of physical and mental health."

"It is my observation and belief that Mr. MacNeill's condition is bad and worsening," Spencer wrote. "He does not seem to care about the pending trial or how it may affect him, which is a completely different mental state for him than my past experience over the last six and a half years of representation."

When Martin next appeared in court, on January 23, his faded inmate clothing hung loosely over his gaunt frame. A scruffy beard covered his drawn, ashen face.

"His mental illness is flaring up," Spencer told Judge McVey. "He needs to be evaluated. Things are getting worse."

Due to a recent decision by the Utah Court of Appeals, if an attorney asked for a mental competency evaluation, the judge was forced to grant the request.

"Any time that trial counsel raises a bona fide doubt as to a defendant's competency to stand trial, the trial court is required to order a full hearing into competency," McVey announced. "So the court has no choice when that has happened."

The ruling derailed Martin's upcoming trial and the sentencing, frustrating Michele's family.

"I think it's ridiculous," Alexis told reporters. "He uses this mental illness card whenever it suits him."

In January, meanwhile, Spencer also filed an appeal requesting a new murder trial, arguing federal inmate Michael Buchanan lied on the stand in exchange for an early release.

Buchanan had insisted under cross-examination that he would not receive an early release in exchange for his testimony. Prosecutors and investigators also told the judge and defense no deal had been negotiated for Buchanan. Weeks after the trial, however, Jeff Robinson wrote to federal prosecutors, calling Buchanan a "very important witness" and stating that he "highly recommended" and encouraged leniency.

Buchanan was subsequently released from prison two years early.

Spencer was disgusted with the prosecutors and filed motions to have the verdict vacated, the charges dismissed, or for prosecutors to be removed from the case.

For the next few months, Martin further delayed the sexual assault trial by refusing to cooperate with doctors for the court-ordered mental health evaluation. By late April, however, he had changed his mind and agreed to participate. Two doctors evaluated Martin and both found he was competent to move forward with the trial.

McVey set a trial date for July and made it clear there would be no further delays.

Throughout the summer of 2014, Martin attended pretrial hearings for the forcible sexual abuse case and the murder appeal.

Despite still being on suicide watch, Martin appeared more at ease in court, smiling and speaking animatedly with his attorneys. By late June, Spencer suggested that his client was open to discussing a plea.

Alexis, however, wanted to confront her father in court. "As a victim of sexual abuse, I felt it a duty to come forward and seek justice for these crimes," Alexis told reporters. "Regardless of the outcome, I think I will sleep a little better tonight knowing I've done everything in my power to protect my family, protect my little sisters and others from my father, who is a murderer and a sexual predator."

50.

In a different courtroom, the same cast of characters assembled for Martin MacNeill's final act. For the second time in less than a year he stood trial, this time for forcible sexual abuse of his very own daughter.

The trial began on July 2, 2014, and would last just two days.

Prosecutor David Sturgill told the jury the case would center on the testimony of Alexis Somers. "There will be other witnesses, there will be additional testimony, but she will be the bulk of the state's case," Sturgill said. "Watch her, listen to her, and eventually we'll talk again."

Once again, the defense attacked Alexis's character. Randall Spencer told the jurors to be careful and evaluate Alexis's testimony because, according to him, she had a reputation of lying.

On the first day of the trial, Alexis took the stand, telling jurors how at the age of twenty-four and just six weeks after her beloved mother's death, she awoke to her father fondling her. His hand was down her pants, his lips on her palm. She'd bolted from the bed, repulsed.

She explained that she made amends with her father after the incident and that she later sent him postcards from Cancún, Mexico, to persuade him to allow her to return to the house. The postcards were entered into evidence by the prosecutor.

On cross, Spencer tried to poke holes in her testimony, questioning why she waited months to call the police. Once again the defense attorney became combative, but Alexis remained calm and resolute on the stand.

On the second day of the trial, Rachel testified about the family meeting her father had called when he informed his children that the younger girls would no longer be allowed in his bedroom for fear he might touch them in his sleep.

Lieutenant Britt Smith of the Pleasant Grove police also took the stand, to discuss taking the report.

Spencer called no witnesses—he based his case exclusively on the theory the prosecution had insufficient evidence.

During closing arguments, Sturgill described the "turmoil" going on inside the MacNeill home during 2007.

"Is there any wonder or any question why Alexis would do what she had to do to get this out in the open and protect those kids?" Sturgill asked the jury. "Yes, she had something to gain by coming forward, but that doesn't mean she lied about it."

Spencer told the jurors Alexis had slanted her testimony out of a desire to gain custody of her sisters. "She's a very sharp woman, but she also has motive to not be truthful," Spencer said. "If she was truly so concerned about the kids being in the home with a sexual predator, is it reasonable to believe she would have gone off with her friends to Cancún?"

On July 3, the case went to the jury. Just before 7 P.M., the five-woman, three-man jury returned a verdict: guilty of one count of forcible sexual abuse.

Martin faced up to fifteen additional years in prison.

After the verdict, Alexis spoke to reporters. "He's a sexual predator," she said. "There's some justice. The jury once again saw the truth."

Sentencing for the sexual abuse conviction was delayed for months due to one of Randall Spencer's trademark motions to dismiss. In the motion, he argued the police had lost a recorded interview between Alexis and officers from 2007, which denied him the opportunity to cross-examine any inconsistent statements Alexis made on the stand "with her own words."

It was similar to an argument Spencer had made before trial when he asked for the case to be tossed due to the lost evidence. McVey had rejected the argument then, and once again denied the motion, stating that deleting the recording was an error but not "gross negligence" or done "in bad faith."

Meanwhile, in another courtroom, Judge Pullan had been mulling over a similar defense motion: to throw out the guilty verdict in the murder trial because prosecutors hadn't disclosed the deal with inmate Michael Buchanan. On Friday, August 29, eight months after the motion had been filed, Judge Derek Pullan gave his ruling.

"The question is whether there is a reasonable likelihood that the false testimony affected the trial," Pullan's forty-page ruling read. "The Court holds no."

Martin would receive no new trial.

Pullan actually agreed with Spencer, stating that prosecutors had "elicited false testimony" about whether Buchanan received any benefits for his testimony, adding that a member of the prosecution knew the testimony was untrue and did nothing to correct it.

Ironically, the judge's reason for denying the motion was Spencer's "long, pointed, and devastating" cross-examination of Buchanan, which proved to the jury the inmate would have done anything to get out of prison early. The judge added Martin was convicted even though the jury didn't trust Buchanan, so a new trial wouldn't change the outcome.

"Jurors understood that the interests of the inmates in the case were different than any ordinary witness, and that both had motive to testify falsely," Pullan wrote in his ruling.

Martin's latest hope for a release had been dashed. Outside the courtroom, Spencer seemed dejected.

"We're obviously very disappointed in the decision," Spencer told reporters outside of court.

It was the defense attorney's final word on the case.

After months of delays, both of Martin MacNeill's trials would conclude the third week of September.

On Monday, September 15, 2014, Martin was sentenced for sexually assaulting his daughter. Wearing a red-and-white-striped jumpsuit, Martin sat in the back row of the jury box, shackled to other inmates. He remained stone-faced as Alexis addressed the judge, pleading for the maximum sentence.

"My father's evil did not begin or end with the murder of my mother. Shortly after my mother's death, my father sexually assaulted me on two different occasions," Alexis told Judge McVey. "He destroyed my world and created a living nightmare in its place."

Alexis held back tears as she stared directly at the judge, never glancing at Martin.

"He made the choice to destroy his family," Alexis said. "He made the choice to murder my mother. He made the choice to sexually assault me."

Alexis insisted she was not the only victim of sex abuse at the hands of Martin. She hoped his conviction in her case would help his other victims heal.

"He has created his own fate," she said. "My father's façade is now crumbled. My father is a monster."

Spencer did not say anything on his client's behalf. Martin also refused to address the judge, as most defendants do during sentencing. He continued to deny guilt and had not cooperated with a postconviction evaluation to offer mitigating factors to possibly reduce his prison term. Instead, he stared straight ahead as the judge handed down the sentence.

"Mr. MacNeill is not only not cooperating, but he has not admitted to misconduct, which would preclude him from being involved in sex offender treatment," McVey told the court.

For those reasons, McVey could not consider parole, and instead gave Martin the maximum sentence: one to fifteen years in Utah State Prison.

Following the sentence, Spencer bolted from the courtroom without addressing reporters.

Martin, meanwhile, was transferred from the Utah County Jail to the Utah State Prison, where he exchanged his red and white stripes for a bright orange jumpsuit.

Seven years, five months, and eight days had passed since Michele's life ended in the bathtub of her home in Pleasant Grove. On Friday, September 19, Martin was finally sentenced for her murder.

Seated at the defense table beside his attorney, Martin appeared gaunt in his orange prison garb. He wore his square-framed glasses, his gray hair closely cropped. Hovering nearby, two Department of Corrections officers monitored their new prisoner's every move.

Throughout the proceedings, Martin chatted and laughed with his attorney. He ignored the three women responsible for putting him in jail, refusing to acknowledge them when they addressed the court to request the maximum sentence.

As Linda Cluff approached the podium, Martin barely looked in her direction. Throughout her statement to the judge, Martin continued whispering in his attorney's ear.

"Martin is a man who believes he is above the law," Linda told Judge Pullan, her voice defiant. "He believes he is above everyone and everything. He is calculating and controlling. Martin is evil."

Linda said several painful questions remained in Michele's murder: Did her sister suffer? Was she scared? What was she thinking? What were her last thoughts? "I shatter thinking of my sister looking at her own husband as he was doing this to her," Linda said.

At one point while addressing the court, she turned and glared directly at her former brother-in-law. For a brief moment, Martin looked back at her, the two locking eyes.

"I can finally look into the eyes of my sister's murderer and say, 'Martin, you haven't gotten away with this,'" she said.

Linda would later say she saw nothing staring back at her, just a blank gaze. "There was no emotion whatsoever. Just a cold, calculated look," she recalled.

Rachel MacNeill sobbed throughout most of her statement, as she spoke of the loss of her mother. "He took the kindest, most caring person I've ever known, and he calculatingly took her from us all," Rachel said, tears clouding her eyes.

Since her mother's murder, her family had been shattered, she said, referencing her brother's suicide. "True justice for my mother does not end with the conviction and sentencing of her murderer," she said. "It begins."

Alexis asked the judge to show her mother's murderer that he "is not above the law" and to sentence Martin to the maximum.

"He has never shown remorse for any of his crimes," Alexis told Judge Pullan. "While we wept, he laughed. He used the date of my mother's funeral as the marriage date of his mistress."

Finally, she described how the loss of her mother had impacted her entire family. "He has destroyed so many lives," Alexis said. "She was taken from us and robbed of her life. We were all robbed of so much happiness and joy."

Prosecutor Chad Grunander then stood to address the court, lamenting that Utah law didn't consider Michele's murder a capital offense, which would have made Martin eligible for the death penalty.

"This was a heinous, heinous, terrible crime—premeditated murder. But in Utah, it doesn't qualify as a capital offense," the prosecutor said. "It's as bad as you can get. Doctor, husband, father, a lawyer—what he did here, using his unique special knowledge, it's as bad as it gets."

Once again, Martin refused to address the court. Spencer also did not speak or make any recommendations for leniency.

Judge Pullan then delivered the sentence, reading from a prepared ruling. "The defendant was a respected doctor and family man, but he was also engaged in an extramarital affair and unwilling to give up his social standing or his paramour," Pullan said. "Divorce was unacceptable to him. Instead, he devised a plan to murder his wife."

In orchestrating the murder, Martin used his knowledge as a physician to secure the drugs, which the judge said was particularly reprehensible. "A man who has taken an oath to do no harm only adds insult to irreparable injury."

Martin's calculated scheme to kill his wife was all part of a "juvenile and bizarre plan" to start a new life with his mistress, the judge said.

"Mr. MacNeill has led a double life, which in the end proved to be unsustainable," Pullan said. "The devastation experienced by the MacNeill family is immeasurable."

THE STRANGER SHE LOVED 315

The crimes committed were done with an "unmitigated selfishness that really shocks the conscience," the judge explained, looking directly at Martin.

"Mr. MacNeill, as you deprived Michele MacNeill of her life, the state of Utah exacts from you today the liberty you otherwise might have enjoyed in your remaining years," Pullan said. "The only restitution that can be made is just punishment."

Pullan then sentenced Martin to the harshest term possible: at least fifteen years and up to life on the murder charge, plus one to fifteen years on the conviction for obstruction of justice.

The sentences would run consecutively, meaning he would not begin serving time on one sentence until the first one was completed. The sexual assault sentence would also run consecutively. He received credit for the 748 days he had spent in jail waiting for trial and sentencing.

Martin would serve seventeen years before he would be eligible for parole, which in this case would not likely be granted. For Martin, it was essentially a life sentence, Grunander later said.

"Given his age, he's fifty-eight years old now, given the circumstances of this crime, the fact that he's not taking any responsibility, if he continues to do that, there's absolutely no hope he's going to be released. I think he dies in prison," explained the prosecutor. "I think even if he does take responsibility, in the interest of justice he will never be free again."

For Michele MacNeill's loved ones, the sentence freed them from the hell they had been living in for the past seven years.

"This is what we were hoping for. We're just happy this chapter is finally closed," Linda Cluff told reporters as she stood outside the courtroom. "It's utter relief. It's indescribable . . . I felt Michele's presence there. It's just a wonderful feeling."

After the sentence was read, Martin rose from the defense table. His hands were cuffed behind him as he was led away by corrections officers, returning to the bleak and isolated prison cell where he would spend each day for the rest of his life.

With that the curtain closed on Martin MacNeill's theater of the macabre. His audience had vanished. His final stage was a prison.

Dr. Martin MacNeill, esquire, had been stripped of all his wealth, pretense, and prosperity.

No longer the doctor, lawyer, Mormon bishop, husband.

Now, and for the rest of his lonely, miserable existence, Martin MacNeill's most prominent title is simply: murderer.

AFTERWORD

SEPTEMBER 19, 2014

The drapes in the vacant house in Pleasant Grove have been pushed back, the sunlight streaming through the windows, casting a stark glow on the remnants of one family's tragedy.

Dust covers the antique furniture Michele so carefully selected and arranged around the home. Boxes packed with framed family photos, albums, and heirlooms crowd the garage.

In the bathroom, Michele's lotions, perfumes, and toiletries have long since vanished from the cabinets and drawers. The tub where she took her last bath is bone dry, droplets of water no longer clinging to the faucet.

During a walk-through of the MacNeill home, the family noticed some of the valuables had gone missing. Yet many rooms remain just as Michele had left them.

Nearly a year after Martin's conviction for murder, ownership of the Pleasant Grove property remains in probate. It will almost certainly end up in Alexis's hands, because of a Utah law known as the Slayer statute, which prevents convicted murderers from benefiting financially from their crimes.

As the executor of her mother's estate, Alexis plans to sell the house and distribute the money among her sisters. With that, the final monument of

Martin's legacy will become the setting for another family to create hope-fully happier memories.

In other homes and apartments across Utah, Michele's children will at-tempt to rebuild from the charred remains of their family.

When I first learned of the disgraced Mormon doctor and the women who helped convict him, I was moved by the strength and determination of Michele's sister and daughters. My publisher had approached me about writing a book on the crimes and trial of Martin MacNeill. Although I was reluctant to write about such a heavy case, I decided to tell the story, in hope that their strength would inspire others. Their determined crusade for jus-tice truly demonstrates how much Michele was loved.

These women sacrificed their own careers, money, mental health, and relationships to fight for Michele. When I asked Linda Cluff what possessed her to dedicate years to seeking justice for her sister, she seemed momen-tarily at a loss for words. It was simply unimaginable to do anything else.

"It was for Michele." She sighed. "If I had to die trying to get someone to listen, that's what I was going to do."

As I researched the case, I often wondered what exactly drove Martin to deconstruct the life he had so carefully built. I wouldn't get the chance to question him—he had consistently declined all media interviews. But even if I was confined in a cell with Martin, I doubt I'd ever learn the truth. Mar-tin was a pathological liar and a textbook sociopath who cared for no one but himself.

What creates such a monster?

Martin often spoke about his dysfunctional background, revealing un-settling stories about growing up in New Jersey. Most of what Martin said about his childhood had no way of being substantiated, and given his pro-pensity for deceit, it's possible it was untrue.

Investigating his background, I was hindered by the fact that nearly all of his relatives were dead. Aside from his sister Mary, who never spoke pub-licly, there was no one left to confirm his accounts of what may have oc-curred during Martin's formative years.

Because so many of Martin's siblings struggled with mental illness, drug use, and suicide, one could easily assume something terrible indeed hap-pened in his childhood. I decided not to dwell on those details, and came to the conclusion that focusing on whatever abuse he may have suffered would only offer an excuse for his behavior.

There should be no sympathy for the devil.

I think that defense attorney Randall Spencer truly believes in his client's innocence. But the jury and I—after writing this book—formed a very different opinion about the dishonorable doctor.

Martin was manipulative, cruel, duplicitous, and deceitful. As a sociopath he was unable to empathize, and feigning emotion day after day was draining. I believe any love or compassion he showed was contrived, designed to obtain something he desired and driven by his calculating agenda.

At church, work, even at home, he had to wear the skin of another man. It must have been exhausting having to act like a caring Mormon bishop, playing the part of a family man, pretending to be a normal person.

He sloughed off the costume of the fictional character he created only when he was alone or with his mistresses. By Gypsy's own admission, Martin found being with her "liberating."

Confronting middle age with a genetic condition, Martin lost all interest in Michele and found her sudden interest in his infidelity a nuisance. He wanted a carefree, sex-filled future with Gypsy.

Divorce was not an option for Martin—it would damage his finances and reputation in the church and community.

He decided Michele had to die.

Investigators suspected murder was not anything new to Martin, believing it possible that he killed patients over the years, possibly the mentally challenged residents of the Developmental Center. He could have tried to kill his mother and may have succeeded in murdering his brother. The details of Rufus Roy MacNeill's death remain murky.

Just as he had when he offered to end Vanessa's drug addiction by ending her life, Martin likely rationalized that the lives he took had no value. It's possible he also convinced himself he would spare his wife the mental anguish of a divorce by providing her a peaceful death.

Or maybe he had such little regard for her that he just didn't care.

The plot to snuff out Michele was sinister.

Lying about having cancer and multiple sclerosis was likely a combination of his obsessive need for attention and a way to later deflect blame for her murder, as investigators theorized. Why would anyone suspect a dying man of killing his wife?

Reflecting back, one may view Martin's actions prior to Michele's death as evidence of premeditation. Did he put the house in Michele's name and take out a life insurance policy on himself to further the subterfuge? Was giving each of his children five thousand dollars a twisted payoff for taking away their mom?

Martin played on Michele's insecurities, coercing her to get a face-lift and requesting extra medication from the surgeon, which he knew could be lethal when combined. The day after the surgery, Martin tried to kill his wife with an overdose of that medication, unsuccessful only because the pills caused her to vomit.

April 11 was the day Martin ultimately chose to end Michele's life— Alexis was gone and he could establish an alibi at the safety fair. One of the first things he did that morning, at 6:48 A.M., was call his mistress. When he later spoke with Gypsy, what did he tell her?

At that point, Michele was wary of her cheating husband. She had been so alarmed the day after he overmedicated her, she had told her daughter the heartbreaking words: "If anything happens to me, make sure it wasn't your dad." To regain Michele's favor, Martin was extra sweet, laying it on thick. "Your dad is being so, so nice to me," Michele told Alexis during their final phone call.

As I worked on the case, I developed a theory of the murder. I doubt at that point Michele would take a handful of pills provided to her by her husband. And I don't think it would be possible for him to slip them in her food undetected. Instead, as one of the jailhouse informants testified, Martin likely delivered the medication in an enema.

At around 8:30 A.M., after dropping off Giselle, Elle, Sabrina, and Ada at school, Martin may have returned home under the guise of assisting his wife with a medical issue. Michele's autopsy later showed she was severely constipated, likely as a result of the pain pills she had been weaning off of, which can produce such an effect.

As a doctor, it wouldn't be unusual for him to administer an enema to help his constipated wife. After all, he was being "so sweet."

Prior to administering it, he may have surreptitiously crushed the Ambien, Valium, Percocet, and Phenergan and funneled the powdered pills into the enema bag. With rectal use, medication has a more powerful and rapid effect, since it bypasses the digestive system. Almost instantly Michele would have become sleepy, confused, and unaware of her surroundings.

Maybe Martin could not re-dress his unconscious wife, who would have had to remove her pants and underwear for the procedure. Or if he had dressed her, the enema may have also produced its intended results and Michele may have defecated, which could explain why Martin stripped her of her pants and underwear.

The pants that matched her black top were not in the bathroom or bedroom and have never been found.

It's possible Martin immediately took her to the bathtub after administering the enema. Or he may have returned to work to establish an alibi, expecting the pills would kill her. About an hour later he could have slipped away from the Developmental Center again and returned to find Michele alive but extremely lethargic and possibly unconscious.

He could have drawn a bath, helped her to the bathroom, bent her over the tub's ledge, and held her face under the water—the position he had described to his children.

Water filled her lungs. She struggled, causing her stitches to split open and bleed, blood-tinged water spilling onto the tile floor.

Michele stopped moving; her heart ceased beating.

Then, Martin swept his dead wife into the tub, her body slumped, head beneath the faucet, facing forward. He then used the towels to clean the floor, depositing them in the laundry room.

Michele's body was left stewing in the water, while Martin rushed back to work and accepted his award at the safety fair, where he demanded his photo be taken to prove his presence.

At 11:35 A.M. he picked up Ada from school. In one of the sickest twists, he allowed his youngest daughter to stumble upon the body of her dead mother.

Once the neighbors arrived, Martin feigned mouth-to-mouth. He was so disconnected from humanity that he thought his rehearsed, dramatic, soap-opera-like display of grief would make him seem innocent.

The autopsy later showed early signs of heart disease, a condition that could be the result of the extreme stress of dealing with Martin's hysterics for thirty years. Although the autopsy also showed Michele's lungs were heavy, during the resuscitation efforts she had expelled the water. There is no definitive way to prove either drowning or an arrhythmia after death. Given no other clues as to what caused Michele to die, the pathologist was quick to rule the death natural.

It was an almost perfect murder. And if not for the determination of Michele's loved ones, Martin would have gotten away with it.

As the jury rightly determined, Martin murdered his wife. But the real question mark in my mind is Gypsy.

No evidence was ever uncovered implicating Gypsy in Michele's slaying and she was never charged with any crime relating to the murder. But, while Gypsy had an alibi, many people, including the MacNeill children, have wondered if she was involved in some way with Michele's death. To find out what she knew, I went directly to Gypsy.

Like most who saw her callous courtroom performance, I was repulsed. To brazenly sit on the witness stand and shield an accused murderer from justice was—as prosecutor Grunander stated during closing arguments—offensive.

When I interviewed Gypsy, however, she surprised me. We spoke at length about her background, her affair with Martin, her involvement as the nanny, and the theft of Giselle's identity. While she was dispassionate about Michele, she seemed forthright and genuine. It appeared she had accepted some degree of accountability for her actions.

"I never thought I would be associated with Martin long term. And I'm sorry for it," she told me. Perhaps she was telling the truth. After all, Martin was a powerful manipulator—it's possible he tricked Gypsy as well.

I decided to set aside personal judgment as to her character and focus on the facts. In the pages of this book I tried to present those details simply and objectively and confine my opinions to the afterword.

Still, as I wrote about the case, creeping doubts and lingering questions consumed me. If she truly believed Martin to be innocent, how could she reconcile the contradictory accounts he gave on his failing health? Did she really find it reasonable that Michele had so much medication in her system?

And, most glaring, if her relationship with the married doctor was casual, why would she e-mail another suitor a month prior to Michele's murder to say her relationship with Martin had grown serious and they were now exclusive?

It made no sense that she would suddenly decide to stop dating other men if her married boyfriend had no intention of leaving his wife. Had Gypsy known of Martin's plans when she committed herself exclusively to their relationship?

I would get no answers.

As Martin's trial garnered widespread media coverage, Gypsy signed with a publicist to field interview requests. The publicity firm she chose is run by Gina Rodriguez, a former porn star who has represented infamous tabloid figures including Joey Buttafuoco, Michael and Dina Lohan, "Tan Mom" Patricia Krentcil, *Teen Mom* Farrah Abraham, Nadya "Octomom" Suleman, Anthony Weiner's sexting partner Sydney Leathers, and Charlie Sheen's onetime companion Capri Anderson, also a porn star.

Many of Rodriguez's scandal makers end up cashing in on their notoriety by later filming pornography. Gypsy's representation was handled by Rodriguez's daughter, Brandi Snail, who costarred with her mother and brother in a 2009 reality program called *Mommy XXX*.

Months after first interviewing Gypsy, following Martin's conviction but prior to his sentencing, I contacted his mistress directly, asking if we could speak again. Gypsy insisted we set up the interview through Brandi Snail. I sent Snail an e-mail.

Her reply came quickly: "I would love to help set this up for you but their [sic] would have to be some sort of incentive for Gypsy to do this."

As I explained to Snail, it's journalistically unethical to pay for interviews with any subject.

Snail's response was audacious. "Gypsy would need a minimum of $1,500 to do this. Gypsy is a big piece of the story and if she cannot get a minimum of $1,500 then I will have to say that we will pass on this."

Needless to say, I was not willing to pay.

Messaging Gypsy directly, I informed her about her publicist's demand of money and explained why it was wrong. Gypsy was unapologetic. Eventually she responded to an e-mail to clarify a few issues, which all benefited her. To my more difficult questions, I received no response. We never spoke again.

"I don't mean to sound like a fainting flower over here, but delving into all this again is so hard," Gypsy said in an e-mail.

But that interaction with Gypsy and her publicist demonstrated to me more about her character than I could have gleaned from a dozen interviews. For sleeping with a married man and stealing the identity of a teenage girl, Gypsy wanted to be rewarded. Gypsy truly was Martin's perfect match—she is equally as cold, heartless, and unscrupulous as he is. Martin found it liberating to be with her because he didn't have to conceal his true nature—she had a dark side, too.

She plotted and schemed with Martin to deceive Michele's grieving children. She attended Michele's funeral and sent her lover provocative photos the following day to keep his interest. She moved into the family home and shamelessly continued to sleep with Martin in the marital bed he had shared with Michele. She participated in the theft of a teenager's identity, knowing the girl had been abandoned in Ukraine. And finally, she shielded Martin from blame on the witness stand by attempting to minimize their relationship.

I don't know exactly what Gypsy knows, but I can't help wondering whether she knows more than she has told me, the investigators, or the media. She has said in many interviews that she was shocked about the guilty verdict and had expected Martin would go free. She has also said she can't imagine that she was the motive for the murder. "The idea that I am an incentive is very appalling to me. It's very hard to swallow," she has said.

Was she truly appalled that she may have been the motive for murder? Or is it possible she was flattered that Martin loved her enough to kill?

Amid all of this, Michele was truly an innocent victim.

It would have been impossible for such a genuine, loving person to imagine the depths of her husband's deception—the affairs, crimes, phony degree, and misconduct as a doctor.

Michele never looked at Martin and considered he had a demon of a mind. She saw only the best in her husband. Her fatal flaw was simply loving him unconditionally. Martin swept Michele into his chaos and eventually took her life. He was a dangerous and destructive force who damaged or destroyed almost everyone he came in contact with.

Dozens of women he had affairs with were left wounded after they say Martin preyed on them sexually. Patients were disregarded and misdiagnosed, unaware he was never qualified to treat their conditions. Nurses and doctors he worked with were bullied and browbeaten by Dr. MacNeill. And there are almost certainly crimes he committed over the years that the investigators never uncovered.

Each of his children has also been left scarred. After growing up in the harsh conditions of Ukraine, his adopted daughters experienced Michele's love for only a few short years. And Ada will be forever haunted by the childhood memory of discovering her mother's body.

Rachel struggles with bipolar disorder. Vanessa battles drug addiction. Alexis has spent thousands of dollars and countless hours fighting to gain custody of her little sisters and to seek justice for her mother.

And most tragically, Damian took his own life, which his family believes happened after he finally came to the disturbing realization that his father killed his mother.

Rather than being torn apart by all the loss they have faced during the past seven years, the MacNeill family has remarkably been united in their quest for justice.

And with Martin's conviction, the darkness has finally receded.

They will each move forward and return to the business of remembering Michele.

Martin, meanwhile, will likely rot in prison every day for the rest of his life. If given the chance, he may again attempt to kill himself to escape the hell he created. Whether by suicide, illness, or old age, one day he will almost certainly die in prison, penniless and alone.

His death will not be mourned. There will be no funeral. He'll probably be buried in a pine box in the prison cemetery.

Martin's legacy will be that of a depraved murderer.

He lied to everyone. But his most dangerous lie was the one he told to himself—that he was untouchable.

His undoing was hubris.

By 2007, Martin's ego had become so bloated he had lost all perspective. He almost always got away with his crimes and affairs. He convinced himself he was invincible and became reckless, risking everything to cheat, lie, and steal from the military.

Slowly he lost touch with the man he pretended to be.

Nothing said to or written about Martin could cause him to have one moment of introspection. In prison, he will never reflect back and question how his own actions led to his downfall. He will never mourn his wife. He will never feel empathy for destroying his family or alienating his children.

For there can be no soul-searching for a man without a soul.

Martin MacNeill is an empty vessel devoid of humanity, his heart blackened by depravity. His entire being revolves around the six-foot-three, 180-pound space his body consumes in this world.

Undeniably, he was a talented actor. He concealed his awful deeds and hid his poisonous thoughts. For years no one ever suspected there was corrosive evil coating his insides.

Reputation always meant so much to Martin—to be known as someone who was accomplished, successful, and good. The man who cared so much about image, who valued the appearance of perfection rather than showing a hint of frailty, will now be defined forever by his faults and deficits.

The world now knows his true wickedness.

Martin MacNeill has been exposed, a stranger no more.

ACKNOWLEDGMENTS

This was my third book but my very first case outside of my home state of Arizona. Stepping outside my comfort zone brought with it unique and interesting complications. There were many times throughout the writing process when I wished I could have walked away. Peering into Martin MacNeill's twisted mind was so dark.

I have nothing but genuine respect and admiration for the determination of Linda Cluff and Alexis, Rachel, Vanessa, Elle, Giselle, Sabrina, Ada, and Noelle. You all have tremendous strength and spirit. For Doug Witney, Jeff Robinson, Chad Grunander, Sam Pead, and Jared Perkins—to watch you fight so passionately to help others was an honor.

Although not all of the subjects involved in this case granted my interview requests, I would like to thank each one who took the time to personally share their stories with me.

I'd especially like to thank the one person who held my hand and kept me going through this book—my former journalism professor, turned colleague, turned friend, who helped pre-edit the book out of order, the remarkable Christia Gibbons. You are a gifted and generous soul.

I owe special gratitude to my literary agent, Sharlene Martin, for her continual support of my career. Additionally, my gratitude goes out to my superb editors at St. Martin's Press: April Osborn and Charles Spicer.

On a personal note, thank you to Kimberly Hundley for your editing advice. To my beloved Carol "Mimi" Hogan, for teaching me to read with Stephen King and Dean Koontz. To my entire family, namely my parents, Dann and Debbie Hogan, as well as my mother-in-law, Joann LaRussa—I truly love and appreciate you.

Most important, I would like to thank the one person who is the most wonderful, remarkable person in my life, my husband, Matt LaRussa.